# THE DICTIONARY OF

# CONCISE

# THE DICTIONARY OF

# CONCISE WRITING

## 10,000
## Alternatives to
## Wordy Phrases

Robert Hartwell Fiske

**Marion Street Press, Inc.**

Library of Congress Cataloging-in-Publication Data

Fiske, Robert Hartwell.
The dictionary of concise writing : 10,000 alternatives to wordy
phrases / by Robert Hartwell Fiske.
    p. cm.
ISBN 0-9665176-6-0
1. English language--Rhetoric--Dictionaries. 2. English
language--Usage--Dictionaries. 3. Report writing--Dictionaries. I.
Title.
PE1464 .F57 2002
808'.042'03--dc21
                                            2002008142

Cover design by Michelle Crisanti

ISBN 0-9665176-6-0
Printed in U.S.A.
Printing 10 9 8 7 6 5 4 3 2

Marion Street Press, Inc.
PO Box 2249
Oak Park, IL 60304
708-445-8330
Toll-free 866-443-7987
www.marionstreetpress.com

# The Vocabula Review

Robert Hartwell Fiske is the editor and publisher of *The Vocabula Review* (www.vocabula.com), an online journal about the English language.

\*\*\*

Along with the evolution of language — the thousands of neologisms that new technologies and new thinking have brought about, for instance — there has been a concurrent, if perhaps less recognizable, devolution of language. The English language has become more precise for some users of it while becoming more plodding for others. Not a small part of this new cumbrousness is due to the loss of distinctions between words, the misuse of words, and other abuses of language.

That a U.S. presidential candidate can cry *Is our children learning*, an admired basketball star can use the word *conversate*, a well-known college professor can say *vociferous* when he means *voracious*, and another can scold a student for using the word *juggernaut* because she believes it means *jigaboo* is disturbing. *The Vocabula Review* strives to combat the degradation of our language.

Equally important, we celebrate its opulence and its elegance. The English language is wonderfully expressive and infinitely flexible. There are many thousands of words and many hundreds of ways in which to use them. *The Vocabula Review* seeks to promote the richness of our language.

In sum, *TVR* battles nonstandard, careless English and embraces clear, expressive English. We hope we can encourage our readers to do as much.

Why not take a look?

*The Vocabula Review*:
www.vocabula.com

*To Brad and Bruce — the one as accomplished and caring as the other*

# CONTENTS

Words are like leaves; and where they most abound,
Much fruit of sense beneath is rarely found.

ALEXANDER POPE, Essay on Criticism


Polonius: What do you read, my lord?
Hamlet: Words, words, words.

WILLIAM SHAKESPEARE, Hamlet, act 2, scene 2


A barren superfluity of words.

SIR SAMUEL GARTH, The Dispensary, canto II


Let thy words be few.

ECCLESIASTES

# About This Book

This is a reference book and, like all such books, is meant to be referred to, not read through. Although I've long thought works of reference, dictionaries in particular, to be among the most spellbinding books, I cannot expect everyone to agree.

I do wish, as any writer would, that this were a work of creation instead of compilation; still, whether you refer to or read through the book, it will help you write and speak more clearly.

*The Dictionary of Concise Writing* consists of two parts. In the first part, I suggest how to identify and correct wordiness. The second part of the book is a compilation of several thousand wordy phrases followed by concise alternative expressions and real-world examples. I show each sentence example in its original, wordy version and then in a revised, concise version.

In replacing a wordy phrase by one less wordy or by a single word or in deleting the phrase altogether, I have tried to show how wordiness can encumber clarity and that it can be corrected. The sentence examples have been edited only to remedy the wordiness diagnosed; rarely are they syntactically and stylistically indefectible.

I don't claim that the entries I've compiled are unfailingly inferior to the alternatives I suggest. All the alternatives are merely proposed; they are not inarguable. In your own writing, you may at times find that an alternative suggested here, though less wordy, does not work so well.

Finally, as sole author of this book, I am solely accountable for any errors or, if I may be so charitable, oversights that these pages may hold. Although I have tried to be as thorough as possible and to include as many entries, and alternatives to them, as time would allow, I don't doubt that I have overlooked some. Anyone who finds an error or omission is welcome to share his discovery with me, and in a revised edition, I will gladly include any correction.

ROBERT HARTWELL FISKE
info@vocabula.com

*The Vocabula Review*
www.vocabula.com

# Foreword

In a letter to a twelve-year-old boy, Mark Twain wrote, "I notice you use plain, simple language, short words, and brief sentences. That is the way to write English — it is the modern way and the best way. Stick to it; don't let fluff and flowers and verbosity creep in."

Alas, with most of us, as we grow older, fluff and flowers and verbosity do creep in. Writing today often has too much fat, too little muscle — bulk without strength. Much of what we read these days ranges from slightly flabby to grossly obese. As children we wrote sentences like "See Dick run." As adults, we are more likely to write, "It is imperative that we assiduously observe Richard as he traverses the terrain at an accelerated rate of speed." We gain girth and lose mirth — and so does our prose.

What happens to people's writing in the years between childhood and maturity? For one thing, their reasons for writing change. The child writes for the best of reasons — to tell somebody something that is worth telling. Little Janie Jones wants her friends to know about her dog, Spot. Her only concern is to share her joy that "Spot is the bestest dog in the whole wide world."

Mr. Jones, Janie's dad, also has something worthwhile to write about — his company's new marketing plan, which may or may not be the "bestest" marketing plan in the industry. But his real reason for writing a long memo about the plan is that he wants to be perceived as having had "input" into the plan's development. As he writes, he worries about the impression his writing might make on his colleagues, especially his boss. He chooses his words carefully — the more and the longer, the better. Even if his instinct tells him to write simply, he's afraid to, lest his memo not be taken seriously.

Janie has no such fear. While she uses a simple, clear, unaffected second-grade vocabulary, her dad draws on marketing terms he learned while earning his MBA. Relying heavily on the jargon of his business, he throws in a couple of "viable alternatives," a "new set of parameters," and a "plan for prioritization that should be implemented at this point in time" — the bureaucrat's way to use seventeen letters to write "now." When it's done, he has produced a bloated, tedious, pompous piece of writing full of sound and fury signifying very little.

As Janie grows older, her writing gradually becomes more like her dad's — lacking in warmth, sincerity, and directness. She begins to worry about impressing her classmates and teachers — or even Dad, just as Dad worries about impressing his boss. In junior high, her teacher assigns the class a theme about summer vacation and insists that the composition be at least 800 words. This encourages Janie to use two or three words where one would do the job, to stretch out her composition to the 800-word minimum set by the teacher. So what might have been an interesting, tightly written 500-word piece about a trip to Disney World turns out to be just another example of dull, flabby, padded prose, wheezing away as it lurches uphill.

In addition, Janie and Mr. Jones read so much bloated writing that they start to emulate the style that seems to be the norm. Even if they were fortunate enough to have good writing instruction in school, they allow hard-learned skills to rust. They lose confidence in their ability to write clearly and convincingly. They underestimate the power and grace of the simple, declarative sentence. To get their points across, they resort to the theory that if one word is good, two words must be twice as good.

Far from contributing to the reader's enlightenment, wordiness enshrouds meaning in a fog of confusion. As William Zinsser, the author, teacher, and journalist, wrote in *On Writing Well*, "Writing improves in direct ratio to the things we can keep out of it that shouldn't be there." Cutting the fat is probably the quickest and surest way to improve. No matter how solid is your grasp of grammar, punctuation, spelling, and other fundamentals, you cannot write well unless you train yourself to write with fewer words.

If you want to create fat-free sentences and paragraphs, you will pay heed to Robert Hartwell Fiske's advice throughout the dictionary you are about to explore. He means what he says, and he says what he means. Give this book a chance, and you will, too.

— RICHARD LEDERER

Richard Lederer is the author of more than 2,000 books and articles about language and humor, including *Anguished English* and *The Bride of Anguished English*. Dr. Lederer's syndicated column, "Looking at Language," appears in newspapers and magazines throughout the United States. He is also a language commentator on public radio, and his website, www.verbivore.com, offers many language resources.

# PART 1

# Words and People

# CHAPTER 1

# The Perfectibility of Words

Words are flawed, but they can easily be fixed. Words exist to be thought and then formed, to be written and then revised, and even to be said and then denied. They can be misused and neglected or cared for and corrected.

Inadequate though they may be, words distinguish us from all other living things. Only we humans can reflect on the past and plan for the future; it is language that allows us to do so. Indeed, our worth is partly in our words. Effective use of language — clear writing and speaking — is a measure of our humanness.

When they do their work best, words help people communicate; they promote understanding between people. And this, being well understood, is precisely the goal we should all aspire to when writing and speaking. As obvious as this seems, it is not a goal we commonly achieve.

Words often ill serve their purpose. When they do their work badly, words militate against us. Poor grammar, sloppy syntax, abused words, misspelled words, and other infelicities of style impede communication and advance only misunderstanding. But there is another, perhaps less well-known, obstacle to effective communication: too many words.

We often believe that many words are better than few. Perhaps we imagine that the more we say, the more we know or the more others will think we know, or that the more obscure our writing is, the more profound our thoughts are. Seldom, of course, is this so. Wordiness is arguably the biggest obstacle to clear writing and speaking. But it is also more than that.

■ *Wordiness is an obstacle to success.* Almost all professional people know that success in business partly depends on good communications skills, on writing and speaking clearly and persuasively. Businesspeople who cannot express themselves well are often at a disadvantage in the corporate world.

■ *Wordiness is an obstacle to companionship.* Few of us enjoy being with someone who speaks incessantly or incoherently. Wordiness in others may make us impatient; it may annoy us, and we may think it rude. Worse than that, when we have difficulty understanding someone, sooner or later we may not care what it is that he tries to convey. We lose interest in what a person says and, ultimately, in who a person is.

■ *Wordiness is an obstacle to self-knowledge.* A superfluity of words conceals more than it reveals. We need time to be silent and still, time to reflect on the past and think about the future; without it, no one is knowable.

Wordiness is an obstacle to these goals and others. Whatever your profession, whatever your personality, wordiness is a condition for which we all should seek a cure.

# Of polish and panache

Usually, in reading someone's writing, we see more words than we need to, and in listening to someone speak, we hear more words than we care to. For example, how often have you heard someone say *at this juncture* or, worse still, *at this moment in the history of my life* when a simple *now* would serve? These two phrases are flawed; they are two and eight words longer than they need be. The extra words are not needed to convey the thought; in truth, they interfere with the conveyance of thought.

These are but two of the wordy phrases that we overindulge in when writing and speaking. Though it may be hard to fathom, the English language contains thousands of wordy phrases that dull our understanding of and interest in whatever is being expressed.

Wordiness is a flaw of style — in how we express our language.

Today, the style is prevailingly shoddy. In almost everything we read and hear, there is complexity instead of simplicity and obscurity instead of clarity. This is particularly inexcusable in written material, where words can be reworked.

Few of us write well effortlessly. Typically, we have a thought, and then we write it down in whatever form it first occurred to us. Looking at our sentence further, though, we are usually able to improve on it. By reducing the number of words in a phrase, substituting a single word for a phrase, or deleting extraneous words or phrases, we are able to polish our sentence, to simplify and clarify our thought.

## Reducing the number of words in a phrase

■ *The real test, however, lies in* _the degree to which_ *the man's performance at his regular job improves.*

*The real test, however, lies in* _how much_ *the man's performance at his regular job improves.*

■ _Insofar as_ *the implementation of bank projects* _is concerned_, *the situation is going back to normal.*

_As for_ *the implementation of bank projects, the situation is going back to normal.*

■ *There is no* _evidence to support that_ *those new mortgages are any more likely to default than those insured by F.H.A. under current law.*

*There is no* _evidence that_ *those new mortgages are any more likely to default than those insured by F.H.A. under current law.*

■ *The MWRA's decision will allow it to* _concentrate its energies on_ *rebuilding the region's water and sewer systems.*

*The MWRA's decision will allow it to* _concentrate on_ *rebuilding the region's water and sewer systems.*

## Substituting a single word for a phrase

■ *The practice* _is in violation of_ *perjury laws requiring candidates to attest that every signature was signed in person.*

*The practice* _violates_ *perjury laws requiring candidates to attest that every signature was signed in person.*

■ *Despite the fact that Hanson PLC has revenues of over $12 billion, its corporate staff is exceedingly lean.*

*Although Hanson PLC has revenues of over $12 billion, its corporate staff is exceedingly lean.*

■ *I think to a large extent this kind of problem is a function of our society's inability to talk about sexuality in a reasonable way.*

*I think this kind of problem is largely a function of our society's inability to talk about sexuality in a reasonable way.*

■ *We're talking about a sports anchor who stands to make in the neighborhood of a half million bucks a year.*

*We're talking about a sports anchor who stands to make around a half million bucks a year.*

# Deleting extraneous words or phrases

■ *The more sophisticated savings institutions were located in places like Boston, New York, and Los Angeles.*

*The more sophisticated savings institutions were in places like Boston, New York, and Los Angeles.*

■ *He or she must develop strategies to resolve potentially disruptive or dysfunctional conflict situations.*

*He or she must develop strategies to resolve potentially disruptive or dysfunctional conflicts.*

■ *The Japanese government is not supplying much in the way of guidance concerning comparative advantages involved in investments in particular countries.*

*The Japanese government is not supplying much guidance concerning comparative advantages involved in investments in particular countries.*

■ *There are a large number of applications that involve manipulating uncertain knowledge.*

*A large number of applications involve manipulating uncertain knowledge.*

A further benefit of applying some polish, of expressing ourselves more concisely, is that mistakes in grammar and word usage often are corrected as well. For example, we *compare* one person or thing *to* or *with* another, not *against* or *versus* another. The correct phrase is *compare to* or *compare with*, not *compare against* or *compare versus*; *to* and *with* both have one syllable fewer than *against* and *versus*. Fewer syllables count; life is short.

■ *The investigators will analyze the new data and <u>compare</u> them <u>against</u> computer models in an effort to link unequivocally the Arctic's perturbed chemistry to its ozone loss.*

*The investigators will analyze the new data and <u>compare</u> them <u>with</u> computer models in an effort to link unequivocally the Arctic's perturbed chemistry to its ozone loss.*

Likewise, the correct expression is *center on*, not *center around*.

■ *Much of their behavior <u>centers around</u> doing things to please others in an attempt to earn approval.*

*Much of their behavior <u>centers on</u> doing things to please others in an attempt to earn approval.*

And the analphabetic *that way there* and *this way here* are correct only without the *there* and *here*.

■ *<u>That way there</u>, I won't have to worry about someone hitting my car.*

*<u>That way</u>, I won't have to worry about someone hitting my car.*

But there are more telling examples.
Say *the reason is* or simply *because* instead of *the reason is because*, and you are at once concise and correct.

■ *A common <u>reason</u> people join groups <u>is because</u> they work near one another.*

*A common <u>reason</u> people join groups <u>is</u> they work near one another.*

■ *The reason* you explore what-ifs sequentially *is because few* solutions to business problems can be achieved by making a single change.

You explore what-ifs sequentially *because few* solutions to business problems can be achieved by making a single change.

The familiar *but rather* or *but instead* is also solecistic. Use *but* or *rather* or *instead*, for each alone does the job.

■ *It was not lack of sales that led to the downsizing of the project but rather the delays caused by a turnover of contractors.*

*It was not lack of sales that led to the downsizing of the project but the delays caused by a turnover of contractors.*

■ *Ericsson has not reduced its investments in the data processing field, but it has, instead, obtained greater resources with which to further develop and strengthen the advanced DP technology that constitutes its communications systems.*

*Ericsson has not reduced its investments in the data processing field; instead, it has obtained greater resources with which to further develop and strengthen the advanced DP technology that constitutes its communications systems.*

One final example is using *for example, for instance, like,* or *such as* along with *and others, and so forth, and so on, and such, and the like, et al.,* or *etc.* You don't need both sets of expressions to convey your meaning; use one or the other.

■ *These codes are used to change formats, for example, fonts, printer colors, etc.*

*These codes are used to change formats, for example, fonts and printer colors.*

■ *We have to give it the serious attention that we give illicit drugs such as heroin, cocaine, and so on.*

*We have to give it the serious attention that we give illicit drugs — heroin, cocaine, and so on.*

I grumble about grammar because mistakes in it invariably vitiate one's style of writing and, like wordiness, often arrest the reader's flow of thought.

A good writing style starts with polish, but it does not stop with it. Style must also have presence and personality. Along with polish, then, a writing style would be a good deal improved by panache, which is as creative as polish is corrective. Panache means writing with variety as well as with balance, writing heedful of sound as well as of sense, and writing interestingly as well as enthusiastically. All this is panache, and it is far more than this.

With a dollop of polish and a dash of panache our words will approach perfection.

# Clues to concision

There are several clues to realizing a clear and concise writing style. By being vigilant, that is, by rereading and rewriting your material, you will become increasingly adept at identifying superfluous words.

Further, the more words you know and have at your command, the more concise you can be. You will repeatedly discover, in the definition of one word, two or three others that you may have faithfully relied on to express a thought. For example, *like* means *in the same way that*, *never* means *under no conditions*, *halve* means *cut in half*, *share* means *have in common*, *with* means *in the company of*, and *cynosure* means *center of attention*. By becoming well acquainted with the meanings of words, you will see that a single word often says as much as a string of words.

The key is to question. Ask yourself whether each word in every sentence that you write is needed. More than that, is it vital? Does it contribute to or interfere with the meaning of your sentence? Does it add anything to your meaning that another, perhaps adjacent, word does not?

Eventually, this constant questioning becomes second nature. Not only will you start writing better, you will start speaking better. As you question, be especially aware of phrases containing prepositions, verbs, and nouns and of extraneous adjectives and adverbs. Euphemisms, circumlocutions, clichés, idioms, and polysyllables are also frequent offenders.

## Preposition phrases

All preposition phrases are suspect, particularly those longer than two words. A preposition phrase usually can be reduced to a single word or deleted altogether. We depend on these three- and four-word preposition phrases because we are unfamiliar with the meanings of so many one-word prepositions.

Consider a few examples.

■ *Over the duration of the project, we expect there will be some disruption due to noise, dirt, and dust.*

*Over the duration of* is one of those four-word preposition phrases; it is an excrescence. *During* is all that is needed.

■ *As a result of last year's ONA process, a host of new network services will become available to providers of enhanced services in the very near future.*

*In the very near future* is certainly a murky preposition phrase. Far better is the more clear *soon* or *shortly.*

■ *I think it is premature to relinquish our destiny to the hands of fate, for indeed much progress has been made in the past, and much more is still possible in the future.*

*In the past,* like *in the future,* is often needlessly used. The context of the sentence usually makes the tense clear.

■ *We have used the MSE and the RMSE for the purpose of measuring how much fluctuation remains after a model has been built.*

*For the purpose of -ing* is unpardonably wordy. Use the simpler *to.*

■ *In the event that you are not sure whether a particular problem is an emergency, we encourage you to call the Plan for advice.*

*In the event that* usually can be reduced to *if* or *should.*

■ *We should be moving in the direction of finding psychotherapeutic measures to help correct this sexual disorder whenever the patient wishes it to be corrected.*

*In the direction of* means *toward* in this sentence though the phrase also can mean a monosyllabic *on, to,* or *with.*

■ *You can even set these switches in such a way that the RAM area can be read from but not written to.*

*In such a way that* is a long-winded way of saying *so* or *so that.*

■ *There are a number of theories as to how firm value is affected by a firm's capital structure design.*

As to, like *as regards, in relation to, with reference to,* and other equally dull devices, usually means an unadorned *about, for, in, of,* or *on.*

# Verb phrases

Many verb phrases are redundant. In these phrases, two words (generally, a verb followed by a noun) do the work of one (the noun made into a verb).

Consider the following examples.

### *to arrive at, to come to,* and *to reach* phrases

■ *Space probers are reluctantly reaching the conclusion that there is little likelihood that intelligent life is out there in the empty spaces beyond our solar system.*

*Space probers are reluctantly concluding that there is little likelihood that intelligent life is out there in the empty spaces beyond our solar system.*

■ *Several economists predict that the expansion will come to an end in what is now its seventh year.*

*Several economists predict that the expansion will end in what is now its seventh year.*

### *to be* phrases

■ *He is lacking in sensitivity.*

*He lacks sensitivity.*

■ *Unlike computers, which depended on the Cold War and the space race for the funds that drove their development, U.S. biotech is dependent on the flow of various health-care payment streams.*

*Unlike computers, which depended on the Cold War and the space race for the funds that drove their development, U.S. biotech depends on the flow of various health-care payment streams.*

## *to express* and *to voice* phrases

■ *In one letter, dated June 15, 1892, Cather <u>expresses regret</u> that friendships between women are looked upon as unnatural.*

In one letter, dated June 15, 1892, Cather <u>regrets</u> that friendships between women are looked upon as unnatural.

■ *The government of Israel <u>voiced disapproval of</u> the decision.*

The government of Israel <u>disapproved of</u> the decision.

## *to give* phrases

■ *The rest of the equation is to give people from diverse backgrounds a chance <u>to give expression to</u> their different views of the world.*

The rest of the equation is to give people from diverse backgrounds a chance <u>to express</u> their different views of the world.

■ *The continuing strong demand for our products and improving trends in component costs <u>give us encouragement</u> that this will be another year of significant growth in revenues and earnings.*

The continuing strong demand for our products and improving trends in component costs <u>encourage us</u> that this will be another year of significant growth in revenues and earnings.

## *to have* phrases

■ *This measure <u>has the appearance of</u> reasonableness, but its application would have to be monitored to make sure it did not induce high turnovers by employers to cut labor costs.*

This measure <u>appears</u> reasonable, but its application would have to be monitored to make sure it did not induce high turnovers by employers to cut labor costs.

■ *Any disruption of normal computer operations may <u>have a considerable impact on</u> the running of the business.*

*Any disruption of normal computer operations may <u>considerably impact</u> the running of the business.*

## to *make* phrases

■ *The code is moved into place by <u>making use of</u> the system Monitor block move subroutine, MOVE.*

*The code is moved into place by <u>using</u> the system Monitor block move subroutine, MOVE.*

■ *The column does not <u>make a distinction</u> between having chronic pain as a symptom and being a "chronic pain patient," that is, having a chronic pain syndrome.*

*The column does not <u>distinguish</u> between having chronic pain as a symptom and being a "chronic pain patient," that is, having a chronic pain syndrome.*

## to *place* and to *put* phrases

■ *As a result, the women's groups now <u>put heavy emphasis on</u> fielding candidates for open seats and on identifying incumbents who might be vulnerable.*

*As a result, the women's groups now <u>heavily emphasize</u> fielding candidates for open seats and identifying incumbents who might be vulnerable.*

■ *Excess supply within the next few years would <u>place pressure on</u> the cartel to maintain production restraint and keep average prices low.*

*Excess supply within the next few years would <u>pressure</u> the cartel to maintain production restraint and keep average prices low.*

## to *present*, to *provide*, and to *show* phrases

■ *The final section of the chapter <u>provides an explanation of</u> how to use most of MathCAD's more popular features.*

*The final section of the chapter explains how to use most of MathCAD's more popular features.*

■ *The middle third of the screen shows a listing of the jobs waiting to be printed.*

*The middle third of the screen lists the jobs waiting to be printed.*

## *to take* phrases

■ *I would like to take this opportunity to thank all of you who aided my candidacy.*

*I would like to thank all of you who aided my candidacy.*

■ *Their forecasts are best prepared when they take the functional area forecasts into consideration.*

*Their forecasts are best prepared when they consider the functional area forecasts.*

# Noun phrases

These are flaccid phrases that often begin with *a* or *the* followed by a noun and end with *of*. They can easily be made firm, as the following examples show.

## *(a; the) -ance of* and *(a; the) -ence of* phrases

■ *Maintenance of this flow is assured by their willingness to rubber-stamp the decisions of their benefactor.*

*Maintaining this flow is assured by their willingness to rubber-stamp the decisions of their benefactor.*

■ *When a number of investment proposals perform essentially the same function so that the acceptance of one proposal necessarily means rejecting the others, we are dealing with mutually exclusive investments.*

*When a number of investment proposals perform essentially the same* *function so that <u>accepting</u> one proposal necessarily means rejecting the others, we are dealing with mutually exclusive investments.*

## *(a; the) -sion of* and *(a; the) -tion of* phrases

■ *<u>The inclusion of</u> families is crucial if nurses are to become a source of help rather than an addition to families' difficulties.*

*<u>Including</u> families is crucial if nurses are to become a source of help rather than an addition to families' difficulties.*

■ *<u>The installation</u> and testing <u>of</u> a new product, <u>the conversion of</u> user files, and training users are not small matters.*

*<u>Installing</u> and testing a new product, <u>converting</u> user files, and training users are not small matters.*

## *(a; the) -ment of* phrases

■ *For more than a decade, Motorola invested in <u>the development</u> and marketing <u>of</u> cellular systems and phones around the world.*

*For more than a decade, Motorola invested in <u>developing</u> and marketing cellular systems and phones around the world.*

■ *To the masses, a good government is one that prevents the strong from exploiting the weak, which is best done by <u>the punishment of</u> transgression.*

*To the masses, a good government is one that prevents the strong from exploiting the weak, which is best done by <u>punishing</u> transgression.*

## *(a; the) -ing of* phrases

■ *Personal computers were meant to give people more flexibility in <u>the processing of</u> information.*

*Personal computers were meant to give people more flexibility in <u>processing</u> information.*

■ *Organizing at the middle level means <u>the making of</u> specific adjust-*

*ments in the organizational structure and <u>the allocating of</u> the resources acquired by top management.*

*Organizing at the middle level means <u>making</u> specific adjustments in the organizational structure and <u>allocating</u> the resources acquired by top management.*

## (a; the) ... of phrases

■ *You have to deal with <u>the issues of</u> betrayal, anger, rejection — all these things.*

*You have to deal with betrayal, anger, rejection — all these things.*

■ *In other situations, <u>the practice of</u> rotating managers of work teams on a normal schedule can stimulate a group.*

*In other situations, rotating managers of work teams on a normal schedule can stimulate a group.*

# Adjectives and adverbs

By coupling adjectives and adverbs to perfectly good nouns, verbs, or adjectives, we often diminish the force and effectiveness of our writing. Powerful writing is taut; it admits no weak word, no superfluous adjective or adverb. Consider these examples.

## active; actively

■ *Individual managers need to be <u>actively</u> involved in the human resource planning process.*

*Individual managers need to be involved in the human resource planning process.*

■ *Suicide attempts by hospitalized patients with "do not resuscitate" orders on their medical charts should be met by <u>active</u> resuscitation efforts unless recovery is unlikely.*

*Suicide attempts by hospitalized patients with "do not resuscitate" orders on their medical charts should be met by resuscitation efforts unless recovery is unlikely.*

## actual; actually; real; really

■ Ideas are exchanged, but there is no _real_ closure or plan of action.

Ideas are exchanged, but there is no closure or plan of action.

■ My sense is that there is some interest, though it's too early to say how many companies will _actually_ submit bids to set up demonstration projects.

My sense is that there is some interest, though it's too early to say how many companies will submit bids to set up demonstration projects.

## total; totally; whole; wholly

■ I was _totally_ overwhelmed by their generosity.

I was overwhelmed by their generosity.

■ The _whole_ color-coding idea is perfect for marketing the books.

The color-coding idea is perfect for marketing the books.

There are other examples: _full potential_ says no more than _potential_ does alone; _completely eliminate_ no more than _eliminate_; _possibly may_ no more than _may_; _close scrutiny_ no more than _scrutiny_; _excruciatingly painful_ no more than _excruciating_; _firm commitment_ no more than _commitment_; and _exactly identical_ no more than _identical_.

# Other common phrases to watch for
## back with _refer, repay, return, revert,_ and the like

■ The second section of the booklet, while occasionally _referring back_ to ideas discussed in the first section, is more or less independent.

The second section of the booklet, while occasionally _referring_ to ideas discussed in the first section, is more or less independent.

■ Type the new text, and then press Return to _return_ the cursor _back_ to the left margin.

*Type the new text, and then press Return to <u>return</u> the cursor to the left margin.*

## *mutual* with *and, between, both, two,* and the like

■ *I think this is <u>mutually</u> beneficial to <u>both</u> sides.*

*I think this is beneficial to <u>both</u> sides.*

■ *The receiver must share in these responsibilities if the <u>two</u> parties are to arrive at a <u>mutual</u> understanding.*

*The receiver must share in these responsibilities if the <u>two</u> parties are to arrive at an understanding.*

## *old* with *adage, cliché, maxim, proverb, saying,* and the like

■ *Children, according to the <u>old adage</u>, are to be seen, not heard.*

*Children, according to the <u>adage</u>, are to be seen, not heard.*

■ *You may have heard the <u>old saying</u>, "the best laid plans of mice and men often go astray."*

*You may have heard the <u>saying</u>, "the best laid plans of mice and men often go astray."*

## *past, previous,* or *prior* with *experience, history,* and the like

■ *From <u>previous experience</u>, we know that a compiler will find many typographical errors.*

*From <u>experience</u>, we know that a compiler will find many typographical errors.*

■ *<u>Past history</u> is full of people who didn't fit in and were left as outcasts.*

*<u>History</u> is full of people who didn't fit in and were left as outcasts.*

### *record* with *all-time, high, new,* and the like

■ *"Knots Landing" has been on for nine years, the <u>all-time record</u> among prime-time soaps.*

*"Knots Landing" has been on for nine years, the <u>record</u> among prime-time soaps.*

■ *The number of days in the 90s in Boston and Washington may set a <u>record high</u>.*

*The number of days in the 90s in Boston and Washington may set a <u>record</u>.*

### *relatively* with *compared (contrasted) to (with), in comparison to, in relation to, relative to,* and the like

■ *Although my proposal has one disadvantage, it is a <u>relatively</u> insignificant one <u>compared to</u> its many advantages.*

*Although my proposal has one disadvantage, it is an insignificant one <u>compared to</u> its many advantages.*

■ *It's a better measure because the nature of many businesses means that earnings may be <u>relatively</u> small <u>in comparison to</u> the overall cash generated.*

*It's a better measure because the nature of many businesses means that earnings may be small <u>in comparison to</u> the overall cash generated.*

### *separate* with *apart, distinct, entity, independent,* and the like

■ *The public permitting process was <u>separate and distinct</u> from the landlord's approval rights under the contract.*

*The public permitting process was <u>separate</u> from the landlord's approval rights under the contract.*

■ *In the biological world, there are many instances in which the same adaptation has evolved separately and independently.*

*In the biological world, there are many instances in which the same adaptation has evolved independently.*

## *together* with *combine, group, join, link,* and the like

■ *Its many parts are linked together by computers and can respond to changing needs more quickly than their aging counterparts.*

*Its many parts are linked by computers and can respond to changing needs more quickly than their aging counterparts.*

■ *We're thousands of Americans who have joined together to lower our cost of living and live better on the money we earn.*

*We're thousands of Americans who have joined to lower our cost of living and live better on the money we earn.*

# Euphemisms

Euphemisms are inoffensive or tasteful words and phrases that we use in place of offensive or distasteful ones. Many well-known euphemisms deal with sex or death, topics long thought too delicate for candor. Other euphemisms, less well known, are expressions of politeness or deception. Euphemisms also mask disagreeable situations. It sounds better, for example, for a company to speak of *downsizing* or, even, *rightsizing* than it does for them to speak of *laying off* or *firing* employees. During wars or dubious governmental policies, euphemisms abound, like *pacification* for *killing, collateral damage* for *wounding* or *killing civilians,* and *ethnic cleansing* for *genocide.* At other times, euphemisms are less recognizable, but only because we are less watchful.

Consider these euphemisms.

| Instead of | Use |
|---|---|
| *advanced in years* | *old* |
| *comfort facilities* | *bathroom* |
| *correctional facility* | *prison* |
| *economic adjustments* | *price hikes* |
| *involuntary severance* | *layoff* |

| | |
|---|---|
| *loss prevention specialist* | *security guard* |
| *no longer with us* | *dead* |
| *put to sleep* | *destroy* |
| *revenue enhancements* | *taxes* |
| *seminal fluid* | *semen* |
| *succumb to injuries* | *die* |
| *unpleasant arousal* | *depression* |

# Circumlocutions

Circumlocutions are roundabout words and phrases. Often they are simply indirect expressions that say in several words what one or two ably would. Occasionally, however, circumlocutions are used to evade an issue. When people do not want to commit themselves to a cause, or when they do not want to be held accountable for either supporting or not supporting a position, they hedge by using ambiguous words. Circumlocutions may mean something far different from what almost anyone would imagine.

Consider these circumlocutions.

| **Instead of** | **Use** |
|---|---|
| *a limited number* | *one* |
| *an overwhelming majority of* | *most* |
| *a significant proportion of* | *some* |
| *a sizable percentage of* | *many* |
| *in the near future* | *soon* |
| *is at variance with* | *differs from* |
| *is of the opinion* | *believes* |
| *make a statement saying* | *say* |
| *on more than one occasion* | *three times* |
| *over the long term* | *ultimately* |
| *to a certain extent* | *in part* |
| *to a large degree* | *largely* |

# Clichés

We should never become too attached to a term for fear that it be reduced to a cliché. Once people start using a word or phrase excessively, its meaning is blunted and its usefulness lost. Clichés are words or phrases that no longer effectively express thought or sentiment.

Consider these clichés.

| Instead of | Use |
|---|---|
| cautiously optimistic | optimistic |
| consensus of opinion | consensus |
| fear and trembling | dread |
| fly in the face of | defy |
| for all intents and purposes | virtually |
| goes to show | proves |
| in a timely fashion | promptly |
| it is imperative that | must |
| kinder and gentler | humane |
| par for the course | typical |
| sick and tired | annoyed |
| window of opportunity | opportunity |

## Idioms

An idiom is an expression that, on the surface, makes little, if any, sense. An idiom's literal meaning, even if decipherable, is frequently different from its actual meaning. Unlike euphemisms and clichés, which usually should be shunned, many popular idioms have their place in the language. Although idioms often say clearly and cleverly what other words cannot, many are wordy expressions that we can find a more economical phrase or particular word for.

Consider these idioms.

| Instead of | Use |
|---|---|
| as a matter of fact | in fact |
| before long | soon |
| day in and day out | every day |
| high and mighty | arrogant |
| in a nutshell | briefly |
| in place of | for |
| on the part of | by |
| put on an act | pretend |
| take exception | object |
| take offense to | resent |
| the long and the short | the gist |

## Polysyllables

The more words you know and can correctly use, the wider your knowledge and understanding of the world and of yourself. Still, there are polysyllabic words that we can, without fear of unrefine-

35

ment, do well without.
Consider these polysyllables.

| Instead of | Use |
| --- | --- |
| *effectuate* | *effect* |
| *eventuality* | *event* |
| *indebtedness* | *debt* |
| *materialize* | *happen* |
| *methodology* | *method* |
| *multiplicity* | *many* |
| *necessitate* | *require* |
| *parameter* | *limit* |
| *remunerate* | *pay* |
| *terminate* | *end* |

## Couples

A couple is two words, on either side of *and*, that have but one meaning. We often feel that two words do the job twice as well as one, that in a couple, the second word reinforces the first. In truth, the second word enfeebles the first. The English language contains scores of couples, and most of them should never have met.
Consider these couples.

| Instead of | Use |
| --- | --- |
| *aid and abet* | *aid* or *abet* |
| *compare and contrast* | *compare* or *contrast* |
| *fair and equitable* | *fair* or *equitable* |
| *first and foremost* | *first* or *foremost* |
| *new and innovative* | *new* or *innovative* |
| *null and void* | *null* or *void* |
| *one and only* | *one* or *only* |
| *peace and quiet* | *peace* or *quiet* |
| *pick and choose* | *pick* or *choose* |
| *plain and simple* | *plain* or *simple* |
| *rules and regulations* | *rules* or *regulations* |
| *various and sundry* | *various* or *sundry* |

## Embarrassments

Embarrassments are found more often in speech than in writing. Of course, these expressions are more embarrassing to the listener than the speaker, who were he embarrassed, wouldn't say them. Embarrassments are best abolished.

Consider these embarrassments.

| **Instead of** | **Use** |
| --- | --- |
| *and everything* | delete |
| *and stuff like that* | delete |
| *anyway* | delete |
| *hopefully* | *I hope* |
| *how's it going?* | *hello* |
| *humongous* | *huge* |
| *I'll tell you* | delete |
| *I mean* | delete |
| *kind of thing* | delete |
| *most definitely* | *yes* |
| *or something* | delete |
| *you know?* | delete |

# Chapter 2

# The Imperfectibility of People

As the several thousand entries in *The Dictionary of Concise Writing* suggest, wordiness is a problem — an omnipresent problem. Though a contagion that nearly all of us suffer from, businesspeople, lawyers, politicians, journalists, and academics seem unusually afflicted with wordiness.

## Wordiness everywhere

### Business jargon

In a survey, 503 top executives at leading U.S. manufacturing and service firms reported that two-thirds of their entry-level managers and professionals wrote unclearly. Entry level or top level, it seems to matter not.

Consider this diffuse phrasing from the president and CEO of a bank, from whom we should expect a style more stately.

> *We've enclosed an informative brochure that includes a map and information on the changes occurring February 17. As you will note, you can continue banking just as you have in the past. There is no action required on your part.*

*Informative* and *information* are redundant, *in the past* is superfluous with *as you have*, and *There is no action required on your part* is much inferior to, for example, *You need do nothing.*

From a real-estate professional, we have this unwieldy wording.

*I'm under the impression, due to the fact that I've not heard from the main office, that your application has been accepted.*

Had this person written *I believe* instead of *I'm under the impression that* and *since* instead of *due to the fact that*, we might have a bit more confidence in his abilities.

Consider this sentence from a letter written by the president of a business.

*The employees of Flagship Press thank you in advance for your past, present, and future business and support.*

The phrase *thank you in advance* is an offensive one, but used in this typically "businesslike" sentence, it is altogether nescient; *thank you for your business and support* would do.

Here is an "explanation" from a credit card company.

*The Minimum Payment Due each month shall be reduced by the amounts paid in excess of the Minimum Payment Due during the previous three months which have not already been so applied in determining the Minimum Payment Due in such earlier months, unless you have exceeded your line of credit or have paid the entire New Balance shown on your billing statement.*

This language is so laborious to understand that many people simply wouldn't bother to try; they would disregard it. Of course, the purpose of a statement like this is less to lucidly convey a policy than to legally protect a company.

Consider this artful sentence from the chairman and CEO of a well-known consulting firm.

*Management, with the participation and concurrence of key professional staff, has determined that we can best serve our shareowners and ourselves by resisting temptation to pursue all of the interesting challenges we are equipped to handle.*

This is typical business bombast. It sounds fairly good, and it is meant to (coming as it does from an annual report). But as is often so in business, sound precedes sense. Though phrases like *participation and concurrence, key professional staff, resisting temptation,* and *all of the interesting challenges we are equipped to handle* may to shareholders sound sweet, the sentence means no more than

*We will focus on only some areas of our expertise.*

Among the verbose phrases valued by those in the business world are *a high level of, component part, course of action, from the standpoint of, game plan, have an impact on, in a timely fashion, in the not-too-distant future, is in receipt of, plan of action, please be advised that, prioritize, time frame, valuable asset,* and *window of opportunity.*

## Legalese

The language of the law is often complicated and unintelligible, but it could be made less so if lawyers would only choose to communicate with laymen in fewer words and syllables.

*Neither party to this Agreement nor any persons to whom either party has disclosed the Proprietary Information pursuant to this paragraph shall disclose the Proprietary Information to any persons, or permit any person access to the Proprietary Information, or use the Proprietary Information or permit it to be used, directly or indirectly, for their own account, or for the account of another, or make any copy of the Proprietary Information without the express prior written consent in each instance of the party from whom it originated, with such consent being granted only by an individual with the capacity to authorize copying, except that each party may disclose and grant access to the Proprietary Information to those members of its staff who (a) need such access in order to effectuate the Arrangement and (b) have agreed not to further disclose or allow access to the Proprietary Information, and not to use it or permit it to be used, directly or indirectly for their own account or for the account of another, but to safeguard the Proprietary Information and treat it as the highly confidential, proprietary and trade secret property of the other party and to use it only to effectuate the Arrangement and only so long as the Arrangement remains in effect.*

And that's just one sentence. Here are several shorter, though no less bewildering, illustrations of lawyers' language.

*This Agreement shall inure to the benefit of the Agent's successors and assigns, and it shall be binding upon Author's successors, assigns, executors, administrators, heirs, and legal representatives.*

Boilerplate like this invariably contains the grandiloquent *inure to the benefit of*; lawyers should one day learn that *inure to* says no less.

*The trust has agreed that in the event the advisory agreement between the investment adviser and the trust is terminated, or if the affiliation between the investment adviser and its parent company is terminated, the trust will eliminate the name "Allstate" from its name if the investment adviser or its parent company so request.*

Legal phraseology frequently is exposed for what it truly is by those who write it. Here the phrase *in the event* in the first line means simply *if*, as the *if* in the second line makes plain.

Lawyers, too, have their preferred wording: *compensate, effectuate, expeditiously, in accordance with, in consideration of, in force and effect, in perpetuity, in the absence of, necessitate, notwithstanding, pursuant to, save and except, subsequent to,* and *until such time as.*

## Political cant

In a poll of 1,513 adults, 70 percent of the respondents considered politicians "not so good" or "poor." The prevailing view was that most politicians make campaign promises they do not intend to fulfill, will lie if the truth would hurt them politically, and are mainly concerned with holding on to power.

Indeed, it is often in the interest of politicians and government officials to conceal their true thoughts from us. Consider this prize display of evasiveness by a political aide to a city mayor.

*I confirm that I said it, but I will neither confirm nor deny that I meant it.*

Of saying as little as possible with as many words as possible, this phrasing by a high-ranking military official is paradigmatic.

*We will benefit from the experience that we've already had about how to implement that, and learning from the lessons of the past in terms of what we've already done.*

Or consider this wording by top presidential aide, the meaning of which is meant to elude us all.

*I think what's important to point out there is that they said they found no evidence of wrongdoing on my part and certainly nothing that indicated anything that he said with evidence to anything that I've done.*

Equally unsettling is how politicians are forever devising new expressions or redefining old ones to serve their own interests. *"I misspoke,"* explained the politico when the committee asked about his stated opinion on abortion.

**mis•speak** (mis spek') *vt., vi. -spoke', -spok'en, -speak'ing* to speak or say incorrectly; *to lie.*

The danger here is that the euphemism will become synonymous with the word it is used for. When a word like *misspeak* is used euphemistically for a word like *lie*, we must all loudly complain. Lest euphemisms become synonyms, dictionaries become undone, and minds become mangled, we must all complain.

There are other illustrations of euphemism; for example, the wordy *it remains to be seen* and *that's an open question*, favored by politicians and their sort, so often truly mean the inadmissible *I don't know.*

Allied to euphemism is circumlocution, another stratagem that politicians depend on.

*The senator, who once was seen as wavering, says he now "is support-ive of the president's nominee" for secretary of defense.*

The verb phrase *is supportive of* is less binding than the verb *supports* and nicely serves the senator his equivocal purpose. Verb phrases are more wordy than verbs, so it seems as though more is being said, but they are less direct and less meaningful. Deception requires more words than truthfulness.

Consider, too, this ineffectual phrasing by a government bureaucrat.

*It remains my hope and cautiously optimistic expectation that neces-sary legislation may be enacted prior to October 1.*

The phrase *hope and expectation* is redundant, but to qualify *expec-tation* with *cautiously optimistic* is witless. Moreover, *cautiously opti-mistic* — one of officialdom's favorite phrases — is oxymoronic. But it is surely the incongruity of the words that so appeals to politicians; juxtaposed, they mean nothing, and politicians generally prefer say-ing nothing to saying something. Still uneasy with his pronounce-ment, the bureaucrat further tempers it with the *may* preceding *be enacted.* He might have written his words more capably had he used fewer of them.

*I expect legislation will be enacted before October 1.*

## Journalese

If politicians are attached to euphemism and circumlocution, journalists are surely attached to cliché and slang: *bear a striking resemblance to, despite the fact that, express concern, in connection with, in the meantime, in the midst of, in the wake of, on the condition that, on the part of, on the verge of, stand in sharp contrast to,* and *the vast majority of* are a few of their frightful phrases.

Moreover, despite the confines of their columns, newspaper and magazine writers have yet to learn much about using the shorter phrase or the single word.

> *Oftentimes, the Senate, as well as the White House, struggles with questions involving what is now being described as lifestyle. The problem is that, in effect, the Senate and the White House sometimes are being asked to put their stamp of approval on lifestyles that, while acceptable in Washington, are not acceptable by general standards elsewhere.*

If we change *oftentimes* to *often, as well as* to *and, involving what is now being described as* to *of,* the Senate and the White House to *both,* put their stamp of approval on to *approve,* and *by general standards* to *generally* and delete *in effect* and *being,* we lose two lines of text but not a word of meaning.

> *Often, the Senate and the White House struggle with questions of lifestyle. The problem is that both sometimes are asked to approve lifestyles that, while acceptable in Washington, are not generally acceptable elsewhere.*

Journalists furnish their newspapers and magazines with quantities of verbiage. Here, though, are just a few more examples.

> *Lack of experience on the part of the firm is also a source of delay and difficulty.*

*Lack of experience* would be better phrased as *the inexperience,* and *on the part of* as, simply, *of.*

> *If sea levels rise to the extent that scientists predict, the Marshall Islands, which are composed of two chains of coral islands rising no more than 5 feet above the sea, would be submerged.*

A more careful journalist might have written *as much as* instead of *to the extent that,* and *comprise* instead of *are composed of.*

*In the course of the debate, legislators complained that the vote was futile, because the governor had the power to freeze spending regardless of what legislators did.*

*In the course of* can be replaced by *during*, and *regardless of what* by *despite what*.

*The law created the Occupational Safety and Health Administration, a federal agency charged with the responsibility of ensuring the safety of workers.*

The phrase *charged with the responsibility of* is repetitious; either *charged with* or *responsible for* is enough.

## Academicspeak

Another area known for its reliance on jargon and gibberish is academia. Academics (especially social scientists, administrators, and self-important students) regularly try to give more prestige to their disciplines, and themselves, by breeding their own vocabularies. The author of a recent book on relationships identifies five levels of commitment.

*1. dating — no commitment*

*2. steady dating — some commitment*

*3. monogamy — seeing yourselves as a couple*

*4. monogamy plus — you're a couple and everyone around you knows it*

*5. living together — you're making plans*

*Monogamy plus* (which we might reasonably think a euphemism for bigamy) is one of their misbegotten idioms. Academics create terms like this so that they may explain the obvious to us. We need them to define their terminology. Of course, most of these words we can happily do without. More than just idioms, academics (and those who would have us think they are) tirelessly create their own spurious systems and subsystems. They categorize what the rest of us have long known and don't need to be reminded of.

From a college preparatory school catalog, here is an entertaining, some might say indecorous, description of a course in human sexuality.

*Human sexuality is a required skills course that teaches sexuality top-*
*ics through the framework of values clarification activities.*

I think most parents would like further explanation of *required*
*skills course* and *values clarification activities,* but better yet would be a
less ambiguous description.

Disturbingly often, the academics' language belies their intellectual standing. Consider this paragraph from the manuscript of a college text on finance.

*Mutual savings banks have grown steadily, but relatively slowly. A*
*major reason for their relatively slow growth is that they are geographi-*
*cally limited. There are less than 500 of them operating in only 16*
*states. They primarily are located only in the Northeastern section of*
*the country — with the sole exception of 6 states, and less than 20*
*mutual savings banks, that operate in the Far West and Midwest.*

There's nothing inherently abstruse about the information in this
paragraph. It is the wordiness of the writing, the fuzziness of the
thinking, that interferes with our understanding.

*Mutual savings banks have grown steadily but slowly. Fewer than 500*
*of them operate in only 16 states. Except for some 20 mutual savings*
*banks in the Far West and Midwest, they are all in the Northeast.*

Here is a lovely example of academicspeak.

*The University in its continuous effort to improve the physical plant,*
*will at this time proceed to implement the window replacement initia-*
*tive in Coburn Hall.*

The university, we can surmise, will have new windows installed.

Finally, here are a few words from a recent college graduate's
commencement address.

*I think back to freshman year when my parents called in those first cou-*
*ple of weeks, and in the course of the conversation they asked, "Well,*
*what have you learned so far?" I think they were a little worried when I*
*said I've learned to write a sentence — a short, simple, concise sentence*
*that was to the point.*

Well they worry.

# The age of shoddiness

To say *at this juncture* or *at this moment in the history of my life* instead of *now* signifies more than mere wordiness. It signifies a perversion of society's values. Since how a person speaks and writes is a fair reflection of how a person thinks and feels, shoddy language may imply a careless or inconsiderate people — a public whose ideals have been discarded and whose ideas have been distorted. A society is generally as lax as its language. And in a society of this sort, easiness and mediocrity are much esteemed.

But why, we must wonder, are we wordy? Why do we say seven words where two will do or write three instead of only one? Understanding why we are wordy may help us reclaim our command of the language.

Habit, ignorance, and imitation are among the most common reasons for our wordiness.

■ *Habit.* People who write and speak wordily may do so out of habit. Habit, though human, means behaving automatically, without question or deliberation. Many of us write and speak habitually, as we always or long have; few of us pay much attention to how we express ourselves. We neither read what we write nor listen to what we say.

■ *Ignorance.* Often people are wordy because they know     no better. They are unaware that the concise phrase is preferable to the prolix and the precise word to the imprecise; indeed, they may assume the reverse. Moreover, people are generally loath to learn. We embrace what is easy or effortless and avoid what is hard or demanding.

■ *Imitation.* As never before, people do as others do, speak as others speak, and think as others think. The cliché is king. Nothing is so reviled as individuality. We imitate one another lest we be left alone. We want to fit in, to be part of the crowd. We want groups to engulf us and institutions to direct us.

Habits can be broken, ignorance overcome, and imitation resisted. But even if we do achieve all this, there are other possible reasons for our wordiness, less understandable and forgivable, perhaps, but human nonetheless.

■ *To enhance our self-importance.* Many of us seek to enhance our self-importance by using ostentatious language. We may believe that the more words we use, or the more elaborate our language, the more intelligent we sound and important we are. We may recognize the thinness of our thoughts and try to give them added weight by using polysyllabic words. Or we may chatter endlessly as though each word were further proof of our presence.

■ *To interfere with others' thoughts.* Some people, not uncommonly, will try to interfere with other people's thoughts. Through expedient, euphemistic, or circumlocutory language, these people strive to conceal their actions, to becloud what they say and do. With words they do whatever they please and, in so doing, manage to confuse our perception of their deeds and, even, their identity.

■ *To interfere with our own thoughts.* If we can interfere with others' thoughts, we can interfere with our own. Some of us do not want to know the meaning of our words. We fear knowing who we truly are, so to shield ourselves from the insight that genuine views and convictions can impart, we write without feeling and speak without thinking. We babble to ward off some specter of self-knowledge with whom we battle.

# PART 2

# The Dictionary of Concise Writing

# A

a bigger (greater; higher; larger) degree (extent) (of) *more.* Whereas the UC-Davis site assumed users want to focus on extensive reading, the American Girls site assumed users want a higher degree of graphics, less external linking, and briefer and simpler sections of text. *Whereas the UC-Davis site assumed users want to focus on extensive reading, the American Girls site assumed users want more graphics, less external linking, and briefer and simpler sections of text.* ■ Politicians and public officials should be required to tolerate a greater degree of criticism than ordinary citizens since, unlike such citizens, they have willingly taken on a public role in a democratic context where their actions are subject to the scrutiny of the public. *Politicians and public officials should be required to tolerate more criticism than ordinary citizens since, unlike such citizens, they have willingly taken on a public role in a democratic context where their actions are subject to the scrutiny of the public.* ■ One can speculate whether concentrating all the army special forces units in one regiment is the most appropriate solution or if rather a bigger degree of force diversification would contribute to achieving more specialization and introduce a competitive factor among the units. *One can speculate whether concentrating all the army special forces units in one regiment is the most appropriate solution or if rather more force diversification would contribute to achieving more specialization and introduce a competitive factor among the units.* ■ A bigger extent of improvement was prevented by the HUF 197 million of cash contribution made by BC Rt. to promote the development of its subsidiaries. *More improvement was prevented by the HUF 197 million of cash contribution made by BC Rt. to promote the development of its subsidiaries.*

about the fact that *because; for; in that; since; that;* delete. Management is also concerned about the fact that Walco has not developed brand identification within the market. *Management is also concerned that Walco has not developed brand identification within the market.* ■ Moscow is worried about the fact that the Israeli side has used heavy arms for the first time since the sides, in principle, approved of the ceasefire working plan. *Moscow is worried because the Israeli side has used heavy arms for the first time since the sides, in principle, approved of the ceasefire working plan.* ■ Are they proud about the fact that over 60% of these students didn't redesignate? *Are they proud that over 60% of these students didn't redesignate?*

about (around) ... to *about (around); to.* He works around 10 to 12 hours a day. *He works 10 to 12 hours a day.*

51

**above and beyond** *above; besides; beyond; more than; over.* The officers were honored for actions that went above and beyond the call of duty. *The officers were honored for actions that went beyond the call of duty.*

**(after; for; in; over; within) a brief (limited; little; short) amount of time (length of time; moment of time; period; period of time; span of time; time; while)** *before long; briefly; directly; momentarily; presently; quickly; shortly; soon; straightaway.* This anxiety will pass after a short time, and you will then be wondering why you felt it in the first place. *This anxiety will pass quickly, and you will then be wondering why you felt it in the first place.* ■ It snowed for a brief period of time. *It snowed briefly.* ■ In a short while, he will be making a speech before the convention delegates. *He will shortly be making a speech before the convention delegates.*

**a (the) broad (extensive; great; vast; wide) array of** *an array of; assorted; broad; countless; different; divers; diverse; extensive; many; numerous; scores of; sundry; untold; varied; various; varying; vast;* delete. In any domestic market, a wide array of official and unofficial sources provides information about the chosen market segments. *In any domestic market, numerous official and unofficial sources provide information about the chosen market segments.*

**a (the) broad (extensive; great; vast; wide) range of** *a range of; assorted; broad; countless; different; divers; diverse; extensive; many; numerous; scores of; sundry; untold; varied; various; varying; vast;* delete. A wide range of products is sold by NTIS as subscriptions or standing orders. *Various products are sold by NTIS as subscriptions or standing orders.*

**a (the) broad (extensive; great; vast; wide) spectrum of** *a spectrum of; assorted; broad; countless; different; divers; diverse; extensive; many; numerous; scores of; sundry; untold; varied; various; varying; vast;* delete.

**a (the) broad (extensive; great; vast; wide) variety of** *a variety of; assorted; broad; countless; different; divers; diverse; extensive; many; numerous; scores of; sundry; untold; varied; various; varying; vast;* delete. A wide variety of templates are available for drawing nuts and bolts. *Various templates are available for drawing nuts and bolts.*

**(a; the) absence of** *dis-; having no; il-; im-; in-; ir-; lacking; -less(ness); mis-; missing; no; non-; not; not any; not having; scant; un-; with no; without.* I wanted to communicate to young people the absence of purpose and how it felt so senseless and wasteful. *I wanted to communicate to young people the purposelessness and how it felt so senseless and wasteful.*

■ The absence of communications in today's business will quickly result in the absence of business. *No communications in today's business will quickly result in no business.*

**absolutely**  *at all;* delete. Rarely am I dissatisfied with purchases of music I know absolutely nothing about. *Rarely am I dissatisfied with purchases of music I know nothing about.*

**absolutely**  *yes.*

**absolutely essential (indispensable)**  *essential (indispensable).* I abhor government regulations except where absolutely indispensable. *I abhor government regulations except where indispensable.*

**absolutely not**  *by no means; no; not at all.*

**absolutely positively**  *absolutely; positively;* delete. Descartes was an introspective man who probed his meditations for things he could be absolutely, positively sure of. *Descartes was an introspective man who probed his meditations for things he could be absolutely sure of.*

**a case in point**  *an (one) example; for example; for instance.* Teachers in the trades and industry program at Queen Anne's County High School are a case in point. *Teachers in the trades and industry program at Queen Anne's County High School are an example.*

**acclimatize**  *acclimate.* Perhaps your company has recently hired several Nigerian accountants, and you want to help them successfully acclimatize to your corporate culture. *Perhaps your company has recently hired several Nigerian accountants, and you want to help them successfully acclimate to your corporate culture.*

**accommodations**  *rooms.*

**accompanied by**  *along with; and; as well as; combined with; coupled with; joined with; paired with; together with; with.* The behavioral implications of this emphasis are an increase in job satisfaction accompanied by a decrease in turnover and absenteeism. *The behavioral implications of this emphasis are an increase in job satisfaction coupled with a decrease in turnover and absenteeism.*

**accomplish**  *achieve; do; perform.* This can be accomplished by assigning consecutive numbers to consecutive periods. *This can be achieved by assigning consecutive numbers to consecutive periods.*

**accordingly** *hence; so; then; therefore; thus.* Accordingly, the board of directors recommends a vote against this stockholder proposal. *Therefore, the board of directors recommends a vote against this stockholder proposal.*

**according to** *by; following; to; under.*

**according to** *affirm; allege; announce; assert; attest; aver; avow; claim; comment; contend; declare; maintain; note; say; state; suggest; vouch.* According to various estimates, the measure would translate into a 10-percent trimming of insurance rates next year. *Various estimates suggest the measure would translate into a 10-percent trimming of insurance rates next year.*

**according to plan (projections)** *as planned (projected).* If everything goes according to plan, five old-fashioned riverboat casinos should begin operating about a year from now on the Mississippi. *If everything goes as planned, five old-fashioned riverboat casinos should begin operating about a year from now on the Mississippi.*

**accumulative** *cumulative.* The proportions reflect accumulative information as one reads the table from left to right. *The proportions reflect cumulative information as one reads the table from left to right.*

**accustomed to** *inured to; used to.* I am accustomed to her sinful ways. *I am inured to her sinful ways.*

**a certain amount of** *much; some;* delete. There's a certain amount of truth to what you say. *There's much truth to what you say.*

**a (the) consequence of** *because of; caused by; due to; owing to; resulting from.* The increase is almost entirely the consequence of rising economic activity. *The increase is almost entirely caused by rising economic activity.*

**a couple of** *a few; two.*

**a couple three (two; two or three)** *a couple of; a few; two; two or three; three.* I've known her for a couple two or three years, and never has she said anything like that to me before. *I've known her for a few years, and never has she said anything like that to me before.*

**(all) across (throughout) the country (nation)** *nationwide.*

**(all) across (throughout) the world** *worldwide.*

**act in accord (accordance) with** *act on; comply with; conform to; follow; obey.* The bankers were responding to a Federal Reserve study that found that they were not acting in accordance with the federal Community Reinvestment Act. *The bankers were responding to a Federal Reserve study that found that they were not complying with the federal Community Reinvestment Act.*

**(a; the) ... action** delete. Jailing Danilov was retaliatory action against the seizure of a Soviet agent in the United States. *Jailing Danilov was retaliation against the seizure of a Soviet agent in the United States.* ■ We are taking steps to revoke the security clearances of individuals who have been involved in illegal actions. *We are taking steps to revoke the security clearances of individuals who have been involved in illegalities.* ■ The innovative actions of the European Regional Development Fund are laboratories of ideas for disadvantaged regions. *The innovations of the European Regional Development Fund are laboratories of ideas for disadvantaged regions.* ■ This implies both preventive actions and rehabilitation of victims. *This implies both prevention and rehabilitation of victims.*

**action (attack; battle; game) plan** *course; formula; method; plan; policy; procedure; scheme; strategy.* The Democratic leadership's action plan is simple: Delay action as long as possible. *The Democratic leadership's strategy is simple: Delay action as long as possible.*

**active (actively)** delete. They are learning to actively participate in their own decisions. *They are learning to participate in their own decisions.* ■ To counteract this, the change agent takes an active role in encouraging new solutions and approaches to problems. *To counteract this, the change agent takes a role in encouraging new solutions and approaches to problems.* ■ Citibank is actively pursuing private banking in numerous domestic markets around the world. *Citibank is pursuing private banking in numerous domestic markets around the world.*

**... activity** delete. There could be some thunderstorm activity as well. *There could be some thunderstorms as well.* ■ Unfortunately, countries where counterfeiting activity is widespread are generally not parties to such treaties. *Unfortunately, countries where counterfeiting is widespread are generally not parties to such treaties.* ■ These thunderstorms have been known to produce some severe tornadic activity. *These thunderstorms have been known to produce some severe tornadoes.* ■

The majority of unemployed were so by choice or because of chil-drearing activities. *The majority of unemployed were so by choice or because of childrearing.*

**actual (actually)**  delete.

**add ... additional (further; more)**  *add.* If I can add any additional information, please do not hesitate to contact me. *If I can add any information, please do not hesitate to contact me.* ■ Please add an additional three days to your schedule if you have oversized images. *Please add three days to your schedule if you have oversized images.*

**(an) additional**  *added; extra; further; more; other.* It supports all KnowledgeMan/2 capabilities and integrates two additional compo-nents. *It supports all KnowledgeMan/2 capabilities and integrates two other components.*

**additionally**  *also; and; as well; besides; beyond that (this); even; further; furthermore; moreover; more than that (this); still more; then; too; what is more.* Additionally, he was an authority on butterflies. *He was also an authority on butterflies.*

**add together**  *add; total.* Add together the first 31 numbers in the sequence 6, 66, 666, 6666, ... . *Add the first 31 numbers in the sequence 6, 66, 666, 6666, ... .* ■ If you add together the workers in all industries who lose jobs, change jobs, or get their first jobs, 37% of the labor force changes its employment status every year. *If you total the work-ers in all industries who lose jobs, change jobs, or get their first jobs, 37% of the labor force changes its employment status every year.*

**a (a certain; some) degree (of)**  *a certain; much (of); some (of); somewhat; delete.* The best results will likely be obtained by firms that exercise some degree of restraint in their offshore activities. *The best results will likely be obtained by firms that exercise some restraint in their offshore activ-ities.* ■ Each of us has a planning method that works with some degree of effectiveness. *Each of us has a planning method that works somewhat effectively.*

**adequate enough**  *adequate; enough.* As important as these rewards may be, no one would suggest that they are adequate enough to inspire the changes anticipated. *As important as these rewards may be, no one would suggest that they are enough to inspire the changes anticipat-ed.*

**(an; the) adequate number (of)** *enough; five (ninety).* Performance tasks appear quite feasible in large-scale assessments as well as in classroom use, provided an adequate number of good tasks are available. *Performance tasks appear quite feasible in large-scale assessments as well as in classroom use, provided enough good tasks are available.*

**a (the) diversity of different** *assorted; a variety of; broad; countless; different; divers; diverse; extensive; many; numerous; scores of; sundry; varied; various; varying.* The diversity of different types of music that the Society now offers would have been unheard of 20 years ago. *The diverse types of music that the Society now offers would have been unheard of 20 years ago.*

**adjacent to** *beside; close to; near; next to.*

**admit to** *admit.* The General Accounting Office found 16 percent of the employers surveyed admitted to engaging in discriminatory hiring practices. *The General Accounting Office found 16 percent of the employers surveyed admitted engaging in discriminatory hiring practices.*

**advance ahead (forward; on; onward)** *advance; continue; go on; move on; proceed; progress.*

**advanced (along) in years** *elderly; old; 72 (90).* She's dating a man who's rather advanced in years. *She's dating a man who's rather old.*

**advance (prior) notice** *notice.* Congress is in the thick of a new stage of the battle over my proposal to require businesses to give advance notice to workers before plants are closed or major layoffs are ordered. *Congress is in the thick of a new stage of the battle over my proposal to require businesses to give notice to workers before plants are closed or major layoffs are ordered.* ■ Since there is no evidence that unannounced quizzes improve performance, it seems reasonable to provide students with as much advance notice about testing as possible. *Since there is no evidence that unannounced quizzes improve performance, it seems reasonable to provide students with as much notice about testing as possible.*

**advance planning (plans)** *planning (plans).* The overhead projector is a powerful aid for demonstrations and is simple to use with a minimum of advanced planning. *The overhead projector is a powerful aid for demonstrations and is simple to use with a minimum of planning.*

**advance preparation** *preparation.* In a meeting designed to solve problems or make decisions, you should include in your advance preparations a statement of the problem and your recommended solution. *In a meeting designed to solve problems or make decisions, you should include in your preparations a statement of the problem and your recommended solution.*

**advance reservations** *reservations.* Participants are strongly advised to make advance reservations for the Athens–Mytilini–Athens leg of their trip, because flights to and from the islands are usually fully booked during this period. *Participants are strongly advised to make reservations for the Athens–Mytilini–Athens leg of their trip, because flights to and from the islands are usually fully booked during this period.*

**advance up** *advance.* As the person's needs are met on one level, the person advances up to the next level of needs. *As the person's needs are met on one level, the person advances to the next level of needs.*

**advance warning** *warning.* Seismologists generally concur that the science of earthquake prediction is such that a region about to be struck by a major quake would have, at best, only a few days' advance warning. *Seismologists generally concur that the science of earthquake prediction is such that a region about to be struck by a major quake would have, at best, only a few days' warning.*

**a (the) ... experience** delete. Just getting up in the morning is a painful experience for her. *Just getting up in the morning is painful for her.* ■ I wasn't afraid; it wasn't a nightmare, but it was a rather startling experience. *I wasn't afraid; it wasn't a nightmare, but it was rather startling.*

**a (the) ... fact** delete. This is an alarming fact, considering that these workers make up the foundation of our service-sector economy. *This is alarming, considering that these workers make up the foundation of our service-sector economy.*

**affiliated with** *belongs to; employed by; works for.*

**affirmative** *yes.* If the answer is affirmative, selecting an optimal dividend policy is a valid concern. *If the answer is yes, selecting an optimal dividend policy is a valid concern.*

**afford (give; offer; present; provide) ... (an; the) opportunity** *allow; give ... (the) chance; let; permit.* Winning the Boston Marathon provided me with an opportunity to make running my career. *Winning the*

*Boston Marathon allowed me to make running my career.* ■ Raising cattle gave him an opportunity to practice genetics on a large scale, though the results weren't always what he expected. *Raising cattle let him practice genetics on a large scale, though the results weren't always what he expected.*

**after all is said and done**  *even so; finally; in the end; still; ultimately; yet;* delete.

**after ... first**  *after.* Any model relying on deseasonalized data should be built after the modified Census II method of deseasonalization is first applied to the data. *Any model relying on deseasonalized data should be built after the modified Census II method of deseasonalization is applied to the data.*

**after ... later (subsequently)**  *after.* After you have created and saved a file on the disk, you can retrieve it later for editing. *After you have created and saved a file on the disk, you can retrieve it for editing.*

**after ... next**  *after.* After you note the spread, next check your stock's level II screen for the depth of the market makers. *After you note the spread, check your stock's level II screen for the depth of the market makers.*

**after the conclusion (end) of**  *after; following.* And 3.25 million women were pushed or persuaded to leave industrial jobs after the end of World War II. *And 3.25 million women were pushed or persuaded to leave industrial jobs after World War II.*

**after the event (incident; occurrence)**  *after; afterward; later; next; then.*

**after ... then**  *after.* After making changes, you can then use the transfer command to save the style sheet. *After making changes, you can use the transfer command to save the style sheet.* ■ Finally, after the additional taxes, if any, are added in, you then arrive at the total tax. *Finally, after the additional taxes, if any, are added in, you arrive at the total tax.*

**again and again**  *frequently; often; recurrently; regularly; repeatedly.*

**again re-**  *re-.* It's an image that again reinforces my belief that we are more interested in pizzazz than performance. *It's an image that reinforces my belief that we are more interested in pizzazz than performance.*

**age (aged)**  delete. Women reach peak fertility at age 25 and then the ability to get pregnant naturally declines. *Women reach peak fertility at 25 and then the ability to get pregnant naturally declines.*

**aggregate together** *aggregate.* The most remarkable aspect of the developmental process of these bacteria is their ability to aggregate together to form a swarm. *The most remarkable aspect of the developmental process of these bacteria is their ability to aggregate to form a swarm.* ■ Wires from individual homes are aggregated together in a hierarchical manner. *Wires from individual homes are aggregated in a hierarchical manner.*

**a good (great) deal of** *great; much; vast.* There is a great deal of disagreement about generations after the first three. *There is great disagreement about generations after the first three.*

**ahead of** *before.* The ambassador departed five minutes ahead of the deadline imposed by the State Department. *The ambassador departed five minutes before the deadline imposed by the State Department.*

**ahead of schedule** *early; too soon.* They arrived in the country two hours ahead of schedule. *They arrived in the country two hours early.*

**ahead of time** *before; beforehand; earlier; in advance; sooner.* The production manager never knew what was in the pipeline, so he could never prepare the materials and staff ahead of time. *The production manager never knew what was in the pipeline, so he could never prepare the materials and staff beforehand.*

**a (whole) host of** *many; numerous.* There are a whole host of reasons why these people resigned from their jobs. *There are many reasons why these people resigned from their jobs.*

**aid and abet** *abet; aid; help.* The NRC, aided and abetted by the industry and most of the press, has chosen to wink at the law. *The NRC, aided by the industry and most of the press, has chosen to wink at the law.*

**aid in -ing** *help.* In order to aid in recharging the groundwater, large spreading basins were constructed along the Santa Ana River. *In order to help recharge the groundwater, large spreading basins were constructed along the Santa Ana River.*

**a (the) ... job of** *delete.* When the banks offer the products of investment entities with a high market profile, the job of introducing the funds to bank customers is much easier. *When the banks offer the prod-*

*ucts of investment entities with a high market profile, introducing the funds to bank customers is much easier.*

**a ... kind (sort; type) (of) thing**  *like;* delete. It became a competition type thing. *It became like a competition.* ■ This type thing happens often. *This happens often.*

**alas and alack**  *regrettably; sadly; sorrowfully; unfortunately; unhappily.*

**albeit**  *although; though.* There appears to be enough fuel to propel stocks higher, albeit irregularly, even if the bond market is waylaid by fears of a too robust economy. *There appears to be enough fuel to propel stocks higher, although irregularly, even if the bond market is waylaid by fears of a too robust economy.*

**a lesser (lower; smaller) degree (extent) (of)**  *less.* Transparent WDM systems offer a lesser degree of monitoring and network capability than TDM systems. *Transparent WDM systems offer less monitoring and network capability than TDM systems.* ■ The less common plants are given a smaller degree of treatment not just because of their limited use in food production but because of their scarcity on sites. *The less common plants are given less treatment not just because of their limited use in food production but because of their scarcity on sites.* ■ Most land areas in China have a lower extent of soil degradation. *Most land areas in China have less soil degradation.*

**a little bit**  *a bit; a little; fairly; rather; slightly; somewhat.* They're a little bit hesitant. *They're a little hesitant.*

**all and sundry**  *all; everybody; everyone; everything; one and all.* He is cheered by all and sundry despite his confession. *He is cheered by everyone despite his confession.*

**all done (finished)**  *complete; done; ended; finished; over; past.* Are you all done with your homework? *Are you done with your homework?*

**alleged suspect**  *suspect.* The detective will next attempt to locate and interview the alleged suspect concerning the allegations. *The detective will next attempt to locate and interview the suspect concerning the allegations.*

**alleviate**  *lessen; reduce.* The proposal is designed to alleviate overcrowding at Framingham State Prison. *The proposal is designed to lessen overcrowding at Framingham State Prison.*

**all in all** *all told; in all; overall.* All in all, it would be difficult to find a less suitable site. *All told, it would be difficult to find a less suitable site.*

**all ... long** *all.* The president, shop chairman, and entire shop committee of UAW Local 422 worked hard all winter long. *The president, shop chairman, and entire shop committee of UAW Local 422 worked hard all winter.*

**all of (the)** *all (the).* Can you do all of them? *Can you do them all?*

**all of (us)** *(we) all.* All of us practice a kind of inventory control. *We all practice a kind of inventory control.*

**all of a sudden** *suddenly.* All of a sudden, I began getting memos from the corporate office criticizing my performance. *Suddenly, I began getting memos from the corporate office criticizing my performance.*

**all over with** *complete; done; ended; finished; over; past.*

**allow of** *allow; permit.* Top does not allow of any user input. *Top does not permit any user input.* ■ The exception is possibly when one wants to "broadcast" video out to a large group such as an online lecture but this often does not allow of any real interaction. *The exception is possibly when one wants to "broadcast" video out to a large group such as an online lecture but this often does not allow any real interaction.*

**allow ... to** *let.* Do it in a way that allows you to look the consumer straight in the eye. *Do it in a way that lets you look the consumer straight in the eye.*

**all (just) the same** *anyhow; even so; still; yet.*

**all the time** *always; ceaselessly; constantly; endlessly; everyday; forever.*

**all things considered** *all in all; all told; altogether; in all; on the whole; overall.*

**all-time record (high)** *record.* International Falls, Minnesota, sometimes called the nation's icebox, tied its all-time record of 98 degrees. *International Falls, Minnesota, sometimes called the nation's icebox, tied its record of 98 degrees.*

**all-time record low** *record low.* Temperatures in Alaska reached 78 degrees below zero, an all-time record low for the area. *Temperatures* *in Alaska reached 78 degrees below zero, a record low for the area.*

**almost without exception**  *almost all; almost every; most; nearly all; nearly every.* Almost without exception, those professionals stated that innovation was of major importance to the continued success of the company. *Almost all those professionals stated that innovation was of major importance to the continued success of the company.*

**alongside of**  *alongside; among; beside; next to; with.* You will work alongside of experienced workers and see what joys and frustrations they undergo. *You will work with experienced workers and see what joys and frustrations they undergo.*

**along that (this) line**  *about (in; on) that (this).* I don't know what the Twins' thinking was along that line. *I don't know what the Twins' thinking was on that.*

**along that (this) line**  *like that (this).* I can see using TrueScan for some work along that line but only if the documents aren't too complex in fonts or layout. *I can see using TrueScan for some work like that but only if the documents aren't too complex in fonts or layout.*

**along the lines of**  *akin to; close to; like; resembling; similar to; such as.* They have no interest in publishing anything along the lines of Microsoft *Bookshelf. They have no interest in publishing anything similar to Microsoft* Bookshelf.

**along the same line**  *alike; likewise; much the same; similar; similarly.* Along the same line, increasing monetary benefits but not expanding opportunities for job variety would be a serious mistake. *Likewise, increasing monetary benefits but not expanding opportunities for job variety would be a serious mistake.*

**(for) a long time (while)**  *long.* She has wanted to travel to Europe for a long time. *She has long wanted to travel to Europe.*

**a long time (while) ago**  *long ago.* These Star Wars pages were created a long time ago. *These Star Wars pages were created long ago.*

**along with (and; combined with; coupled with; plus; together with) the fact that**  *and that.* U.S. Labor Department figures show that most minimum-wage employees work part time coupled with the fact that 60 percent are between 16 and 24 years old. *U.S. Labor Department figures show that most minimum-wage employees work part* *time and that 60 percent are between 16 and 24 years old.* ■ One of the largest impediments to getting CFS recognized were the vast and varied symptoms that accompany it, along with the fact that many practitioners refused to accept it as a verifiable disease. *One of the largest impediments to getting CFS recognized were the vast and varied symptoms that accompany it, and that many practitioners refused to accept it as a verifiable disease.*

**a lot** *much.* It also makes assembly-language programs that use GS/OS a lot easier to read. *It also makes assembly-language programs that use GS/OS much easier to read.*

**a lot of** *many; much; numerous.* In a lot of people's minds, there was no question of his quilt. *In many people's minds, there was no question of his guilt.*

**a lot of (the) time** *frequently; often.* We went into the city a lot of times. *We went into the city often.*

**alphabetical** *alphabetic.*

**alphanumerical** *alphameric; alphanumeric.*

**also ... as well** *also; as well.* They also agreed to other demands as well. *They also agreed to other demands.* ■ But also the content needs to be protected as well. *But the content needs to be protected as well.*

**also ... too** *also; too.* We also know that Marilyn Monroe was one of his lovers, too. *We know that Marilyn Monroe was one of his lovers, too.*

**alternative choice** *alternative.* Herbs are an alternative choice for modern day medicines and stress. *Herbs are an alternative for modern day medicines and stress.* ■ In the event that BMP are unable to provide you with the hotel room you have requested for circumstances beyond our control BMP reserve the right to provide you with an alternative choice. *In the event that BMP are unable to provide you with the hotel room you have requested for circumstances beyond our control BMP reserve the right to provide you with an alternative.*

**(what is) a (the) manner (means; mechanism; method; procedure; process; technique) by which** *how.* What is the means by which a nation can increase investment? *How can a nation increase investment?* ■ The manner by which the man ultimately inflicts himself on his companion is, of course, immaterial. *How the man ultimately inflicts* *himself on his companion is, of course, immaterial.* ■ We will now examine the process by which natural and global marketing activities are controlled. *We will now examine how natural and global marketing activities are controlled.* ■ The answer should describe a process by which all corners are equally likely to be chosen. *The answer should describe how all corners are equally likely to be chosen.*

**a matter of** *a;* delete. The issue of automobile insurance has been a matter of concern to me since my early years as a legislator. *The issue of automobile insurance has been a concern to me since my early years as a legislator.*

**a matter of** *a few; some;* delete. In a matter of seconds, SpinRite determines the interleave characteristics of the entire system. *In seconds, SpinRite determines the interleave characteristics of the entire system.*

**a (a certain; some) measure (of)** *a certain; much; some;* delete. With the employer-employee relationship should come a certain measure of understanding. *With the employer-employee relationship should come a certain understanding.*

**ameliorate** *heal; help; improve; make better.* As medical technology and surgical procedures increase in their ability to ameliorate, they unfortunately also increase in their ability to harm. *As medical technology and surgical procedures increase in their ability to heal, they unfortunately also increase in their ability to harm.*

**(8:00) a.m. ... morning** *(8:00) a.m.; in the morning.* I want the cost estimates by 9:00 a.m. tomorrow morning. *I want the cost estimates by 9:00 a.m. tomorrow.* ■ At the start of the week, everyone was predicting strong winds and rain, but who would have thought that at 11 a.m. this morning there would be a pleasant breeze and the April sun burning through the clouds? *At the start of the week, everyone was predicting strong winds and rain, but who would have thought that at 11 a.m. there would be a pleasant breeze and the April sun burning through the clouds?*

**(a; the) ... amount of** delete. If you have any amount of intelligence, you know what's right and what's wrong. *If you have any intelligence, you know what's right and what's wrong.* ■ In reality, it takes a considerable amount of political skill and perseverance to get anything of significance through this process. *In reality, it takes considerable political skill and perseverance to get anything of significance through this process.*

**amount (quantity; sum) of cash (money)** *sum*. When the Soviets spent enormous amounts of money improving their antiaircraft systems, the United States responded not by giving up on its bomber program but rather by improving it with cruise missiles, electronic jammers, and so on. *When the Soviets spent enormous sums improving their antiaircraft systems, the United States responded not by giving up on its bomber program but rather by improving it with cruise missiles, electronic jammers, and so on.*

**(a; the) ... amount of time (length of time; period of time; span of time)** *period; time; while*; delete. They filmed our arguments over a three-month period of time. *They filmed our arguments over three months.* ■ You can get to know someone very well if you date him or her for a long enough period of time. *You can get to know someone very well if you date him or her for a long enough while.* ■ But over the same length of time, inflation averaged 3 percent a year. *But over the same period, inflation averaged 3 percent a year.*

**amounts to** *is; totals*. The number of prisoners released amounts to less than one-third of those held. *The number of prisoners released is less than one-third of those held.*

**an (the) abundance of** *abundant; ample; copious; countless; legion; liberal; many; myriad; numerous; plentiful; plenty of; profuse*. Among the educated, there is an abundance of people trained in these occupations. *Among the educated, there are plenty of people trained in these occupations.*

**an accomplished (established) fact** *accomplished (established); a fact*; delete. It is an established fact that reaction times and vision deteriorate with age. *It is established that reaction times and vision deteriorate with age.*

**an acknowledged (known) fact** *acknowledged (known); a fact*; delete. It is an acknowledged fact that well-trained and highly skilled construction craftsmen are not willing to work for wages substandard to the prevailing wage rates. *It is acknowledged that well-trained and highly skilled construction craftsmen are not willing to work for wages substandard to the prevailing wage rates.*

**analytical** *analytic*.

**analyze in depth (in detail)** *analyze; detail*. He analyzes in detail the three nativist eruptions that occurred during the era of mass immigration. *He details the three nativist eruptions that occurred during the era of mass immigration.*

**an array of** *assorted; countless; different; divers; diverse; extensive; many; numerous; scores of; sundry; varied; various; varying;* delete. Lately, however, an array of new troubles has surfaced — troubles like radon. *Lately, however, many new troubles have surfaced — troubles like radon.*

**(a; the) -ance (-ence) of** *-ing.* With such asset and liability opportunities, the avoidance of large credit losses was a practical management consideration in ensuring attractive profitability. *With such asset and liability opportunities, avoiding large credit losses was a practical management consideration in ensuring attractive profitability.* ■ In the performance of their routines, they are acting as extensions of your position. *In performing their routines, they are acting as extensions of your position.* ■ A recent variation on providing version protection has been liquidation of the product on site by issuance of a credit to the retailer. *A recent variation on providing version protection has been liquidation of the product on site by issuing a credit to the retailer.*

**and ... also** *also; and.* The Winters' models are more complex and also more potentially rewarding. *The Winters' models are more complex and more potentially rewarding.*

**and ... as well** *and; as well.* It is being done by some of the women whose careers you chronicled and by a growing number of working women as well. *It is being done by some of the women whose careers you chronicled and by a growing number of working women.*

**and etc. (et cetera)** *and so forth; and so on; and the like; etc.* He talked to us about the projection lens, the mirror, orientation and parity, the parallel plate, the prism, and etc. *He talked to us about the projection lens, the mirror, orientation and parity, the parallel plate, the prism, and so on.*

**and everything** delete.

**and everything (stuff; things) like that** *and so forth; and so on; and the like; etc.;* delete.

**and ... further (furthermore; in addition; moreover; what is more)** *also; and; as well; besides; beyond that (this); even; further; furthermore; in addition; moreover; more than that (this); still more; then; too; what is more.* And furthermore, the company is seeking to cooperate with other companies with expertise for mutual advancement. *The company is also seeking to cooperate with other companies with expertise for mutual advancement.* ■ You can restore the database to its state at the time of any available backup, and in addition you can reapply subsequent committed transactions up to some desired time. *You can restore the database to its state at the time of any available backup; in addition, you can reapply subsequent committed transactions up to some desired time.*

**and so** *and; so.* Thank you for submitting your pieces to *Critical Inquiry;* however, they are inappropriate for our journal, and so we are returning them to you. *Thank you for submitting your pieces to* Critical Inquiry; *however, they are inappropriate for our journal, so we are returning them to you.*

**and so as a result** *as a result; consequently; hence; so; then; therefore; thus.*

**and so on and so forth** *and so forth; and so on; and the like; etc.* We believe our neighbor started the conflict with propaganda, espionage, assassinations, bombings, and so on and so forth. *We believe our neighbor started the conflict with propaganda, espionage, assassinations, bombings, and so on.*

**and ... too** *and; too.* I have become acutely aware of the epidemic of abuse suffered by children in this country — and elsewhere, too. *I have become acutely aware of the epidemic of abuse suffered by children in this country — and elsewhere.*

**and yet** *and; yet.*

**an estimated** *about; around; close to; more or less; near; nearly; or so; roughly; some.* An estimated 50,000 people lined up yesterday to register to vote. *Nearly 50,000 people lined up yesterday to register to vote.*

**(after; for; in; over; within) an extended (lengthy; long; prolonged; protracted) amount of time (length of time; period; period of time; span of time; time; while)** *at last; at length; eventually; finally; in due time; in time; over the months (years); over time; ultimately; with time.*

**an (a certain; some) extent of** *a certain; much; some; somewhat;* delete.

**an integral part of** *a part of; integral to.* Keeping abreast of these developments is an integral part of successful EFT strategy development. *Keeping abreast of these developments is integral to successful EFT* *strategy development.*

**an (the) open question**   *a (the) question; arguable; debatable; disputable; doubtful; dubious; in doubt; in question; moot; open; questionable; uncertain; unclear; undecided; unknown; unsettled; unsure.* That remains an open question. *That remains questionable.*

**an order of magnitude**   delete. While the first CD-ROM copy costs an order of magnitude more than a WORM disk, subsequent copies cost much less, making CD-ROM practical for applications requiring many copies of document disks. *While the first CD-ROM copy costs more than a WORM disk, subsequent copies cost much less, making CD-ROM practical for applications requiring many copies of document disks.* ■ The MFC development cycle remains an order of magnitude faster and still represents the better development method to use for desktop application components. *The MFC development cycle remains faster and still represents the better development method to use for desktop application components.*

**anterior to**   *before; earlier than.* What is now called administrative tutelage was an institution in France anterior to the Revolution. *What is now called administrative tutelage was an institution in France before the Revolution.*

**a (a fair; any) number (of)**   *a few; almost all; dozens (of); hundreds (of); many; most; nearly all; scores (of); several; sixty-seven (twenty); some;* delete. A fair number of stores were either sited incorrectly or in the wrong markets and weren't producing the kind of profits they needed to. *Some stores were either sited incorrectly or in the wrong markets and weren't producing the kind of profits they needed to.*

**any and all**   *any; all.* This certificate replaces any and all insurance certificates that may have been issued previously to the Insured under the Group Policy and is subject to the terms of the Group Policy. *This certificate replaces all insurance certificates that may have been issued previously to the Insured under the Group Policy and is subject to the terms of the Group Policy.*

**anybody (anyone) and everybody (everyone)**   *all; anybody (anyone); everybody (everyone).* They told anyone and everyone that you are the one we want to use in our ads. *They told everyone that you are the one we want to use in our ads.*

**anyplace (anywhere) else**   *elsewhere.* This is an invaluable resource that you will not find anywhere else. *This is an invaluable resource that you will not find elsewhere.*

**anything and everything** *all; all things; anything; anything at all; everything.* These kids lie about anything and everything. *These kids lie about everything.*

**anything (something) in the way of** *any; some;* delete. It has yet to accomplish anything in the way of practical benefits. *It has yet to accomplish any practical benefits.*

**anyway** delete.

**anywhere (somewhere) between ... and** *between ... and.* Upjohn says Minoxidil's success rate ranges anywhere between 24 and 40 percent. *Upjohn says Minoxidil's success rate ranges between 24 and 40 percent.*

**anywhere (somewhere) in the range of ... to** *in the range of ... to.*

**anywhere near** *nearly.* You are not anywhere near as dumb as some of this material will make you feel. *You are not nearly as dumb as some of this material will make you feel.*

**a (the) ... one** delete. It remains to be seen, however, if this view will turn out to be the correct one. *It remains to be seen, however, if this view will turn out to be correct.*

**apart from** *besides; beyond.* Apart from looking like the original, the counterfeit product often performs as well as the original. *Besides looking like the original, the counterfeit product often performs as well as the original.*

**apart from ... also (as well)** *apart from; besides; beyond.* Apart from being expensive, the international development process is also very risky. *Besides being expensive, the international development process is very risky.*

**a (a certain; some) part (of)** *almost all (of); many (of); most (of); much (of); nearly all (of); (a) part (of); some (of).*

**a (a certain; some) percentage (of)** *almost all (of); many (of); most (of); much (of); nearly all (of); (a) part (of); (45) percent (of); some (of).* I own a certain percentage of Caesar's Palace. *I own some of Caesar's Palace.*

**a (the) ... period (of)**  delete. The FBI conducted its investigation over a two-year period. *The FBI conducted its investigation over two years.* ■ Total contract value, excluding database licensing fees, was approximately $2 million over a six-year period. *Total contract value, excluding database licensing fees, was approximately $2 million over six years.*

**a (the) ... point**  *a (the)*; delete. Identifying a need is the beginning point of the process. *Identifying a need is the beginning of the process.*

**a (the) point of (that)**  *a (the)*; delete. Is this a point of concern for the rest of the pack? *Is this a concern for the rest of the pack?*

**a (a certain; some) portion (of)**  *almost all (of); many (of); most (of); much (of); (a) part (of); nearly all (of); some (of).* To print only a portion of the document, select the block. *To print only part of the document, select the block.* ■ Analysts say that the high employment in the state deserves a portion of the credit. *Analysts say that the high employment in the state deserves some of the credit.*

**appear (arrive) on (upon) the scene**  *appear (arrive).* Several bands will appear on the scene such as Implant and of course a special show by Suicide Commando himself. *Several bands will appear such as Implant and of course a special show by Suicide Commando himself.*

**appellation**  *name; title.*

**appertain (appertaining) to**  *pertain to; relate to.* Moneys therefor having been deposited with the Trustee from and after June 12, 1989, interest thereon shall cease to accrue and coupons appertaining to said bonds payable after that date will be void. *Moneys therefor having been deposited with the Trustee from and after June 12, 1989, interest thereon shall cease to accrue and coupons pertaining to said bonds payable after that date will be void.*

**appoint as**  *appoint.* Harding was succeeded by Calvin Coolidge, who appointed Harlan Fiske Stone as attorney general. *Harding was succeeded by Calvin Coolidge, who appointed Harlan Fiske Stone attorney general.*

**appreciate**  *admire; applaud; approve of; enjoy; (be) grateful (for); like; prize; (be) thankful (for); thank you (for); value; welcome.* We appreciate it. *We are grateful.* ■ I appreciate your coming. *I thank you for coming.* ■ Your concern is very much appreciated. *Your concern is very much welcomed.*

**appreciate in value** *appreciate.* Due to the overall rise of the stock market, many individuals have securities which have appreciated considerably in value. *Due to the overall rise of the stock market, many individuals have securities which have appreciated considerably.* ■ Another effective tax strategy is to make a charitable contribution with long-term assets that have substantially appreciated in value. *Another effective tax strategy is to make a charitable contribution with long-term assets that have substantially appreciated.*

**appreciation** *gratefulness; gratitude; thankfulness; thanks.* I would like to express my appreciation for Meals on Wheels. *I would like to express my thanks for Meals on Wheels.*

**apprehend** *arrest; capture; catch; seize.* Daniel Mahoney, 30, was apprehended near Los Lunas shortly before 1:00 a.m. *Daniel Mahoney, 30, was captured near Los Lunas shortly before 1:00 a.m.*

**approbation** *approval; praise.*

**(for) approximately** *about; around; close to; more or less; near; nearly; or so; roughly; say; some.* It will last for approximately two hours. *It will last about two hours.*

**a (the) preponderance (of)** *almost all (of); (nine) in (ten) (of); many (of); more (of); most (of); nearly all (of); (43) of (48) (of); (67) percent (of); delete.* The preponderance of short selling is done by market professionals engaged in the day-to-day provision of liquidity to the market. *Almost all short selling is done by market professionals engaged in the day-to-day provision of liquidity to the market.*

**a (a certain; some) proportion (of)** *almost all (of); many (of); most (of); much (of); nearly all (of); (a) part (of); some (of).*

**a (a certain; some) quantity (of)** *almost all (of); many (of); most (of); much (of); nearly all (of); (a) part (of); some (of).*

**a range of** *assorted; countless; different; divers; diverse; extensive; many; numerous; scores of; sundry; varied; various; varying; delete.* It has been tested in a range of working situations in large manufacturing plants. *It has been tested in diverse working situations in large manufacturing plants.*

**a ... ratio (of)** *delete.* When you add in those with subsyndromal SAD, the figure is closer to one in four, with women outnumbering men by a ratio of three or four to one. *When you add in those with sub-syndromal SAD, the figure is closer to one in four, with women outnumbering men by three or four to one.*

**(a; the) area (locale; locality; location; place; point; position; region; site; spot)** *where; wherever.*

**(after; for; in; over; within) a reasonable amount of time (length of time; period; period of time; span of time; time; while)** *by next week (tomorrow); fast; in (within) a day (year); promptly; quickly; rapidly; shortly; soon; speedily; swiftly;* delete. Unlike corporate sales, which can be tied up in a relatively reasonable period of time, government sales tend to be drawn out. *Unlike corporate sales, which can be tied up relatively quickly, government sales tend to be drawn out.*

**(a; the) area (locale; locality; location; place; point; position; region; site; spot) where** *where; wherever.* The COMSPEC line will show the place where COMMAND.COM is expected. *The COMSPEC line will show where COMMAND.COM is expected.* ■ If you click your mouse on the map, it will show you the area where ATM Mega Link Service is available or planned. *If you click your mouse on the map, it will show you where ATM Mega Link Service is available or planned.*

**argumentation** *argument; debate; dispute.* Some members may take unyielding positions, leading to unproductive argumentation and bickering. *Some members may take unyielding positions, leading to unproductive arguments and bickering.*

**arithmetical** *arithmetic.*

**around about** *about; around.* It was around about then that he left for East Africa. *It was around then that he left for East Africa.*

**arrive at (an; the) accord (about; as to; concerning; of; on; regarding)** *agree; compromise; concur; decide; resolve; settle.* AT&T and unions representing about 160,000 employees arrived at an accord on a new three-year national contract. *AT&T and unions representing about 160,000 employees agreed on a new three-year national contract.*

**arrive at (an; the) agreement (about; as to; concerning; of; on; regarding)** *agree; compromise; concur; decide; resolve; settle.* I'm confident that we will arrive at an agreement on how to proceed jointly on that operation. *I'm confident that we will decide on how to proceed jointly on that operation.* ■ Several small color sketches may be produced in an effort to arrive at an agreement on the look of the final work. *Several small color sketches may be produced in an effort to agree on the look of the final work.*

**arrive at (a; the) compromise (about; as to; concerning; of; on; regarding)** *agree; compromise; concur; decide; resolve; settle.* Nearly 10 months since negotiations began, it seems as though the two may not arrive at a compromise any time soon. *Nearly 10 months since negotiations began, it seems as though the two may not agree any time soon.* ■ Either arrive at a compromise or agree to maintain your differences but respect them. *Either compromise or agree to maintain your differences but respect them.* ■ It seems highly unlikely that she would want to arrive at a compromise and lose the opportunity to impeach Mr. Wahid. *It seems highly unlikely that she would want to settle and lose the opportunity to impeach Mr. Wahid.*

**arrive at (a; the) conclusion (about; as to; concerning; of; on; regarding)** *conclude; decide; deduce; determine; infer; judge; reason; resolve; settle.* I think they have arrived at the conclusion that he is now a neutralized force. *I think they have concluded that he is now a neutralized force.* ■ Tennessee officials have told him to take all the time he needs to arrive at a conclusion. *Tennessee officials have told him to take all the time he needs to decide.*

**arrive at (a; the) decision (about; as to; concerning; of; on; regarding)** *conclude; decide; deduce; determine; infer; judge; reason; resolve; settle.* The democratic process requires discussion and debate for people to arrive at a decision on a course of action. *The democratic process requires discussion and debate for people to decide on a course of action.* ■ The details of a particular case must be used to arrive at a decision about what is best for the specific patient being considered. *The details of a particular case must be used to deduce what is best for the specific patient being considered.*

**arrive at (a; the) determination (about; as to; concerning; of; on; regarding)** *conclude; decide; deduce; determine; infer; judge; reason; resolve; settle.* Sampling from an elderly population of bereaved spouses, the authors used various psychological measures to arrive at a determination of the principle elements of complicated grief. *Sampling from an elderly population of bereaved spouses, the authors used various psychological measures to determine the principle elements of complicated grief.*

**arrive at (an; the) estimate (estimation) (about; as to; concerning; of; on; regarding)** *approximate; assess; estimate; evaluate; rate.* Since information from subsequent steps in an assessment is needed to arrive at an estimate of what the firm's actual marketing effort will be, the assessment from this point on is reiterative. *Since information from subsequent steps in an assessment is needed to estimate what the firm's actual marketing effort will be, the assessment from this point on is reiterative.*

**arrive at (an; the) opinion (about; as to; concerning; of; on; regarding)** *conclude; decide; deduce; determine; infer; judge; reason; resolve; settle.* Through analysis of verbal, physical and sexual behavior, we arrive at an opinion whether a series of crimes was committed by the same offender or not. *Through analysis of verbal, physical and sexual behavior, we conclude whether a series of crimes was committed by the same offender or not.* ■ Each property is unique, and the appraiser relies on his or her general expertise and specific research to arrive at an opinion of its value. *Each property is unique, and the appraiser relies on his or her general expertise and specific research to decide its value.*

**arrive at (a; the) resolution (about; as to; concerning; of; on; regarding)** *agree; conclude; decide; resolve; settle.* If the parties arrive at a resolution of their dispute, they, with the help of the mediator, typically write an agreement that captures their chosen course of action. *If the parties settle their dispute, they, with the help of the mediator, typically write an agreement that captures their chosen course of action.*

**arrive at (a; the) settlement (about; as to; concerning; of; on; regarding)** *agree; conclude; decide; resolve; settle.*

**arrive at (an; the) understanding (about; as to; concerning; of; on; regarding)** *agree; compromise; concur; decide; resolve; settle.* Where the Commission fails to arrive at a settlement of the complaint, the Commission will then request the appointment of a tribunal, referred to as a board of inquiry. *Where the Commission fails to resolve the complaint, the Commission will then request the appointment of a tribunal, referred to as a board of inquiry.*

**as a consequence** *consequently; hence; so; then; therefore; thus.* As a consequence, there are a lot of charlatans, zealots, and incompetents offering their services. *Thus, there are a lot of charlatans, zealots, and incompetents offering their services.*

**as a consequence of** *after; because of; by; due to; following; for; from; in; out of; owing to; through; with.* As a consequence of the 43 million babies born in the years immediately following World War II, a middle-aged bulge is forming and eventually the 35- to 45-year-old age group will increase by 80 percent. *Because of the 43 million babies born in the years immediately following World War II, a middle-aged bulge is forming and eventually the 35- to 45-year-old age group will increase by 80 percent.*

**as a consequence of the fact that** *because; considering; for; given; in that; since.* Expectations were low as a consequence of the fact that screen technology was fairly grim. *Expectations were low because screen technology was fairly grim.* ■ As a consequence of the fact that the IPA is a global organization, a number of details regarding ethics are viewed differently in different practice locales. *Since the IPA is a global organization, a number of details regarding ethics are viewed differently in different practice locales.*

**as against** *against; to.* Total investments in property, plant and equipment amounted to SEK 1,592 m. in 1987, as against SEK 1,643 m. in the preceding year. *Total investments in property, plant and equipment amounted to SEK 1,592 m. in 1987, against SEK 1,643 m. in the preceding year.*

**as a general rule** *almost all; as a rule; chiefly; commonly; customarily; generally; greatly; in general; largely; mainly; most; mostly; most often; much; nearly all; normally; overall; typically; usually.* As a general rule, interest payments are made every six months. *Typically, interest payments are made every six months.*

**as a matter of course** *commonly; customarily; habitually; naturally; normally; ordinarily; regularly; routinely; typically; usually.* Most veterinarians do it as a matter of course because it is a money-making procedure. *Most veterinarians do it routinely because it is a money-making procedure.*

**as a matter of fact** *actually; indeed; in fact; in faith; in reality; in truth; really; truly;* delete. As a matter of fact, there are some rumors of discontent. *In fact, there are some rumors of discontent.*

**as a matter of fact** *also; and; as well; besides; beyond that (this); even; further; furthermore; moreover; more than that (this); still more; then; too; what is more.*

**as a means for (of; to) (-ing)** *for (-ing); so as to; to.* I have found the spelling checker extremely useful as a means for proofreading text. *I have found the spelling checker extremely useful for proofreading text.*

**as and when**  *as; when.* At the same time, they have substantial outflows, ongoing expenses which cannot be shifted but must be paid as and when they become due. *At the same time, they have substantial outflows, ongoing expenses which cannot be shifted but must be paid as they become due.*

**as an example**  *for example; for instance.*

**as ... apply to**  *about; as for; as to; concerning; for; in; of; on; over; regarding; respecting; to; toward; with;* delete. I've always been intrigued by the concept of marketing as it applies to health care. *I've always been intrigued by the concept of health care marketing.*

**as a result**  *consequently; hence; so; then; therefore; thus.* The IDA was working to make jobs available to the graduates of these schools, and as a result, the educational climate in Ireland has changed dramatically. *The IDA was working to make jobs available to the graduates of these schools, and thus, the educational climate in Ireland has changed dramatically.*

**as a result of**  *after; because of; by; due to; following; for; from; in; out of; owing to; through; with.* More people die as a result of drinking alcohol than as a result of smoking marijuana. *More people die from drinking alcohol than from smoking marijuana.* ■ Much pain and resentment was rekindled as a result of recent political maneuverings between the Turkish and U.S. governments. *Much pain and resentment was rekindled following recent political maneuverings between the Turkish and U.S. governments.* ■ Other citizens have closed minds to rehabilitation programs as a result of what they refer to as its failures. *Other citizens have closed minds to rehabilitation programs because of what they refer to as its failures.*

**as a result of the fact that**  *because; considering; for; given; in that; since.* This is clearly an area of growing importance to BOCs, particularly as a result of the fact that a recent court decision allows them to enter in certain segments of enhanced services. *This is clearly an area of growing importance to BOCs, particularly since a recent court decision allows them to enter in certain segments of enhanced services.* ■ As a result of the fact that this law was not passed earlier, the judge had to return the confiscated photos. *Because this law was not passed earlier, the judge had to return the confiscated photos.*

**as a rule**  *almost all; chiefly; commonly; generally; greatly; in general; largely; mainly; most; mostly; most often; much; nearly all; normally; over-*

*all; typically.* As a rule, I wouldn't dream of doing something like this. *Normally, I wouldn't dream of doing something like this.*

**as a way for (of; to) (-ing)** *for (-ing); so as to; to.* More and more professionals are using dating services as a way of meeting the perfect mate. *More and more professionals are using dating services to meet the perfect mate.*

**as a whole** *complete; entire; whole;* delete. It's an embarrassment to the administration as a whole. *It's an embarrassment to the administration.*

**ascend up** *ascend.* As you ascend up the status hierarchy, you get to select more expensive furnishings. *As you ascend the status hierarchy, you get to select more expensive furnishings.*

**as compared to (with)** *against; alongside; beside; compared to (with); -(i)er than; less; less than; more; more than; next to; over; than; to; versus; vis-à-vis.* The governments of developing countries give low priority to these skills as compared to technological skills and knowledge. *The governments of developing countries give lower priority to these skills than to technological skills and knowledge.* ■ The Japanese can design and build a car in about 3 1/2 years as compared to U.S. auto makers' average of 5 years. *The Japanese can design and build a car in about 3 1/2 years against U.S. auto makers' average of 5 years.* ■ Data communications is not very familiar ground to the operating companies as compared to their expertise in voice. *Data communications is not very familiar ground to the operating companies compared to their expertise in voice.*

**as compared to (with) ... relatively** *compared to (with); -(i)er than (less than; more than).* As compared to Western Europeans and the Japanese, Americans save a relatively small proportion of their disposable income. *Compared to Western Europeans and the Japanese, Americans save a small proportion of their disposable income.*

**as concerns** *about; as for; as to; concerning; for; in; of; on; over; regarding; respecting; to; toward; with.* As concerns the judicial control of the proceedings of a selection board, the commission stated that one has to distinguish between two kinds of decisions. *As for the judicial control of the proceedings of a selection board, the commission stated that one has to distinguish between two kinds of decisions.*

**as contrasted to (with)** *against; alongside; beside; compared to (with); -(i)er than; less; less than; more; more than; next to; over; than; to; unlike; versus; vis-à-vis.* Epidemiologists find that people who eat a lot of fish have much lower rates of both cholesterol-caused heart disease and cholesterol gallstones as contrasted to people who don't. *Epidemiologists find that people who eat a lot of fish have much lower rates of both cholesterol-caused heart disease and cholesterol gallstones than people who don't.*

**a (the) score of**  delete. Sweden is on top by a score of 6 to 1. *Sweden is on top by 6 to 1.*

**ascribable to**  *because of; caused by; due to; owing to; resulting from.* Likewise, WIG may not be held liable for any loss or damage ascribable to computer viruses when users call up or download data from this website. *Likewise, WIG may not be held liable for any loss or damage due to computer viruses when users call up or download data from this website.*

**as (the) days (decades; months; weeks; years) go on**  *at length; eventually; in time; later; one day; over the months (years); over time; someday; sometime; ultimately; with time; yet;* delete. As the years go on, customers will look to Nynex and others to give them more than just the transmission of information — they'll also need the software and the systems integration to run their businesses and homes more efficiently. *Over time, customers will look to Nynex and others to give them more than just the transmission of information — they'll also need the software and the systems integration to run their businesses and homes more efficiently.*

**a second time**  *again; once more.*

**as (so) far as ... (goes; is concerned)**  *about; as for; as to; concerning; for; in; of; on; over; regarding; respecting; to; toward; with;* delete. The effect of lead is particularly traumatic as far as young children are concerned. *The effect of lead is particularly traumatic on young children.* ■ In fact, as far as the "secrets of entrepreneurial success" go, it's impossible to recognize that a little bit of luck helps and a lot of luck is even better. *In fact, concerning the "secrets of entrepreneurial success," it's impossible to recognize that a little bit of luck helps and a lot of luck is even better.* ■ The general view seems to be that infectious agents transmitted by rodents are not of particular relevance as far as public health goes. *The general view seems to be that infectious agents transmitted by rodents are not of particular relevance to public health.* ■ As far as fish are concerned, the optimal Hct theory appears to be too simplistic to account for our present state of knowledge. *As for fish, the optimal Hct theory appears to be too simplistic to account for our present state of knowledge.*

79

**as follows** delete. The quote is as follows: "I never met a man who had better motives for all the trouble he's causing." *The quote is "I never met a man who had better motives for all the trouble he's causing."*

**as ... for example (for instance)** *as; for example (for instance); like; say; such as.* No such close match is necessary if the intent of the assessment is to monitor the general state of student knowledge and competence in science, as for example in past assessments conducted by NAEP. *No such close match is necessary if the intent of the assessment is to monitor the general state of student knowledge and competence in science, as in past assessments conducted by NAEP.*

**as for (in; with) the case of** *as for (in; with); like.* Even when countries adopt state religions, as in the cases of the United Kingdom, Spain, and Italy, the religious context of the country is not necessarily monolithic. *Even when countries adopt state religions, as in the United Kingdom, Spain, and Italy, the religious context of the country is not necessarily monolithic.*

**as how** *that.* He allowed as how he could further explore the idea. *He allowed that he could further explore the idea.* ∎ Not having a mistress I explained as how I didn't see the problem. *Not having a mistress I explained that I didn't see the problem.*

**aside from** *besides; beyond.* Aside from the lack of restraints, there are other differences a foreign investor must get used to. *Besides the lack of restraints, there are other differences a foreign investor must get used to.*

**aside from ... also (as well)** *aside from; besides; beyond.*

**as, if, and when** *if; when.* The Company will be deemed to have purchased tendered Shares as, if, and when it gives oral and written notice to the Depositary of its acceptance for payment of such Shares. *The Company will be deemed to have purchased tendered Shares when it gives oral and written notice to the Depositary of its acceptance for payment of such Shares.*

**a single one** *a single; one.* Not a single one of the dire accusations or predictions made in that article has come true. *Not one of the dire accusations or predictions made in that article has come true.*

**a single solitary (one)** *a single; one.*

**(even) as I (we) speak** *(just; right) now;* delete. As we speak, New

York state is starting a drug education program. *New York state is now starting a drug education program.*

**as is the case** *as; like.* As is the case with all of our new words, they sound terribly impressive at cocktail parties. *Like all of our new words, they sound terribly impressive at cocktail parties.*

**as it turned out** *by chance; luckily; unluckily.*

**ask (a; the) question (on)** *ask.* We need to ask ourselves the question if animals are necessary for medical training. *We need to ask ourselves if animals are necessary for medical training.* ■ If you would like to ask a question on how magnets may possibly help a condition, we will do our best to answer your question as soon as possible. *If you would like to ask how magnets may possibly help a condition, we will do our best to answer your question as soon as possible.*

**as long as (so long as) (that)** *if.* This program, as well as others like it, will make a difference as long as we have strong public support for changing the plight of these children. *This program, as well as others like it, will make a difference if we have strong public support for changing the plight of these children.*

**as luck would have it** *by chance; luckily; unluckily.*

**as many (much) as** *up to.* There are nearly 300 individual fund managers, ranging from those with a single fund to the very large mutual fund families that offer as many as 100 different funds. *There are nearly 300 individual fund managers, ranging from those with a single fund to the very large mutual fund families that offer up to 100 different funds.*

**as of** *on; delete.* The plant will shut down as of November 1. *The plant will shut down November 1.*

**as often as not** *commonly; customarily; generally; normally; often; ordinarily; typically; usually.*

**as opposed to** *against; alongside; beside; compared to (with); -(i)er than; less; less than; more; more than; next to; over; than; to; unlike; versus; vis-à-vis.* Thanks to the recent strength of the dollar, the U.S. markets remain attractive, as opposed to their foreign counterparts. *Thanks to the recent strength of the dollar, the U.S. markets remain more attractive than their foreign counterparts.* ■ You should experience better results with the cool white as opposed to the warm white because the cool white approximates natural sunlight. *You should experience better results with the cool white than the warm white because the cool white approximates natural sunlight.*

**as opposed to** *instead of; not; rather than; whereas.* Why do customers choose one brand as opposed to another? *Why do customers choose one brand rather than another?* ■ This typically includes name, e-mail address, and home address, as opposed to anonymous demographic information such as country, gender, and Web service preferences. *This typically includes name, e-mail address, and home address, not anonymous demographic information such as country, gender, and Web service preferences.*

**as opposed to ... relatively** *compared to (with); -(i)er than (less than; more than).* As opposed to the organization and access rules of network and hierarchical data models, those of the relational model are relatively simple. *Compared to the organization and access rules of network and hierarchical data models, those of the relational model are simple.*

**a spectrum of** *assorted; countless; different; divers; diverse; extensive; many; numerous; scores of; sundry; varied; various; varying;* delete.

**as regards** *about; as for; as to; concerning; for; in; of; on; over; regarding; respecting; to; toward; with.* He promises to be less tightfisted in the future as regards training. *He promises to be less tightfisted in the future about training.* ■ There are significant differences across countries as regards the use of on-site and off-site supervisory techniques. *There are significant differences across countries regarding the use of on-site and off-site supervisory techniques.*

**assemble together** *assemble.* Proteins are constructed by assembling together several modules or domains. *Proteins are constructed by assembling several modules or domains.*

**assistance** *aid; help; succor.*

**assist in -ing** *help.* This view assists you in visualizing the problem. *This view helps you visualize the problem.*

**associated with** *for; in; linked to; of; related to; -'s; with.* The greater the required accuracy, the greater the cost associated with generating a plan. *The greater the required accuracy, the greater the cost of generating a plan.* ■ Because of the rugged terrain associated with mountainous areas, you will frequently encounter fractures and sprains. *Because of the rugged terrain of mountainous areas, you will frequently encounter fractures and sprains.* ■ One of the essential reasons for this is the high cost associated with owning and maintaining the infrastructure required to create a common global platform. *One of the essential reasons for this is the high cost of owning and maintaining the infrastructure required to create a common global platform.*

**associated with** *belongs to; employed by; works for.*

**association** *connection; link; relation; tie.* The CDC study concluded there was no association between use of the pill and breast cancer. *The CDC study concluded there was no link between use of the pill and breast cancer.*

**as soon as** *once; when.* I'll call you as soon as I can. *I'll call you when I can.*

**(most; very) assuredly** *yes.*

**assure (ensure; insure) ... guarantee** *ensure; guarantee.* There must be a way to ensure that their privacy is guaranteed. *There must be a way to ensure their privacy.*

**a (the) stage of** delete. Other products take a long time to gain acceptance and may never reach a stage of widespread adoption. *Other products take a long time to gain acceptance and may never reach widespread adoption.*

**as the basis for (-ing)** *for (-ing); so as to; to.* Data is any information used as the basis for discussing or deciding something. *Data is any information used to discuss or decide something.* ■ The purpose of the course is to provide an understanding of physics as a basis for successfully launching new high-tech ventures. *The purpose of the course is to provide an understanding of physics so as to successfully launch new high-tech ventures.* ■ We can use their modern ecological requirements as a basis for interpreting what past environments must have been like. *We can use their modern ecological requirements to interpret what past environments must have been like.*

**as the case (situation) may be** delete. When both are used on the same drawing, the parts list is placed directly above and in contact with the title block or the title strip, as the case may be. *When both are used on the same drawing, the parts list is placed directly above and in contact with the title block or the title strip.*

**as the need arises (develops)** *as needed.* Corrections and adjustments can be made as the need arises. *Corrections and adjustments can be made as needed.*

**as the saying goes** delete.

**as time goes on** *at length; in due time; in time; later; one day; over time; someday; sometime; ultimately; with time; yet;* delete. As time goes on, maintenance revenues will rise for the average distributor. *Maintenance revenues will yet rise for the average distributor.*

**as time progresses (forward; on; onward)** *at length; eventually; in due time; in time; later; one day; over the months (years); over time; someday; sometime; ultimately; with time; yet;* delete. As time progressed, she decided to divorce him. *At length, she decided to divorce him.*

**as to** *about; by; for; from; in; of; on; over; to; with;* delete. I'm curious as to why you would choose to be in that situation. *I'm curious why you would choose to be in that situation.* ■ People have different ideas as to what is sexually acceptable to them. *People have different ideas on what is sexually acceptable to them.* ■ Once you know your skills, aptitudes, interests, and motivations, you will have a good idea as to what you have going for you and what you want. *Once you know your skills, aptitudes, interests, and motivations, you will have a good idea of what you have going for you and what you want.* ■ We were bewildered as to what was taking place. *We were bewildered by what was taking place.* ■ Different or missing sounds can be a clue as to what's malfunctioning. *Different or missing sounds can be a clue to what's malfunctioning.*

**as to whether** *whether.* It's too early to speculate as to whether the two stabbings are connected. *It's too early to speculate whether the two stabbings are connected.* ■ In the past, Internet Explorer used to guess as to whether data stored in the cache was actually stale. *In the past, Internet Explorer used to guess whether data stored in the cache was actually stale.*

**as well as** *and.* Banks have added to their capital by retaining a higher share of current earnings, in some cases selling their undervalued real estate as well as business assets. *Banks have added to their capital by retaining a higher share of current earnings, in some cases selling their undervalued real estate and business assets.*

**as (of) yet** *yet.* I haven't mastered the sport as of yet. *I haven't mastered the sport yet.* ■ Listen to a tape, or jot down ideas that you haven't put on paper as yet. *Listen to a tape, or jot down ideas that you haven't yet put on paper.*

**at about (around)** *about (around).* We got there at about 7:00. *We got there about 7:00.*

**at a certain (any; one; some) point in my history (point in my life; point in the history of my life; point in time)** *at one time; ever; once; one day; someday; sometime;* delete. At one point in the history of my life, I was a high school English teacher. *I was once a high school English teacher.*

**at a (some) future (later; subsequent) date (time)** *at length; eventually; in due time; in time; later; one day; over the months (years); over time; someday; sometime; ultimately; with time; yet.* These guidelines also apply to other reading materials that you will need to reread and study at a later date. *These guidelines also apply to other reading materials that you will later need to reread and study.*

**at all** delete. You're unwilling to make any sort of compromise at all. *You're unwilling to make any sort of compromise.*

**at a (the) juncture (juncture in time; moment; moment in time; period; period in time; point; point in time; stage; stage in time; time)** *when.* At the point in time this book was published, several other titles were also available. *When this book was published, several other titles were also available.*

**at a (the) juncture (juncture in time; moment; moment in time; period; period in time; point; point in time; stage; stage in time; time) when** *when.* On a computer, the design is created on the screen, and the scale can be decided, and changed, at the time when the final drawing is printed out on a printer or plotter. *On a computer, the design is created on the screen, and the scale can be decided, and changed, when the final drawing is printed out on a printer or plotter.*

**at an (some) earlier (former; past; previous) date (time)** *before; earlier; formerly; once.*

**at an end** *complete; done; ended; finished; over; past.* Barring the unexpected, the 25-year search for a new arena is at an end. *Barring the unexpected, the 25-year search for a new arena is over.*

**at any date (hour; time)** *any time.*

**at any minute (moment)** *directly; momentarily; momently; presently; soon.*

**at any rate** *anyhow; even so; still; yet.*

**at (from; in; on; to) (a; the) area (locale; locality; location; place; point; position; region; site; spot)** *where; wherever.* The program is temporarily interrupted, and can be restarted any time at the exact place it left off. *The program is temporarily interrupted, and can be restarted any time exactly where it left off.*

**at (from; in; on; to) (any; each; every; some) area (locale; locality; location; place; point; position; region; site; spot)** *anyplace; anywhere; ever; everyplace; everywhere; one day; someday; someplace; sometime; somewhere; where; wherever.* If at any point I felt I was an embarrassment to the president, I would resign. *If I ever felt I was an embarrassment to the president, I would resign.*

**at (from; in; on; to) (a; the) area (locale; locality; location; place; point; position; region; site; spot) where** *where; wherever.* The voodoo doctor told me to put them in a location where no one would ever find them. *The voodoo doctor told me to put them where no one would ever find them.*

**at (from; in; on; to) (any; each; every; some) area (locale; locality; location; place; point; position; region; site; spot) where** *anyplace; anywhere; ever; everyplace; everywhere; one day; someday; someplace; sometime; somewhere; where; wherever.* At every place where food was available, people went hungry for lack of dry fuel. *Wherever food was available, people went hungry for lack of dry fuel.*

**at (for) (a; the) cost (price; sum) of** *at (for).* The Tower was built from 1970 to 1974 at a cost of more than $150 million. *The Tower was built from 1970 to 1974 for more than $150 million.*

**at every turn** *always; ceaselessly; consistently; constantly; endlessly; eternally; everyday; forever; unfailingly.*

**at frequent (periodic; regular) intervals (periods)** *frequently; periodically; regularly.* At periodic intervals, the entries made in the journals are posted to the general ledger. *Periodically, the entries made in the journals are posted to the general ledger.*

**at (a; the) ... level** -*(al)ly;* delete. Prices at the wholesale level will go up 6 cents per gallon. *Wholesale prices will go up 6 cents per gallon.*

**at long last** *at last; finally.*

**at (for) no charge (cost)** *free.* It will be available at no charge through Avatar dealers nationwide. *It will be available free through Avatar dealers nationwide.*

**at no time** *never.* At no time was it this union's position to oppose the Emerson College proposal or deprive fellow workers of jobs made available by this project. *Never was it this union's position to oppose the Emerson College proposal or deprive fellow workers of jobs made available by this project.*

**at one time (in the past)** *once.*

**atop of** *atop.*

**a (the) total ... (of)** delete. The United States sent a total of 3.4 million men and women to serve in Southeast Asia during the period. *The United States sent 3.4 million men and women to serve in Southeast Asia during the period.* ■ The status line displays the total number of words that were checked. *The status line displays the number of words that were checked.*

**at (a; the) ... pace (of)** *at; by;* -*(al)ly;* delete. We've had fairly stable interest rates and an economy that continues to grow at a moderate pace. *We've had fairly stable interest rates and an economy that continues to grow moderately.*

**at (the) present** *(just; right) now; nowadays; these days; today; (just) yet;* delete. At present, nothing indicates that South Africa is prepared to completely dismantle apartheid. *Nothing yet indicates that South Africa is prepared to completely dismantle apartheid.*

**at (a; the) ... rate (of)** *at; by;* -*(al)ly;* delete. Crime on college campuses is growing at a geometric rate. *Crime on college campuses is growing geometrically.*

**at some point (time) along the line (the way)** *at some point; at some time.*

**at specific (specified; timed) intervals (periods)** *periodically; regularly.*

**at (a; the) ... speed (of)** *at; by; -(al)ly;* delete. Loosened by rain or melting snow, ordinary soil on a steep hillside can suddenly turn into a lethal wave sweeping downward at speeds of more than 30 miles per hour. *Loosened by rain or melting snow, ordinary soil on a steep hillside can suddenly turn into a lethal wave sweeping downward at more than 30 miles per hour.*

**attach together** *attach.* There are four separate graphics panels which attach together to form a display. *There are four separate graphics panels which attach to form a display.*

**attack by assailants** *assail; assault; attack.* They were departing a local discotheque and entering their vehicle when they were attacked by assailants. *They were departing a local discotheque and entering their vehicle when they were attacked.*

**attempt** *try.* My ex-wife and I attempted to have a child for six years. *My ex-wife and I tried to have a child for six years.*

**attention ... focused on (upon)** *attention on; focus on.* In presidential politics, everyone's attention is now focused on the South. *In presidential politics, everyone is now focused on the South.*

**at that (this) juncture** *at present; at that (this) time; current; currently; (just; right) now; nowadays; present; presently; then; these days; today; (just) yet;* delete. For nimble investors, a little buying may be appropriate at this juncture. *For nimble investors, a little buying may now be appropriate.*

**at that (this) juncture (juncture in time; moment; moment in time; period; period in time; point; point in time; stage; stage in time; time) in my history (in my life; in the history of my life)** *at present; at that (this) time; current; currently; (just; right) now; nowadays; present; presently; then; these days; today; (just) yet;* delete. At that point in my life, death seemed vague and romantic. *Death seemed vague and romantic then.* ■ At this point in time in our history, that can be a subtle and tricky distinction. *Today, that can be a subtle and tricky distinction.*

**at that (this) juncture (moment; period; point; stage) in time** *at present; at that (this) time; current; currently; (just; right) now; nowadays; present; presently; then; these days; today; (just) yet;* delete. At this moment in time, he must abide by the way I want things to be. *He now must abide by the way I want things to be.*

**at that (this) moment** *at present; at that (this) time; current; currently; (just; right) now; nowadays; present; presently; then; these days; today; (just) yet;* delete. Did you know at that moment that your father had killed the rest of the family? *Did you know then that your father had killed the rest of the family?*

**at that (this) point** *at present; current; currently; (just; right) now; nowadays; present; presently; then; these days; today; (just) yet;* delete. At that point, we will discontinue our aid to them. *We will then discontinue our aid to them.*

**at that (this) stage** *at present; at that (this) time; current; currently; (just; right) now; nowadays; present; presently; then; these days; today; (just) yet;* delete. It's hard to tell at this stage. *It's hard to tell now.*

**at that (this) time** *at present; current; currently; (just; right) now; nowadays; present; presently; then; these days; today; (just) yet;* delete. The potential return on the investment is uncertain at this time. *The potential return on the investment is presently uncertain.*

**at (in) the blink of an eye** *abruptly; apace; briskly; directly; fast; forthwith; hastily; hurriedly; posthaste; presently; promptly; quickly; rapidly; right away; shortly; soon; speedily; straightaway; swiftly; wingedly.* All this happens at the blink of an eye, as it would with a standard desktop application. *All this happens swiftly, as it would with a standard desktop application.*

**at (on) the brink of** *about to; approaching; close to; near; nearly; verging on.* Some 10,000 Sudanese are on the brink of starving to death in a southern town under siege by armed guerrillas. *Some 10,000 Sudanese are close to starving to death in a southern town under siege by armed guerrillas.*

**at the corner (intersection) of** *at.* The site is located at the intersection of Buffum and Blake Streets in the Central Square Historic District. *The site is located at Buffum and Blake Streets in the Central Square Historic District.*

**at the current (present) time** *at present; at this time; current; currently; (just; right) now; nowadays; present; presently; these days; today; (just) yet;* delete. What is the value of Digital's stock at the present time? *What is the current value of Digital's stock?*

**at the hands of** *by; from; through.* I am enraged by the second-class treatment we are receiving at the hands of those who legislate for and govern us. *I am enraged by the second-class treatment we are receiving from those who legislate for and govern us.*

**at the (very) minimum** *at least.*

**at the (current; present) moment** *at present; current; currently; (just; right) now; nowadays; present; presently; these days; today; (just) yet;* delete. At the moment, this effort is being left largely to individual state colleges and universities to initiate. *This effort is now being left largely to individual state colleges and universities to initiate.*

**at (on) the point of** *about to; approaching; close to; near; nearly; verging on.*

**at the same time** *as one; at once; collectively; concurrently; jointly; together.* If too many things happened at the same time, data would be lost in the process. *If too many things happened at once, data would be lost in the process.*

**(and) at the same time (as; that)** *as; while.* In many cases, Soviet interest in smoothing East-West relations has been complicated by conflicting diplomatic priorities, such as improving ties with China and maintaining relations with Vietnam at the same time. *In many cases, Soviet interest in smoothing East-West relations has been complicated by conflicting diplomatic priorities, such as improving ties with China while maintaining relations with Vietnam.* ■ A similar dilemma faces Cray Research Inc., which relies on Japanese-made chips at the same time it fends off Japanese challenges to its role as the world's leading maker of supercomputers. *A similar dilemma faces Cray Research Inc., which relies on Japanese-made chips as it fends off Japanese challenges to its role as the world's leading maker of supercomputers.*

**attired** *dressed.*

**(a; the) ... attitude (of)** delete. He had a very cavalier attitude about money. *He was very cavalier about money.*

**at (on) (the) top (of)** *atop; on.* It removes the dead cells that accumulate on top of the skin. *It removes the dead cells that accumulate on the skin.*

**attributable to** *because of; caused by; due to; owing to; result from.* These increases were primarily attributable to a variety of merchant banking activities. *These increases were primarily caused by a variety of merchant banking activities.*

**attributable to the fact that**  *because; considering; for; given; in that; since.* The differing performance of black and white incomes is primarily attributable to the fact that white-married-couple families did significantly better last year than black-married-couple families. *The differing performance of black and white incomes is primarily because white-married-couple families did significantly better last year than black-married-couple families.* ■ The low recovery rate in these cases is largely attributable to the fact that the nature of art theft will involve thieves who know both their art and where to find markets for the sale of stolen works. *The low recovery rate in these cases is largely because the nature of art theft will involve thieves who know both their art and where to find markets for the sale of stolen works.*

**at what (which) juncture (juncture in time; moment; moment in time; period; period in time; point; point in time; stage; stage in time; time)**  *when.* At what point will you know if the business is profitable? *When will you know if the business is profitable?* ■ A term to age 65 policy provides protection to age 65, at which time the policy expires. *A term to age 65 policy provides protection to age 65, when the policy expires.* ■ My research of racial oppression began over 50 years ago, at which time I experienced a traumatic incident that left me with the first of many racial scars that have not healed until this day. *My research of racial oppression began over 50 years ago, when I experienced a traumatic incident that left me with the first of many racial scars that have not healed until this day.*

**at your earliest convenience**  *as soon as possible; at once; presently; quickly; right away; shortly; soon; without delay;* delete. Please return the signed and completed application to this office at your earliest convenience. *Please return the signed and completed application to this office.*

**audible to the ear**  *audible.* CDRs burned below this standard are very likely to be rejected by the CD manufacturing facility on account of too many "uncorrectable errors" (data flow inconsistencies that are not audible to the ear but could result in glitches on replicated discs). *CDRs burned below this standard are very likely to be rejected by the CD manufacturing facility on account of too many "uncorrectable errors" (data flow inconsistencies that are not audible but could* *result in glitches on replicated discs).*

**authentic replica**  *replica.* These archaeology kits contain an authentic replica of an artifact representing an ancient culture. *These archaeology kits contain a replica of an artifact representing an ancient culture.*

**author** *(v)*  *write.*

**authoress**  *author.*

**a variety of**  *assorted; countless; different; divers; diverse; extensive; many; numerous; scores of; sundry; varied; various; varying;* delete. Today, a variety of pricing approaches are used. *Today, various pricing approaches are used.*

**a (the) variety of different**  *assorted; a variety of; countless; different; divers; diverse; extensive; many; numerous; scores of; sundry; varied; various; varying.* The children's museum will have a variety of different events. *The children's museum will have a variety of events.*

# B

**background of experience** *background; experience.* It is, then, from a background of experience in communication that I want to present two ideas. *It is, then, from a background in communication that I want to present two ideas.*

**back in** *in; last.* My daughter disappeared back in January. *My daughter disappeared last January.*

**back (before) in the past** *before; earlier; formerly; in the past; once; delete.* Dealing with irrational people is something my father has done well back in the past and is something he'll do well in the future. *Dealing with irrational people is something my father has done well in the past and is something he'll do well in the future.*

**backward and forward** *completely; entirely; fully; thoroughly; totally; utterly; wholly.*

**badge (mark; sign; symbol) of authenticity (distinction; honor; prestige; rank)** *cachet.* Basler says the bumps, which appear on the foot and are regarded as a badge of distinction among serious surfers, result from long hours spent in contact with a surfboard. *Basler says the bumps, which appear on the foot and are regarded as a cachet among serious surfers, result from long hours spent in contact with a surfboard.*

**balance out** *balance.* Because seasonal forces are relative, they balance each other out by the completion of a full year. *Because seasonal forces are relative, they balance each other by the completion of a full year.*

**bald-headed** *bald.*

**-based** *from; in; of; -'s; delete.* Sharon Howard, an Atlanta-based attorney, has given a lot of thought to the way she is treated in the courtroom. *Sharon Howard, an Atlanta attorney, has given a lot of thought to the way she is treated in the courtroom.*

**based in** *from; in; of; -'s; delete.* PCE is a privately held company based in Portland, Oregon. *PCE is a privately held company in Portland, Oregon.*

**based on (upon)** *after; by; for; from; in; on; through; with; delete.* Based on what I hear, everyone thinks Fan Pier has lost its moment of opportunity. *From what I hear, everyone thinks Fan Pier has lost its moment of opportunity.*

**based on (upon) my personal judgment (opinion)** *I assert; I believe; I claim; I consider; I contend; I feel; I hold; I judge; I maintain; I regard; I say; I think; I view; to me;* delete. Based on my personal judgment, I think tax revenues will grow by 8.3 percent. *I think tax revenues will grow by 8.3 percent.*

**based on the fact that** *because; considering; for; given; in that; since.* I'm not in favor of it based on the fact that a lot of small businesses will suffer. *I'm not in favor of it because a lot of small businesses will suffer.* ■ Based on the fact that no single timing rule works well all the time, AIQ incorporates many rules that work together in a powerful synergism to signal when the overall market, and individual securities, are ready to move. *Since no single timing rule works well all the time, AIQ incorporates many rules that work together in a powerful synergism to signal when the overall market, and individual securities, are ready to move.*

**baseless (groundless; unfounded; unsubstantiated) rumor** *hearsay; rumor.* A Foreign Ministry spokesman characterized the reports as unfounded rumors. *A Foreign Ministry spokesman characterized the reports as rumors.*

**basic** delete. In this section, we introduce you to the basic procedures to control page breaks and page numbers. *In this section, we introduce you to the procedures to control page breaks and page numbers.*

**basically** *chiefly; largely; mainly; most; mostly;* delete. Basically, the social service groups involved are either indifferent or corrupt. *The social service groups involved are either indifferent or corrupt.* ■ The rest of the day will be basically partly cloudy. *The rest of the day will be partly cloudy.* ■ What basically began as an experiment to determine whether a family-type YMCA would survive quickly evolved into a challenge to serve a very enthusiastic community. *What began as an experiment to determine whether a family-type YMCA would survive quickly evolved into a challenge to serve a very enthusiastic community.* ■ Basically, the next step is adding the molasses. *The next step is adding the molasses.*

**basic (and) fundamental** *basic; fundamental.* Our basic, fundamental values are the same. *Our fundamental values are the same.* ■ At the same time, by advancing basic and fundamental research and development, MEXT strives to ensure the promotion of research through-out the nation. *At the same time, by advancing fundamental research and development, MEXT strives to ensure the promotion of research throughout the nation.*

**basic principle** *principle.* We feel there are two basic principles to successful advertising. *We feel there are two principles to successful advertising.*

**basis in fact (reality; truth)** *basis; fact; reality; reason; truth; veracity.* About the only statement in the article that has any basis in fact is "I want to build the biggest film group in the world." *About the only statement in the article that has any truth is "I want to build the biggest film group in the world."*

**bathroom facilities** *bathroom; toilet.*

**(please) be advised (informed) that** delete. Please be advised that we must be notified at least two weeks prior to your closing date in order to issue your 6(d) certificate. *We must be notified at least two weeks prior to your closing date in order to issue your 6(d) certificate.* ■ However, please be advised that this person is out of town until next week; I am sure she will then respond to you at her earliest possible convenience. *However, this person is out of town until next week; I am sure she will then respond to you at her earliest possible convenience.*

**bear (have; hold) a grudge (against)** *dislike; resent.* He and Latin America aide Janice O'Connell bear a grudge against the Cuban-American. *He and Latin America aide Janice O'Connell resent the Cuban-American.*

**(please) bear in mind** *consider; heed; note; realize.*

**bear (a; the) ... resemblance (similarity) to** *be like; be similar to; look like; resemble.* The Lumina's body bears a similarity to Chevrolet's Corsica and Beretta. *The Lumina's body resembles Chevrolet's Corsica and Beretta.* ■ Jay argues that the protesters of the '60s and today's campus left bear a resemblance to the deranged militias of today. *Jay argues that the protesters of the '60s and today's campus left resemble the deranged militias of today.*

**bear witness to** *affirm; attest to; certify to; declare; testify to; verify.* A splendid perennial garden surrounds the house and bears witness to the collaboration in the family. *A splendid perennial garden surrounds* *the house and attests to the collaboration in the family.*

**because of** *after; by; for; from; in; out of; through; with.* Such a model would be inappropriate because of two reasons. *Such a model would be inappropriate for two reasons.*

**because of the fact that** *because; considering; for; given; in that; since.* Because of the fact that they are still monopoly suppliers of local exchange, I also see a discouraging prospect for the operating companies in this area. *Since they are still monopoly suppliers of local exchange, I also see a discouraging prospect for the operating companies in this area.* ■ I discounted these things because of the fact that I cared so much for you. *I discounted these things because I cared so much for you.* ■ We know there is a game because of the fact that there are a lot of people waiting in line. *We know there is a game because there are a lot of people waiting in line.*

**because why** *why.* You say you are a submissive wife, but you are that way because why? *You say you are a submissive wife, but why are you that way?*

**become known** *emerge; surface; transpire.*

**before (earlier; previously) -ed (-en)** *-ed (-en).* As we previously noted, the high-cost load funds distributed through a salesperson have dominated the industry. *As we noted, the high-cost load funds distributed through a salesperson have dominated the industry.*

**before ... first** *before.* Before you use the delete option, first extract the records you are considering deleting. *Before you use the delete option, extract the records you are considering deleting.*

**before (very) long** *shortly; soon.*

**begin (start) at ... and end (finish) at** *(be) between ... and; range from ... to.* Price tags for the condos will start at $350,000 and end at $1.75 million. *Price tags for the condos will range from $350,000 to $1.75 million.*

**begin ... first** *begin.* You should begin by sketching the centerline and guidelines first. *You should begin by sketching the centerline and guidelines.*

**behavior pattern** *behavior.*

**(a; the) ... being** delete. What sets teachers apart from other mortal beings is that they never have first names. *What sets teachers apart from other mortals is that they never have first names.*

**being (as; as how; that)** *because; considering; for; given; in that; since.* They usually deliver by noontime, and being that you're local, it'll probably be before noon. *They usually deliver by noontime, and because you're local, it'll probably be before noon.* ■ I'm afraid that is an impossibility being as how we don't have a copying machine. *I'm afraid that is an impossibility since we don't have a copying machine.*

**besides ... also (as well)** *besides; beyond.* Besides providing the high-end AI tools, they have shells for IBM PCs and compatibles as well. *Besides providing the high-end AI tools, they have shells for IBM PCs and compatibles.*

**beside the point** *immaterial; inapt; irrelevant; not pertinent.*

**best (biggest; greatest; largest; most) ... single** *best (biggest; greatest; largest; most).* Great Britain, where annual production capacity was increased to 700,000 lines a year, is the largest single market. *Great Britain, where annual production capacity was increased to 700,000 lines a year, is the largest market.*

**be that as it may** *all (just) the same; anyhow; even so; still; still and all; yet.*

**between the two of them (us)** *between them (us).*

**between you and me (us)** *between us.* Enclosed is a basic proposal which should lay the groundwork for future discussions between you and us. *Enclosed is a basic proposal which should lay the groundwork for future discussions between us.*

**betwixt and between** *in between; undecided.*

**beverage** *drink.*

**beyond (out of) all reason** *unreasonable.*

**beyond a (the) shadow of a doubt** *assuredly; certainly; doubtless; indisputably; irrefutably; no doubt; surely; undoubtedly; unquestionably.*

**beyond number** *countless; endless; infinite; millions (of); myriad; numberless; untold.*

**beyond (outside) the realm of possibility** *impossible; inconceivable; undoable; unthinkable.* So it's not beyond the realm of possibility that corporate performance could be improved if directors surveyed other areas of corporate activity, like manufacturing and marketing. *So it's not inconceivable that corporate performance could be improved if directors surveyed other areas of corporate activity, like manufacturing and marketing.*

**biased opinion** *bias; prejudice.* It merely expressed a biased opinion about a so-called problem without any indication of the extent and consequences of the problem. *It merely expressed a bias about a so-called problem without any indication of the extent and consequences of the problem.*

**big, huge (large)** *big; huge; large.* I packed a big, huge picnic lunch for us. *I packed a huge picnic lunch for us.*

**biographical** *biographic.*

**biological** *biologic.*

**biometrical** *biometric.*

**biophysiological** *biophysiologic.*

**bit by bit** *gradually; slowly.*

**bits and pieces** *bits; pieces.* Bits and pieces of segregation have been jettisoned or have rotted away. *Bits of segregation have been jettisoned or have rotted away.*

**blend of both** *blend.* Management is a blend of both science and art. *Management is a blend of science and art.*

**blend together** *blend.* Blend this WordStar expertise together in a book, and you have the definitive resource to the most widely used word processing software. *Blend this WordStar expertise in a book, and you have the definitive resource to the most widely used word processing software.*

**block out** *block.* Other conversations, the sound of machinery, and traffic noises can block out messages from being received. *Other conversations, the sound of machinery, and traffic noises can block messages from being received.*

**bode (ill; well) for the future**  *bode (ill; well).* The fact that electric companies had to institute such emergency procedures does not bode well for the future. *The fact that electric companies had to institute such emergency procedures does not bode well.*

**botch up**  *botch.* In my first transplant session, the doctor botched up the job. *In my first transplant session, the doctor botched the job.*

**both ... alike**  *alike; both.* The adherence of career-oriented women to the masculine prototype has led both men and women alike to undermine the value of female qualities and responsibilities. *The adherence of career-oriented women to the masculine prototype has led men and women alike to undermine the value of female qualities and responsibilities.*

**both ... as well as**  *as well as; both ... and.* Both the source .PAS file as well as the compiled .PEN file are available. *Both the source .PAS file and the compiled .PEN file are available.* ■ Netscape engineers originally designed server-side JavaScript to provide both the database object as well as a set of state maintenance objects. *Netscape engineers originally designed server-side JavaScript to provide both the database object and a set of state maintenance objects.* ■ This failure to remember encompasses both product consumption as well as product purchase. *This failure to remember encompasses both product consumption and product purchase.*

**both equally**  *both; equally.* We're both equally attractive. *We're equally attractive.* ■ The poem speaks of two paths, both equally beautiful in their nature and both equally tempting to take, however a decision was made by the traveler to take the road that was less traveled. *The poem speaks of two paths, equally beautiful in their nature and equally tempting to take, however a decision was made by the traveler to take the road that was less traveled.*

**both ... in combination**  *both; in combination.* Both analytic techniques and judgmental methods might be used in combination to verify each other. *Analytic techniques and judgmental methods might be used in combination to verify each other.*

**both of (the)**  *both.* Both of the boys suffer from Tourette syndrome. *Both boys suffer from Tourette syndrome.*

**both share**  *both; share.* We both share a deep commitment to the welfare of the American people. *We share a deep commitment to the welfare of the American people.*

**both together**  *both; together.* Both of the products together cost $117.95. *Together, the products cost $117.95.*

**bound and determined**  *determined; resolute; resolved.* We are still bound and determined that we are going to build a new arena. *We are still determined that we are going to build a new arena.*

**brand new**  *new.* With a brand new product, there is a significant educational need. *With a new product, there is a significant educational need.*

**breadth and depth**  *ambit; area; breadth; compass; degree; extent; field; magnitude; range; reach; scope; sphere; sweep.*

**briefly in passing**  *briefly; in passing.* Let me say briefly in passing that I am opposed to women not having control of their own bodies. *Let me say briefly that I am opposed to women not having control of their own bodies.*

**brief (concise; short; succinct) summary**  *summary.* A concise summary of the scope of the international product manager's task has been provided by Wind. *A summary of the scope of the international product manager's task has been provided by Wind.*

**brief (concise; short; succinct) synopsis**  *synopsis.* I just wondered if I could give you a brief synopsis of the long-distance services that MCI offers. *I just wondered if I could give you a synopsis of the long-distance services that MCI offers.*

**bring about**  *begin; cause; effect; occasion; produce.* Rather than bring about the death of Yellowstone, the fires triggered natural processes of change that are a normal part of the ecosystem. *Rather than cause the death of Yellowstone, the fires triggered natural processes of change that are a normal part of the ecosystem.*

**bring (to) a close (to)**  *cease; close; complete; conclude; end; finish; halt; settle; stop.* How would you bring this meeting to a close? *How would you close this meeting?*

**bring (to) a completion (to)**  *cease; close; complete; conclude; end; finish; halt; settle; stop.* In their final year at St. Valentine Elementary School, students bring to a completion their academic and spiritual foundation for high school and beyond. *In their final year at St. Valentine Elementary School, students complete their academic and spiritual foundation for high school and beyond*

**bring (to) a conclusion (to)** *cease; close; complete; conclude; end; finish; halt; settle; stop.* In December 1997, First Ministers requested that Social Services Ministers bring to a conclusion the development of a vision statement and national framework to guide future collaborative work in this area. *In December 1997, First Ministers requested that Social Services Ministers conclude the development of a vision statement and national framework to guide future collaborative work in this area.*

**bring (to) a halt (to)** *cease; close; complete; conclude; end; finish; halt; settle; stop.* The timber industry said the decision could bring logging to a halt throughout much of the Pacific Northwest within 30 days and cause the loss of as many as 160,000 jobs. *The timber industry said the decision could halt logging throughout much of the Pacific Northwest within 30 days and cause the loss of as many as 160,000 jobs.*

**bring (to) an end (to)** *cease; close; complete; conclude; end; finish; halt; settle; stop.* That comment well describes the work that is yet to be done to bring an end to the pain and suffering. *That comment well describes the work that is yet to be done to end the pain and suffering.*

**bring attention to** *advertise; announce; blazon; broadcast; disclose; divulge; expose; herald; indicate; make known; make public; mention; point out; point to; present; proclaim; promote; publicize; reveal; show; tell; uncover; unveil.* They were demonstrating at the bank branch in order to bring attention to community lending and banking service issues. *They were demonstrating at the bank branch in order to disclose community lending and banking service issues.*

**bring (give) forth** *bear; effect; produce; yield.*

**bring into being (existence)** *conceive; conjure; create; devise; fashion; forge; form; invent; make; mold; plan; produce; shape.* He says that reason itself is a ladder that can now be dispensed with — and should be dispensed with — to help bring the liberal utopia into existence. *He says that reason itself is a ladder that can now be dispensed with — and should be dispensed with — to help fashion the liberal utopia.*

**bring into question** *challenge; contradict; dispute; doubt; question.* The issue goes beyond sexual politics and brings into question how the orthodox verities of an ancient religion fit into the modern world. *The issue goes beyond sexual politics and challenges how the orthodox verities of an ancient religion fit into the modern world.*

**bring into the open** *advertise; announce; blazon; broadcast; disclose;*

*divulge; expose; herald; indicate; make known; make public; mention; point out; point to; present; proclaim; promote; publicize; reveal; show; tell; uncover; unveil.* These experiences are designed to bring into the open some of the students' preconceptions and enable the students to explore ideas related to the topics under discussion. *These experiences are designed to uncover some of the students' preconceptions and enable the students to explore ideas related to the topics under discussion.*

**bring into the world**  *bear; give birth to; produce.*

**bring pressure to bear on (upon)**  *coerce; compel; force; press; pressure.* No matter who is president, the international community must bring pressure to bear on the government to end apartheid. *No matter who is president, the international community must pressure the government to end apartheid.*

**bring to a standstill**  *cease; close; complete; conclude; end; finish; halt; settle; stop.* It should seek to bring to a standstill the international flow of arms to the various Khmer factions. *It should seek to halt the international flow of arms to the various Khmer factions.*

**bring to ... attention (of)**  *advertise; announce; blazon; broadcast; disclose; divulge; expose; herald; indicate; make known; make public; mention; point out; point to; present; proclaim; promote; publicize; reveal; show; tell; uncover; unveil.* He was determined to bring to the world's attention the devastation of the innocents. *He was determined to publicize the devastation of the innocents.*

**bring to bear (on; upon)**  *apply; employ; exercise; exert; influence; use.* Whether such influence can be brought to bear now is of vital importance to the bottom half in the schools. *Whether such influence can be applied now is of vital importance to the bottom half in the schools.*

**bring together**  *ally; bond; connect; join; unite.*

**bring together**  *amass; assemble; collect; gather; join.*

**bring to light**  *advertise; announce; blazon; broadcast; disclose; divulge; expose; herald; indicate; make known; make public; mention; point out; point to; present; proclaim; promote; publicize; reveal; show; tell; uncover; unveil.* Many uncertainties are brought to light when a bank makes a number of changes. *Many uncertainties are revealed when a bank makes a number of changes.*

**bring (back) to mind**  *recall; recollect.*

**bring to pass**  *begin; cause; start.*

**build a bridge across (between)**  *bridge.* Is it not time for you to use these tools to build a bridge across the gulf of knowledge that separates the Islamic world from the West? *Is it not time for you to use these tools to bridge the gulf of knowledge that separates the Islamic world from the West?*

**(a; the) burgeoning (growing; increasing; rising) amount (degree; extent; number; part; percentage; portion; proportion; quantity) (of)**  *increasingly; more; more and more.* A growing number of attorneys are bringing this up of their own initiative in the course of estate planning reviews. *Increasingly, attorneys are bringing this up of their own initiative in the course of estate planning reviews.* ■ A burgeoning number of HIV / AIDS clients require frequent primary medical visits to stay healthy. *More and more HIV/AIDS clients require frequent primary medical visits to stay healthy.*

**but all (just) the same**  *all (just) the same; but.*

**but however**  *but; however.* But however, this is what we do on an everyday basis. *However, this is what we do on an everyday basis.*

**but instead**  *but; instead.* A child's mind is not a tabula rasa, but instead is filled with ideas generated through continuous interaction with the environment. *A child's mind is not a tabula rasa but is filled with ideas generated through continuous interaction with the environment.*

**but nevertheless**  *but; nevertheless.*

**but nonetheless**  *but; nonetheless.*

**but on the other hand**  *but; on the other hand.*

**but rather**  *but; rather.* Behavior is not an isolated event, but rather it is influenced by the past, present, and future. *Behavior is not an isolated event; rather it is influenced by the past, present, and future.*

**but whereas**  *but; whereas.*

**by and large**  *chiefly; commonly; generally; largely; mainly; most; mostly; normally; typically; usually.* But members involved argue the furor is by and large a phony one. *But members involved argue the furor is largely a phony one.*

**by any means** *at all.*

**by (in) comparison** *but; however; whereas; yet;* delete. In comparison, about one-third of the patients whose vessels remained partly blocked showed late potentials on their EKGs. *Whereas about one-third of the patients whose vessels remained partly blocked showed late potentials on their EKGs.*

**by comparison (to; with)** *against; alongside; beside; compared to (with); -(i)er than; less; less than; more; more than; next to; over; than; to; versus; vis-à-vis.* By comparison with the electronic speed of computers, the postal service and the telephone are slow. *Compared with the electronic speed of computers, the postal service and the telephone are slow.*

**by comparison (to; with) ... relatively** *compared to (with); -(i)er than (less than; more than).* By comparison with the rational method, the incremental method uses relatively little quantitative analysis. *Compared to the rational method, the incremental method uses little quantitative analysis.* ■ The figures are prominent even by comparison to the relatively high accident rate for Glasgow as a whole. *The figures are prominent even compared to the high accident rate for Glasgow as a whole.*

**by consequence of** *after; because of; by; due to; following; for; from; in; out of; owing to; through; with.*

**by (a; the) considerable (good; great; huge; large; overwhelming; sizable; vast; wide) margin** *by far; far and away; much.* The leader by a considerable margin was the deep-water lake trout. *The leader by far was the deep-water lake trout.*

**by (in) contrast** *but; however; whereas; yet;* delete. Post-modernism, by contrast, is indifferent to consistency and continuity altogether. *Yet post-modernism is indifferent to consistency and continuity altogether.*

**by contrast to (with)** *against; alongside; beside; compared to (with); -(i)er than; less; less than; more; more than; next to; over; than; to; unlike; versus; vis-à-vis.* And, by contrast with the governor and some younger politicians, Crane has always seen politics as an essential part of the job. *And, unlike the governor and some younger politicians, Crane has always seen politics as an essential part of the job.*

**by definition**  delete. Collaboration, by definition, is a two-way venture. *Collaboration is a two-way venture.*

**(all) by itself (themselves)**  *alone*. Each microcomputer has its own computational ability, so it can function either by itself or as a part of the network. *Each microcomputer has its own computational ability, so it can function either alone or as a part of the network.*

**by (a; the) little (narrow; nominal; slender; slight; slim; small; tiny) margin**  *marginally; narrowly; nominally; slightly*. Blue-chip stocks closed higher by a small margin in a listless session as many participants were absent because of the Jewish New Year holiday. *Blue-chip stocks closed marginally higher in a listless session as many participants were absent because of the Jewish New Year holiday.*

**by (a; the) ... margin (of)**  *by; -(al)ly*; delete. Advancing issues outpaced losers by a margin of more than 2 to 1 among issues listed on the New York Stock Exchange. *Advancing issues outpaced losers by more than 2 to 1 among issues listed on the New York Stock Exchange.*

**by (the) means of**  *by; from; in; on; over; through; with*. It retains control over product decisions and generally markets a standardized product and attempts to influence local decisions by means of persuasion. *It retains control over product decisions and generally markets a standardized product and attempts to influence local decisions through persuasion.* ■ He was convicted of assault and battery by means of a dangerous weapon. *He was convicted of assault and battery with a dangerous weapon.*

**by (its; their) nature**  delete. The truth is that genuine debt crises are, by their nature, almost impossible to predict. *The truth is that genuine debt crises are almost impossible to predict.*

**by no means**  *far from; hardly; scarcely*. Though this advice is extremely helpful to many families, it is by no means the only thing they need to know. *Though this advice is extremely helpful to many families, it is far from the only thing they need to know.*

**by occupation**  delete. He's a day laborer by occupation. *He's a day laborer.*

**by one means or another**  *anyhow; anyway; by some means; however; in any way; in some way; in whatever way; somehow; somehow or another; someway(s)*.

**by reason of**  *after; because of; by; due to; following; for; from; in; out of;*

105

*owing to; through; with.* Nomura, by reason of its size, capital, research abilities, and leading position in the largest creditor nation, should certainly be in the top group. *Nomura, because of its size, capital, research abilities, and leading position in the largest creditor nation, should certainly be in the top group.*

**by reason of the fact that** *because; considering; for; given; in that; since.* Property the decedent had interest in includes dividends payable to the decedent by reason of the fact that, on or before the date of death, the decedent was a shareholder of record. *Property the decedent had interest in includes dividends payable to the decedent because, on or before the date of death, the decedent was a shareholder of record.* ■ This was made inevitable by reason of the fact that the IWW was the result of a later and more mature period of industrial development. *This was made inevitable given that the IWW was the result of a later and more mature period of industrial development.*

**(all) by -self (-selves)** *alone.* She lives all by herself. *She lives alone.*

**by ... standards** *-(al)ly;* delete. By historical standards, these relative prices for thrifts are extremely low. *Historically, these relative prices for thrifts are extremely low.*

**by the fact that** *because; considering; for; given; in that; since.* By the fact that they are using state capital, there can be no free competition. *Considering they are using state capital, there can be no free competition.*

**by the result of** *after; based on; because of; by; due to; following; for; from; in; on; owing to; through; with.* In the United States, policies are determined mainly by the result of discussion and debate, whereas in Europe they are determined on the basis of authority and position. *In the United States, policies are determined mainly from discussion and debate, whereas in Europe they are determined on the basis of authority and position.*

**by the same token** *also; and; as well; besides; beyond that (this); even; further; furthermore; likewise; moreover; more than that (this); similarly; still more; then; too; what is more;* delete. By the same token, northeastern and southeastern banks, which have been the fastest growing, could witness slower loan growth. *Similarly, northeastern and southeastern banks, which have been the fastest growing, could witness slower loan growth.*

**by (in) virtue of** *after; because of; by; due to; following; for; from; in; out* *of; owing to; through; with.* The U.S. hockey team is up by one by virtue of their win over Austria. *The U.S. hockey team is up by one following their win over Austria.* ■ The immiscible units attempt to separate, but by virtue of their connectivity they can never get very far from each other. *The immiscible units attempt to separate, but because of their connectivity they can never get very far from each other.*

**by (in) virtue of the fact that** *because; considering; for; given; in that; since.* People who can be helpful to you are attracted to you by virtue of the fact that you're a person who is doing interesting things and initiating activity yourself. *People who can be helpful to you are attracted to you because you're a person who is doing interesting things and initiating activity yourself.* ■ Enterprise programmers have the most control over their environment by virtue of the fact that they have personal access to every machine that will use the program they create. *Enterprise programmers have the most control over their environment because they have personal access to every machine that will use the program they create.*

**by (the) way of** *by; from; in; on; over; through; with;* delete. By way of conclusion, here are four salient facts. *In conclusion, here are four salient facts.* ■ We will not be ambushed by way of impromptu telephone calls for the purposes of any interview. *We will not be ambushed by impromptu telephone calls for the purposes of any interview.*

**by way of (-ing)** *by (-ing); for (-ing); so as to; through (-ing); to.* All of this is by way of making a point. *All of this is to make a point.* ■ It is today possible to cure the disease by way of performing a bone marrow transplant. *It is today possible to cure the disease through performing a bone marrow transplant.* ■ We would do this by way of creating more awareness in your communities and through grants. *We would do this by creating more awareness in your communities and through grants.*

**by way of being** *by being; for being; so as to be; through being; to be;* delete. Today's column is by way of being a commentary on a column that appeared in this space a week ago. *Today's column is a commentary on a column that appeared in this space a week ago.* ■ James is going out to SLAC pretty straight after the Edinburgh meeting, so it's by way of being a farewell party as well. *James is going out to SLAC pretty straight after the Edinburgh meeting, so it's a farewell party as well.* ■ Yesterday I met with Gregg, a new acquaintance; this was by way of being a blind date. *Yesterday I met with Gregg, a new acquaintance; this was a blind date.*

**by way of comparison (contrast)** *but; however; whereas; yet.* The volume directory for a ProDOS-formatted disk can hold up to 51 files, and by way of contrast, a DOS 3.3 directory can hold 105 files. *The volume directory for a ProDOS-formatted disk can hold up to 51 files, whereas a DOS 3.3 directory can hold 105 files.*

**by way of example (illustration)** *for example; to illustrate.* By way of illustration, here are the main points of a speech about Thailand given by a Thai student. *To illustrate, here are the main points of a speech about Thailand given by a Thai student.* ■ By way of illustration, existentialism could be considered a humanistic form of individualism. *For example, existentialism could be considered a humanistic form of individualism.*

**by whatever (whichever) manner (means)** *despite how; however.* By whatever means they have been brought to our attention, they have been corrected. *However they have been brought to our attention, they have been corrected.* ■ By logging on to our site, by whichever manner you choose, you accept these terms and conditions. *By logging on to our site, however you choose, you accept these terms and conditions.*

**by what (which) means (mechanism)** *how.* Still a mystery is by what mechanism insulin resistance might cause heart disease. *Still a mystery is how insulin resistance might cause heart disease.* ■ By what means does the church secure financial support? *How does the church secure financial support?*

# C

**call a halt to** *cease; close; complete; conclude; end; finish; halt; settle; stop.* We asked them to call a halt to the violence and harassment. *We asked them to stop the violence and harassment.*

**call an end to** *cease; close; complete; conclude; end; finish; halt; settle; stop.* We should call an end to the national ID card debate. *We should end the national ID card debate.*

**call a stop to** *cease; close; complete; conclude; end; finish; halt; settle; stop.* We must call a stop to this madness now. *We must stop this madness now.*

**call ... attention to** *advertise; announce; blazon; broadcast; disclose; divulge; expose; herald; indicate; make known; make public; mention; point out; point to; present; proclaim; promote; publicize; reveal; show; tell; uncover; unveil.* She said the sole purpose of the program was to call attention to what happened in Mexico. *She said the sole purpose of the program was to disclose what happened in Mexico.* ■ Today, many fire fighters are marching in Philadelphia to call attention to this serious, and deadly, occupational disease. *Today, many fire fighters are marching in Philadelphia to publicize this serious, and deadly, occupational disease.*

**called** delete. A set is a collection of objects, and the objects in the set are called the elements. *A set is a collection of objects, and the objects in the set are the elements.*

**call into being (existence)** *conceive; create; devise; fashion; forge; form; invent; make; mold; plan; produce; shape.* This new future requires people to call into existence a new humanity. *This new future requires people to create a new humanity.*

**call into question** *challenge; contradict; dispute; doubt; question.* Whether the magazine has accurately interpreted what those interests are is a point some former staffers call into question. *Whether the magazine has accurately interpreted what those interests are is a point some former staffers dispute.*

**call to ... attention (of)** *advertise; announce; blazon; broadcast; disclose; divulge; expose; herald; indicate; make known; make public; mention; point out; point to; present; proclaim; promote; publicize; reveal; show; tell; uncover; unveil.* The results were called to the attention of the town's building inspector, who forced the ferry service to shut down. *The results were shown to the town's building inspector, who forced the ferry service to shut down.*

**call to mind**  *recall; recollect.*

**call up**  *call.*

**calm, cool, and collected**  *calm; collected; cool.* She is calm, cool, and collected now, but you should have seen her Friday night. *She is calm now, but you should have seen her Friday night.*

**candor and frankness**  *candor; frankness.*

**capability**  *ability.* No two managers are equal in their abilities, and their subordinates will have differing capabilities and levels of experience. *No two managers are equal in their abilities, and their subordinates will have differing abilities and levels of experience.*

**capacity**  *job; position.*

**cast about for**  *look for; search for; seek.* Toymakers have been casting about for something exciting enough to pull parents and children back into the toy stores. *Toymakers have been searching for something exciting enough to pull parents and children back into the toy stores.*

**cast doubt on (upon)**  *challenge; contradict; dispute; doubt; question.*

**catch by surprise**  *startle; surprise.* He says the association was caught by surprise by the House's action. *He says the association was surprised by the House's action.*

**cause ... to be (become)**  *make; render.* Reading his performance appraisal caused him to become angry. *Reading his performance appraisal made him angry.*

**cause to happen (occur; take place)**  *bring about; cause; effect; produce.* Although policy cannot in and of itself cause improvement to happen in the classroom, it can impede or facilitate improvement. *Although policy cannot in and of itself cause improvement in the classroom, it can impede or facilitate improvement.*

**cease and desist**  *cease; desist.*

**center around** *center on.* All these fears center around the loss of control, which may result in being embarrassed or ridiculed by others. *All these fears center on the loss of control, which may result in being embarrassed or ridiculed by others.* ■ The USER subsystem includes a lot of new input options, many of which appear to center around the mouse. *The USER subsystem includes a lot of new input options, many of which appear to center on the mouse.*

**center of attention (attraction)** *cynosure; focus.*

**(of) central (critical; vital) importance** *central; critical; important; vital.* Although these contextual factors are often ignored by domestic firms, they are of central importance to international firms. *Although these contextual factors are often ignored by domestic firms, they are central to international firms.* ■ This information will be critically important to researchers and to the quality of health care for all Americans well into the next century. *This information will be critical to researchers and to the quality of health care for all Americans well into the next century.*

**(a; the) central ... in (of; to)** *central to.* His experience is a central part of the resume on which he is running for office. *His experience is central to the resume on which he is running for office.* ■ As such, religion (or its traces) is a central element of a culture. *As such, religion (or its traces) is central to a culture.*

**characterize as** *call; name; term.* What percentage of your work would you characterize as consulting? *What percentage of your work would you call consulting?*

**charge with the responsibility for (of)** *charge with; responsible for.* The organization might have a management information system that is charged with the responsibility for gathering and processing data. *The organization might have a management information system that is responsible for gathering and processing data.* ■ Does it matter if the people we charge with the responsibility of protecting our nation believe in God? *Does it matter if the people we charge with protecting our nation believe in God?*

**check to see** *check; examine; inspect; look; see.* You should also check to see if the original warranty is still in effect. *You should also check if the original warranty is still in effect.*

**christen as** *christen.* She was later raised by the Confederates, covered with armor plating, and rechristened as the C.S.S. *Virginia. She* *was later raised by the Confederates, covered with armor plating, and rechristened the C.S.S.* Virginia.

**climb up** *climb.* Young Americans have become increasingly disillusioned with their ability to successfully climb up the corporate ladder. *Young Americans have become increasingly disillusioned with their ability to successfully climb the corporate ladder.*

**close (near; rough) approximation (estimate; estimation)** *approximation (estimate; estimation).* Powers of two roughly approximate powers of ten. *Powers of two approximate powers of ten.*

**close (near) at hand** *close by; close to; near; nearby.*

**close down** *close.* Both health plans will close down as of December 31 because of projected financial losses. *Both health plans will close as of December 31 because of projected financial losses.*

**close scrutiny** *scrutiny.* The interest deduction is likely to receive close scrutiny when the chairman of the House Ways and Means Committee looks into the matter this month. *The interest deduction is likely to receive scrutiny when the chairman of the House Ways and Means Committee looks into the matter this month.*

**cluster together** *cluster.* Groups of chapters in textbooks may be clustered together into units or parts. *Groups of chapters in textbooks may be clustered into units or parts.*

**cobble together** *cobble.* This might scan articles on a computerized news service to cobble together a personalized daily news bulletin containing articles of interest to a particular individual. *This might scan articles on a computerized news service to cobble a personalized daily news bulletin containing articles of interest to a particular individual.*

**cohabit together** *cohabit.* Studies show that people who cohabit together first and then get married have a higher rate of getting divorced than people who don't live together first. *Studies show that people who cohabit first and then get married have a higher rate of getting divorced than people who don't live together first.*

**collaborate together** *collaborate.* Generally, a gang can be considered to be a loosely organized group of individuals who collaborate together for social reasons. *Generally, a gang can be considered to be a loosely organized group of individuals who collaborate for social reasons.*

**collect together**  *collect*. Collect together your word processing, desktop publishing, document conversion, and text search programs under one main menu entry. *Collect your word processing, desktop publishing, document conversion, and text search programs under one main menu entry.* ■ A comprehensive set of papers that cover the multiplexing standards, network topologies, and performance and management is collected together in SS96. *A comprehensive set of papers that cover the multiplexing standards, network topologies, and performance and management is collected in SS96.*

**(a; the) combination (of)**  *both*; delete. Architects use a combination of feet and inches, but the inch units are omitted (e.g., 7'2). *Architects use feet and inches, but the inch units are omitted (e.g., 7'2).*

**(a; the) combination of ... along with (combined with; coupled with; joined with; paired with; together with)**  *along with (combined with; coupled with; joined with; paired with; together with)*. The combination of the Relaxation Response coupled with the person's particular belief will work. *The Relaxation Response coupled with the person's particular belief will work.*

**(a; the) combination of both**  *both (of them); combination*. A combination of both whites and blacks are members of these groups. *Both whites and blacks are members of these groups.* ■ Even when children understand questions, they may be reluctant to answer out of fear, misguided love, or a combination of both. *Even when children understand questions, they may be reluctant to answer out of fear, misguided love, or both.*

**(a; the) combination of the two**  *both (of them); combination*. You may use either technique or a combination of the two. *You may use either or both techniques.* ■ The investigation may be done by corporate security personnel, by a private investigator, or by a combination of the two. *The investigation may be done by corporate security personnel, by a private investigator, or by both of them.*

**combine both**  *combine*. The latest development is to combine both record and programming so you can record and then edit macros. *The latest development is to combine record and programming so you can record and then edit macros.*

**combine into one**  *combine*. The single justice noted that combining the two motions into one was a minor procedural discrepancy. *The single justice noted that combining the two motions was a minor procedural discrepancy.*

**combine together** *combine.* The mixed chart allows you to combine different types of charts together. *The mixed chart allows you to combine different types of charts.* ■ No one has yet been able to produce a lichen in the laboratory by combining the two partners together. *No one has yet been able to produce a lichen in the laboratory by combining the two partners.* ■ The signals at the different wavelengths are combined together into a single fiber by means of an optical multiplexer. *The signals at the different wavelengths are combined into a single fiber by means of an optical multiplexer.* ■ The ability to combine various kinds of data together into one application is a very powerful capability, but one that can also lead the programmer into trouble. *The ability to combine various kinds of data into one application is a very powerful capability, but one that can also lead the programmer into trouble.*

**come about** *befall; happen; occur; result; take place.*

**come as a disappointment (to)** *disappoint.* I know this may come as a disappointment to some of you, but my husband is not going to be running for office. *I know this may disappoint some of you, but my husband is not going to be running for office.*

**come as a relief (to)** *relieve.* The pronunciation system of the former OED, a frequent source of criticism, has been replaced by the International Phonetic Alphabet, which should come as a relief to many. *The pronunciation system of the former OED, a frequent source of criticism, has been replaced by the International Phonetic Alphabet, which should relieve many.*

**come as a surprise (to)** *startle; surprise.* It came as a surprise to all the women who work with the senator to learn that his wife left him. *It surprised all the women who work with the senator to learn that his wife left him.*

**come close (near) to** *approach; resemble.* The results of a true national probability sample would most likely come close to these findings. *The results of a true national probability sample would most likely approach these findings.*

**come equipped (furnished) with** *come with; equipped (furnished) with.* All computers come equipped with a keyboard. *All computers come with a keyboard.*

**come in contact (with)** *come across; contact; discover; encounter; find; locate; meet (with); spot; touch.* If the part is designed to come in contact with another surface, the rough surface must be machined. *If the part is designed to touch another surface, the rough surface must be machined.*

**come into being** *appear; arise; evolve; exist.*

**come into existence** *appear; arise; evolve; exist.* In the chain network, the possibility of screening by levels comes into existence. *In the chain network, the possibility of screening by levels arises.*

**come into play** *appear; arise; come about; develop; emerge; happen; occur; result; surface; take place; turn up; unfold.* When they act out their depression, thoughts of suicide can come into play. *When they act out their depression, thoughts of suicide can surface.*

**come into (to) (a; the) ... (of)** delete. Eventually they came to the recognition that the supercomputer business is a high stakes poker game. *Eventually they recognized that the supercomputer business is a high stakes poker game.* ■ It neither glosses over the true historical picture nor attempts to come to the defense of any individuals. *It neither glosses over the true historical picture nor attempts to defend any individuals.*

**come to (an; the) accord (about; as to; concerning; of; on; regarding)** *agree; compromise; concur; decide; resolve; settle.* Croatia, Bosnia-Herzegovina and Yugoslavia have come to an accord on how to deal with the still remaining 1.2 million refugees and displaced persons in their countries. *Croatia, Bosnia-Herzegovina and Yugoslavia have resolved how to deal with the still remaining 1.2 million refugees and displaced persons in their countries.*

**come to a close** *cease; close; complete; conclude; end; finish; halt; stop.*

**come to a (the) conclusion (about; as to; concerning; of; on; regarding)** *cease; close; complete; conclude; end; finish; halt; stop.* In August, the first wave of exploration of the solar system came to a conclusion with Voyager 2's swoop past the present outermost planet, Neptune. *In August, the first wave of exploration of the solar system concluded with Voyager 2's swoop past the present outermost planet, Neptune.*

**come to (an; the) agreement (about; as to; concerning; of; on; regarding)** *agree; compromise; concur; decide; resolve; settle.* The parents and the school board have not yet come to an agreement on whether the child should be in regular classes. *The parents and the school board have not yet agreed on whether the child should be in regular classes.*

**come to a halt** *cease; close; complete; conclude; end; finish; halt; stop.* Suddenly, all activity came to a halt. *Suddenly, all activity stopped.*

**come to an end** *cease; close; complete; conclude; end; finish; halt; stop.* He sees himself as the last survivor of the so-called Bengal Renaissance, the vital and creative cultural movement that was initiated by Ram Mohan Roy (c. 1774-1833) and that came to an end with the death of Rabindranath Tagore in 1941. *He sees himself as the last survivor of the so-called Bengal Renaissance, the vital and creative cultural movement that was initiated by Ram Mohan Roy (c. 1774-1833) and that ceased with the death of Rabindranath Tagore in 1941.*

**come to a standstill** *cease; close; complete; conclude; end; finish; halt; stop.* A spokesman for the Export-Import Bank of Japan said talks with China have come to a standstill. *A spokesman for the Export-Import Bank of Japan said talks with China have ceased.*

**come to (a; the) compromise (about; as to; concerning; of; on; regarding)** *agree; compromise; concur; decide; resolve; settle.* The best situation would be to come to a compromise now so both parties can salvage what is left of the Traveler heritage. *The best situation would be to compromise now so both parties can salvage what is left of the Traveler heritage.*

**come to (a; the) conclusion (about; as to; concerning; of; on; regarding)** *conclude; decide; deduce; determine; infer; judge; reason; resolve; settle.* We came to the conclusion that she should start with antibiotics. *We decided that she should start with antibiotics.*

**come to (a; the) decision (about; as to; concerning; of; on; regarding)** *conclude; decide; deduce; determine; infer; judge; reason; resolve; settle.* It was during the counseling session that we came to the decision to let Allison move in with us. *It was during the counseling session that we decided to let Allison move in with us.*

**come to (a; the) determination (about; as to; concerning; of; on; regarding)** *conclude; decide; deduce; determine; infer; judge; reason; resolve; settle.* While the Board has not come to a determination on the viability of the TPA baseline under current funding scenarios, limited consideration of alternatives is warranted. *While the Board has not determined the viability of the TPA baseline under current funding scenarios, limited consideration of alternatives is warranted.*

**come to (an; the) estimate (estimation) (about; as to; concerning; of; on; regarding)** *approximate; assess; estimate; evaluate; rate.* Thanks to radiometric dating, scientists have come to an estimate that the earth is 4.65 billion years old. *Thanks to radiometric dating, scientists have estimated that the earth is 4.65 billion years old.*

**come together** *assemble; congregate; converge; gather.* In the days before mass immunizations when compulsory education began, disease could spread quickly as large numbers of children came together in unsanitary, poorly heated, poorly ventilated buildings. *In the days before mass immunizations when compulsory education began, disease could spread quickly as large numbers of children gathered in unsanitary, poorly heated, poorly ventilated buildings.*

**come to grips with** *accept; comprehend; cope with; deal with; face; struggle with; understand.* The systems software maker is now coming to grips with a period of rapid growth. *The systems software maker is now struggling with a period of rapid growth.*

**come to light** *emerge; surface; transpire.* In the past year, a few new clues have come to light. *In the past year, a few new clues have transpired.*

**come to (a; the) opinion (of)** *conclude; decide; deduce; determine; infer; judge; reason; resolve; settle.* I came to the opinion that it was an electrical fire, not arson. *I deduced that it was an electrical fire, not arson.*

**come to pass** *befall; happen; occur; result; take place.* If this should come to pass, it would benefit everybody. *If this should happen, it would benefit everybody.*

**come to (a; the) resolution (about; as to; concerning; of; on; regarding)** *agree; conclude; decide; determine; resolve; settle.* I don't understand why they did what they did, and I hope we can come to a resolution about it. *I don't understand why they did what they did, and I hope we can resolve it.*

**come to (a; the) settlement (about; as to; concerning; of; on; regarding)** *agree; conclude; decide; resolve; settle.*

**come to terms (about; as to; concerning; of; on; regarding)** *agree; arbitrate; compromise; concur; decide; settle.* What they can't come to terms on is whether selling the profitable Eastern Shuttle will cure the airline or kill it. *What they can't agree on is whether selling the profitable Eastern Shuttle will cure the airline or kill it.*

**come to terms with** *accept; comprehend; cope with; deal with; face; strug-*

*gle with; understand.* Fitzwater said the president has come to terms with the constant press attention. *Fitzwater said the president has accepted the constant press attention.*

**come to (an; the) understanding** *agree; compromise; concur; decide; resolve; settle.*

**come to (an; the) understanding (about; as to; concerning; of; on; regarding)** *appreciate; comprehend; grasp; understand.* Through this, we will come to an understanding of our own concepts of the primitive and industrial worlds. *Through this, we will understand our own concepts of the primitive and industrial worlds.*

**come up with** *craft; create; design; devise; draft; fashion; find; form; make; map (out); mold; plan; plot; prepare; produce; propose; shape; sketch; suggest.* The NRC has given the nuclear plant a month to come up with a workable plan. *The NRC has given the nuclear plant a month to devise a workable plan.*

**comfortably ensconced** *ensconced.* He is comfortably ensconced as head of the national guard of Panama. *He is ensconced as head of the national guard of Panama.*

**comfort facilities** *bathroom; toilet.* It seems to me that the required visitor-information services, tour departments, and comfort facilities could be provided in a leased ground-floor space in an existing nearby building. *It seems to me that the required visitor-information services, tour departments, and bathrooms could be provided in a leased ground-floor space in an existing nearby building.*

**comical** *comic.*

**commence** *begin; start.* If the candidate accepts the employment offer, the next phase commences. *If the candidate accepts the employment offer, the next phase begins.*

**commencement** *start.* Investment of the net proceeds will take place during a period which will not exceed six months from the commencement of operations. *Investment of the net proceeds will take place during a period which will not exceed six months from the start of operations.*

**commit (a; the) ... (of)** delete. You could not give it to your spouse without committing a violation of federal law. *You could not give it to* *your spouse without violating federal law.*

**common (and) everyday** *common; everyday.*

**communicate (with)** *call; call or write; phone; speak (with); talk (to); write (to).* Please communicate with us at your first opportunity. *Please call us at your first opportunity.*

**communicate in writing** *communicate; write.* To communicate in writing is a very complex process and represents the capturing of an abstract thought in a permanent manner in space and time. *To write is a very complex process and represents the capturing of an abstract thought in a permanent manner in space and time.* ■ Be sure to communicate in writing to the Village Communities staff regarding withdrawal of an application and/or cancellation of an agreement. *Be sure to write to the Village Communities staff regarding withdrawal of an application and/or cancellation of an agreement.*

**communication** *dialogue; letter; message; note; report; speech; talk; text; words.* Nurses frequently make the assumption that their communication has been listened to and understood by patients. *Nurses frequently make the assumption that their words have been listened to and understood by patients.*

**comparatively** *-(i)er; less; more.* Computing what happens to stars and gas in a galactic cube, 100 cells on a side, turns out to be comparatively straightforward. *Computing what happens to stars and gas in a galactic cube, 100 cells on a side, turns out to be more straightforward.*

**comparatively ... compared (contrasted) to (with)** *compared (contrasted) to (with); -(i)er than (less than; more than).* The muscle mass is comparatively small compared to other ruminants. *The muscle mass is small compared to other ruminants.* ■ Although FFWs increased 71 percent from PD, this was comparatively small compared to other short-fuse warnings. *Although FFWs increased 71 percent from PD, this was smaller than other short-fuse warnings.*

**comparatively -(i)er than (less than; more than)** *-(i)er than (less than; more than).* U.S. experts say the Soviet budget deficit that Moscow has finally acknowledged is comparatively larger than that of America. *U.S. experts say the Soviet budget deficit that Moscow has finally acknowledged is larger than that of America.* ■ Comparatively, Benin is slightly smaller than the state of Pennsylvania. *Benin is slightly smaller than the state of Pennsylvania.*

**compare against (versus)**  *compare to (with).* Compare the printout carefully against Figure 50. *Compare the printout carefully with Figure 50.*

**compare and contrast (versus)**  *compare (to); contrast (to).* Perhaps it should have appeared in the Living section, where lifestyles of women from other Arab populations could be compared and contrasted to those living in the occupied territories under Israeli control. *Perhaps it should have appeared in the Living section, where lifestyles of women from other Arab populations could be contrasted to those living in the occupied territories under Israeli control.* ■ Compare and contrast logical versus physical organization. *Compare logical to physical organization.*

**compared to (with)**  *against; alongside; beside; -(i)er than; less; less than; more; more than; next to; over; than; to; versus.* Smoking prevalence has declined across all educational groups, but the decline has occurred five times faster among the higher educated compared with the less educated. *Smoking prevalence has declined across all educational groups, but the decline has occurred five times faster among the higher educated than the less educated.* ■ Volume on the Big Board averaged 153.57 million shares a day compared to 153.39 million in the first week of 1989. *Volume on the Big Board averaged 153.57 million shares a day against 153.39 million in the first week of 1989.* ■ Heavy buying of dollars by traders, or governments, on exchange markets drives up its price, making it strong compared to other currencies. *Heavy buying of dollars by traders, or governments, on exchange markets drives up its price, making it stronger than other currencies.* ■ Star networks have better link budget characteristics compared to bus networks. *Star networks have better link budget characteristics than bus networks.* ■ There is an expectation that electronic books should be considerably less expensive compared to print editions. *There is an expectation that electronic books should be considerably less expensive than print editions.*

**compared (contrasted) to (with) ... relatively**  *compared (contrasted) to (with); -(i)er than (less than; more than).* Compared to the advantages, there are relatively few disadvantages for a sole proprietorship. *Compared to the advantages, there are few disadvantages for a sole proprietorship.* ■ The primary effect appears to be a loss of plutonium from a diseased liver with possible redistribution to the skeleton when compared to relatively healthy individuals. *The primary effect appears to be a loss of plutonium from a diseased liver with possible redistribution to the skeleton when compared to healthy individuals.*

**compartmentalize**  *compartment.* People who compartmentalize their feelings can be trustworthy, dependable, wise, and trusted. *People who compartment their feelings can be trustworthy, dependable, wise, and trusted.*

**compensate**  *pay.*

**compensation**  *cash; fee; money; pay; payment; reward; wage.*

**competency**  *competence.* I feel this would be a good way of assessing his competency. *I feel this would be a good way of assessing his competence.*

**compile together**  *compile.* A database is a compilation of data, such as PsychLit, which compiles all psychological journal abstracts together. *A database is a compilation of data, such as PsychLit, which compiles all psychological journal abstracts together.* ■ Even while busy with these duties, he found time to compile together the legal statements of the popes and councils. *Even while busy with these duties, he found time to compile the legal statements of the popes and councils.*

**complete and utter**  *complete; utter.* It is going to be a complete and utter mess for people to figure out. *It is going to be an utter mess for people to figure out.*

**completely**  delete. The car was completely destroyed in the fire. *The car was destroyed in the fire.*

**completely and utterly**  *completely; utterly; wholly.*

**completely (entirely; exclusively; fully; solely; thoroughly; totally; utterly; wholly) dedicated to**  *dedicated to.* SDS recently moved into a new facility exclusively dedicated to EWSD development for the U.S. market. *SDS recently moved into a new facility dedicated to EWSD development for the U.S. market.*

**completely (entirely; exclusively; fully; solely; thoroughly; totally; utterly; wholly) devoted to**  *devoted to.* The store was devoted entirely to consumer-oriented systems of racks, shelves, bins and hooks, largely of European manufacture, all designed to make a small space more serviceable. *The store was devoted to consumer-oriented systems of racks, shelves, bins and hooks, largely of European manufacture, all designed to make a small space more serviceable.*

**completely (entirely; fully; thoroughly; totally; utterly; wholly) eliminate**  *eliminate.* Computer specialists at MIT said it would take several more days to entirely eliminate the virus. *Computer specialists at MIT said it would take several more days to eliminate the virus.* ■ In some cases, you may even want to completely eliminate certain log entries simply because you don't want to monitor them. *In some cases, you may even want to eliminate certain log entries simply because you don't want to monitor them.*

**completely (entirely; fully; thoroughly; totally; utterly; wholly) eradicate** *eradicate.* Dr. Carlos said he expects the trend to continue, although completely eradicating the decay is probably not possible. *Dr. Carlos said he expects the trend to continue, although eradicating the decay is probably not possible.*

**completely (entirely; fully; thoroughly; totally; utterly; wholly) unanimous** *unanimous.*

**complete monopoly** *monopoly.*

**component** *part.* Two-tier coverage was cited as an important component of successful marketing. *Two-tier coverage was cited as an important part of successful marketing.*

**component (and) part (piece)** *component; part; piece.* The plants manufacture electrical appliances or component parts for the appliances. *The plants manufacture electrical appliances or parts for the appliances.*

**concatenate together** *concatenate; connect; link.* Input lines are concatenated together until a semicolon is encountered, and the result is handled as one statement. *Input lines are concatenated until a semicolon is encountered, and the result is handled as one statement.* ■ Strings can easily be concatenated together using the + operator. *Strings can easily be concatenated using the + operator.*

**concentrate ... attention on (upon)** *concentrate on; focus on.* Eastern has decided to concentrate most of its attention on keeping its shuttle going. *Eastern has decided to concentrate on keeping its shuttle going.*

**concentrate (media; people's; public) attention on (upon)** *advertise; announce; blazon; broadcast; disclose; divulge; expose; herald; indicate; make known; make public; mention; point out; point to; present; proclaim; promote; publicize; reveal; show; tell; uncover; unveil.* She never became president of the American Economics Association — perhaps because of her relentless work concentrating attention on the low status of women in the profession. *She never became president of the American*

*Economics Association — perhaps because of her relentless work exposing the low status of women in the profession.*

**concentrate ... effort on (upon)** *concentrate on; focus on.* If we concentrate our effort on the areas of most need, we might be able to make a difference. *If we concentrate on the areas of most need, we might be able to make a difference.*

**concentrate ... energy on (upon)** *concentrate on; focus on.* Students need to concentrate their energies on their studies, extracurricular activities, and work. *Students need to focus on their studies, extracurricular activities, and work.*

**concentrate ... time and energy on (upon)** *concentrate on; focus on.* We still have 10 million gallons of oil in the water, and we ought to be concentrating our time and energy on minimizing the damage that that does. *We still have 10 million gallons of oil in the water, and we ought to be concentrating on minimizing the damage that that does.*

**concerning** *about; as for; as to; for; in; of; on; over; to; toward; with;* delete. The Federal Reserve Board makes available various indexes, including one concerning industrial production. *The Federal Reserve Board makes available various indexes, including one about industrial production.*

**conclusive end** *conclusion; end.*

**concurrently** *as one; at once; jointly; together.*

**concurrently ... while** *while.* Schools need better tools to help them concurrently diagnose their level of functioning while establishing developmental plans for improvement. *Schools need better tools to help them diagnose their level of functioning while establishing developmental plans for improvement.*

**concurrent (concurrently) with** *while; with.* Concurrent with rejecting the tender offer, Prime's directors approved a series of defensive measures. *While rejecting the tender offer, Prime's directors approved a series of defensive measures.*

**(a; the) ... condition** delete. Congruency is a necessary condition for clients to develop trust in nurses. *Congruency is necessary for clients to develop trust in nurses.*

**conduct (a; the) ... (into; of; on; to; with)** delete. We conducted interviews with EFT industry experts early in the study. *We interviewed EFT industry experts early in the study.* ■ Another method of collecting information is to conduct research on hunters' opinions about the merits of introducing a hunting seat on the market. *Another method of collecting information is to research hunters' opinions about the merits of introducing a hunting seat on the market.* ■ They should conduct an investigation into how these scholarships were awarded with no set criteria for selection, and explain why linguistic minorities are seemingly underrepresented. *They should investigate how these scholarships were awarded with no set criteria for selection, and explain why linguistic minorities are seemingly underrepresented.* ■ I am grateful to you for agreeing to conduct an inquiry into the circumstances giving rise to the current situation at the Equitable Life Assurance Society. *I am grateful to you for agreeing to inquire into the circumstances giving rise to the current situation at the Equitable Life Assurance Society.*

**congregate together** *congregate.* We feel that the five baby dinosaurs were congregating together behind a sand dune in a sandstorm. *We feel that the five baby dinosaurs were congregating behind a sand dune in a sandstorm.*

**connected with** *for; in; linked to; of; -'s; with.* Obviously, the most profitable method of investing would be to buy low and sell high; however, there are several problems connected with this method. *Obviously, the most profitable method of investing would be to buy low and sell high; however, there are several problems with this method.*

**connect together** *connect; link.* A network is two or more computers connected together with cables so that they can exchange files and share resources. *A network is two or more computers connected with cables so that they can exchange files and share resources.* ■ The nuclear material appears as fibrous patches scattered about the cytoplasm; however, it is all connected together. *The nuclear material appears as fibrous patches scattered about the cytoplasm; however, it is all connected.*

**consecutive** *straight.*

**consensus (of) opinion** *consensus.* There is a consensus of opinion in this country against executing our young. *There is a consensus in this country against executing our young.*

**consequence** *import; moment.*

**consequence** *effect; outcome; result.*

**consequence (effect; outcome) resulting from** *consequence (effect; outcome) of; result of.* The potential long-term outcomes resulting from their reactions are destroyed creativity and stifled initiative. *The potential long-term outcomes of their reactions are destroyed creativity and stifled initiative.*

**consequently** *hence; so; then; therefore; thus.* They were victims of misfortune or of circumstances beyond their control, and consequently, they live in shelters or on the streets. *They were victims of misfortune or of circumstances beyond their control, and thus, they live in shelters or on the streets.*

**(a; the) considerable (good; great; huge; large; sizable; vast) amount (of)** *a good (great) deal (of); a good (great) many (of); almost all (of); considerable; many (of); most (of); much (of); nearly all (of); vast;* delete. It's operationally complex and requires a large amount of resources. *It's operationally complex and requires vast resources.*

**(a; the) considerable (good; great; huge; large; sizable; vast) degree (of)** *a good (great) deal (of); considerable; great; much (of); vast;* delete. They now realize they showed a considerable degree of insensitivity toward small businesses. *They now realize they showed great insensitivity toward small businesses.*

**(a; the) considerable (good; great; huge; large; sizable; vast) element (of)** *a good (great) deal (of); considerable; great; much (of); vast;* delete. True to the spirit of covert operations, there was a large element of deception and dissembling in this struggle. *True to the spirit of covert operations, there was much deception and dissembling in this struggle.*

**(a; the) considerable (good; great; huge; large; overwhelming; vast; sizable; wide) majority (of)** *a good (great) deal (of); a good (great) many (of); almost all (of); (nine) in (ten) (of); many (of); most (of); much (of); nearly all (of); (43) of (48) (of); (67) percent (of); three-fourths (two-thirds) (of);* delete. The two own the vast majority of the stock. *The two own almost all the stock.*

**(a; the) considerable (good; great; huge; large; overwhelming; sizable; vast) number (of)** *a good (great) many (of); almost all (of); countless; dozens (of); hundreds (of); many (of); millions (of); most (of); nearly all (of); numerous; scores (of); six hundred (twelve hundred); thousands (of).* The language provides a large number of primitive data types. *The language provides dozens of primitive data types.*

125

**(a; the) considerable (good; great; huge; large; sizable; vast) part (of)** *a good (great) deal (of); a good (great) many (of); almost all (of); (nine) in (ten) (of); many (of); most (of); much (of); nearly all (of); (43) of (48) (of); (67) percent (of); three-fourths (two-thirds) (of)*; delete. What may surprise you, however, is that a large part of this analysis is within your reach at little or no cost. *What may surprise you, however, is that much of this analysis is within your reach at little or no cost.*

**(a; the) considerable (good; great; huge; large; overwhelming; sizable; vast) percentage (of)** *a good (great) deal (of); a good (great) many (of); almost all (of); (nine) in (ten) (of); many (of); most (of); much (of); nearly all (of); (43) of (48) (of); (67) percent (of); three-fourths (two-thirds) (of)*; delete. We know that a large percentage of IRA contributors had been saving very little before IRAs were created. *We know that one-third of IRA contributors had been saving very little before IRAs were created.*

**(a; the) considerable (good; great; huge; large; sizable; vast) portion (of)** *a good (great) deal (of); a good (great) many (of); almost all (of); (nine) in (ten) (of); many (of); most (of); much (of); nearly all (of); (43) of (48) (of); (67) percent (of); three-fourths (two-thirds) (of)*; delete. It will be unseasonably cool over a considerable portion of the United States today. *It will be unseasonably cool over much of the United States today.*

**(a; the) considerable (good; great; huge; large; sizable; vast) proportion (of)** *a good (great) deal (of); a good (great) many (of); almost all (of); (nine) in (ten) (of); many (of); most (of); much (of); nearly all (of); (43) of (48) (of); (67) percent (of); three-fourths (two-thirds) (of)*; delete. They may squander huge proportions of their purchasing power by paying high instead of low prices on each purchase. *They may squander much of their purchasing power by paying high instead of low prices on each purchase.*

**(a; the) considerable (good; great; huge; large; sizable; vast) quantity (of)** *a good (great) deal (of); a good (great) many (of); almost all (of); dozens (of); hundreds (of); many (of); millions (of); most (of); much (of); nearly all (of); scores (of); six hundred (twelve hundred) (of); thousands (of)*. Students often fail to remember or understand large quantities of their elementary calculus. *Students often fail to remember or understand much of their elementary calculus.*

**considerably** *a good (great) deal; amply; far; greatly; largely; mostly; much; vastly*. This is considerably different from the past, when information was printed and approved before being passed up the hierarchy. *This is far different from the past, when information was printed and* *approved before being passed up the hierarchy.*

**consider as**   *consider.* It could be considered as false advertising. *It could be considered false advertising.* ■ Do you have an estimation which mean rate per hour, day or month you would consider as a reasonable fee for your services? *Do you have an estimation which mean rate per hour, day or month you would consider a reasonable fee for your services?*

**consider as being**   *consider.* In many ways, software engineering may be considered as being similar to various other sciences and branches of engineering. *In many ways, software engineering may be considered similar to various other sciences and branches of engineering.*

**considering the fact that**   *because; considering; for; given; in that; since; when.* Considering the fact that the average person uses 77 gallons of water a day, we can estimate that each person uses close to 26 gallons of water every day simply by flushing the toilet. *Since the average person uses 77 gallons of water a day, we can estimate that each person uses close to 26 gallons of water every day simply by flushing the toilet.* ■ Considering the fact that some 6,400 hospitals endured a lengthy and intensive evaluation, analyzing everything from new technology to nurse-to-bed ratio, our ranking is something to be proud of. *Because some 6,400 hospitals endured a lengthy and intensive evaluation, analyzing everything from new technology to nurse-to-bed ratio, our ranking is something to be proud of.*

**consolidate together**   *consolidate.* Cooperatives are independent firms that have consolidated parts of their operations together into one organization. *Cooperatives are independent firms that have consolidated parts of their operations into one organization.*

**constitute**   *be; compose; form; make up.* Corporate debt issues constitute the largest segment, totaling more than $341 billion in 1986. *Corporate debt issues make up the largest segment, totaling more than $341 billion in 1986.*

**contact**   *call; phone; reach; write (to).* She contacted the state agency that helps welfare recipients. *She called the state agency that helps welfare recipients.*

**contain (a; the) ... of**   delete. Chapter 15 contains a formal discussion of the theoretical underpinnings of these formulas. *Chapter 15 formally discusses the theoretical underpinnings of these formulas.* ■ Table 4-3 contains a list of all 26 ProDOS commands and command numbers. *Table 4-3 lists all 26 ProDOS commands and command numbers.*

**continue in existence (to exist)** *continue; endure; exist; last; persevere; persist; prevail; remain; survive.* The possibility of becoming an independent company continues to exist. *The possibility of becoming an independent company persists.*

**continue into the future** *continue.* The rate of growth in the market is expected to continue into the future. *The rate of growth in the market is expected to continue.*

**continue on** *continue.* If he doesn't raise enough money, he won't be able to continue on. *If he doesn't raise enough money, he won't be able to continue.*

**continue to be** *be still; remain; stay.* This was the case before the New York state law and continues to be the case after the New York state law. *This was the case before the New York state law and remains the case after the New York state law.*

**continue to remain** *be still; remain; stay.* Sex stereotypes continue to remain a problem in the military. *Sex stereotypes remain a problem in the military.*

**contractual agreement** *agreement; contract.* Contractual agreements with independent distributors in Indonesia are required by law to be for a minimum of three years. *Contracts with independent distributors in Indonesia are required by law to be for a minimum of three years.*

**contrariwise** *but; conversely; however; instead; not so; rather; still; whereas; yet.*

**contrary to** *after all; apart (from); aside (from); despite; even with; for all; with all.* Contrary to some of the things you've heard, I am the same man I was when I came to Washington. *Despite some of the things you've heard, I am the same man I was when I came to Washington.*

**contrasted to (with)** *against; alongside; beside; compared to (with); -(i)er than; less; less than; more; more than; next to; over; than; to; unlike; versus; vis-à-vis.*

**contribute to** *add to.*

**converge together** *converge.* We both could not tell the resolution reading since the lines seemed to converge together. *We both could not tell the resolution reading since the lines seemed to converge.*

**(in) conversation** *talk.*

**converse** *speak; talk.* She has multiple personalities, and I was able to converse with all of them. *She has multiple personalities, and I was able to talk with all of them.*

**convicted felon** *felon.* There are concerns over the fact that the bank loaned money to convicted felons. *There are concerns over the fact that the bank loaned money to felons.*

**cooperate together** *cooperate.* And there's no question in my mind that as we cooperate together, the people of both our countries will benefit. *And there's no question in my mind that as we cooperate, the people of both our countries will benefit.*

**core essence** *core; crux; essence; gist; pith; substance.* Issues are supposed to be the core essence of a political convention. *Issues are supposed to be the core of a political convention.*

**correctional (prison) facility** *jail; prison.* Opponents complained that a prison facility for 500 inmates and several hundred staff members would overwhelm the town of barely 800 people. *Opponents complained that a prison for 500 inmates and several hundred staff members would overwhelm the town of barely 800 people.*

**correspondence** *letter; memo; note; report.*

**(a; the) countless number (of)** *countless; endless; infinite; millions (of); myriad; numberless; untold.* The congestion has resulted in interminable delays and countless numbers of accidents for motorists. *The congestion has resulted in interminable delays and countless accidents for motorists.*

**couple together** *couple.* Channels up to 150 THz (125 nm) apart will be coupled together with SRS. *Channels up to 150 THz (125 nm) apart will be coupled with SRS.*

**course of action** *action; course; direction; intention; method; move; plan; policy; procedure; route; scheme; strategy.* The coalition has urged a boycott of tuna, but strengthening existing laws — and enforcing them —

would be a better course of action. *The coalition has urged a boycott of tuna, but strengthening existing laws — and enforcing them — would be a better course.*

**cover over** *cover.*

**criminal act** *crime.* Certainly if a public official commits a criminal act, he or she must face full consequences. *Certainly if a public official commits a crime, he or she must face full consequences.*

**criminal offense** *crime; offense.* Mr. Hurd said he had misgivings about making drinking on the streets a criminal offense. *Mr. Hurd said he had misgivings about making drinking on the streets an offense.*

**criminal record** *record.*

**criminal wrongdoing** *crime; wrongdoing.* McNamara may not be guilty of any criminal wrongdoing, but he is a terrible U.S. attorney. *McNamara may not be guilty of any crime, but he is a terrible U.S. attorney.*

**critically (crucially; vitally) important** *critical; crucial; important; vital.* This is crucially important to the investigators since any compromise of the scene lessens its investigative value. *This is crucial to the investigators since any compromise of the scene lessens its investigative value.*

**(a; the) critical ... in (of; to)** *critical to.* A critical ingredient in a manager's philosophy of change is how much emphasis is placed on trust in the work environment. *Critical to a manager's philosophy of change is how much emphasis is placed on trust in the work environment.* ■ Active cooperation between all industry groups is a critical factor to the success of EFT and POS. *Active cooperation between all industry groups is critical to the success of EFT and POS.* ■ The entire landscape of faculty will change, and a critical part of our strategy is bringing new faces to U of T. *The entire landscape of faculty will change, and critical to our strategy is bringing new faces to U of T.*

**(a; the) crucial ... in (of; to)** *crucial to.* He believes hostility is a crucial component of the Type A personality and a potent predictor of heart trouble. *He believes hostility is crucial to the Type A personality and a potent predictor of heart trouble.* ■ Although a crucial part of the equation, this limited view fails to take into account the large number of high achievers who also possess chronic low self-esteem. *Although crucial to the equation, this limited view fails to take into account the large number of high achievers who also possess chronic low self-esteem.*

**currently** *(just; right) now; today; (just) yet;* delete. It's the only spreadsheet currently on the market that has the look and feel of WordPerfect. *It's the only spreadsheet now on the market that has the look and feel of WordPerfect.*

**current (present) status** *status.* Nothing material to date can be reported on the current status of these negotiations. *Nothing material to date can be reported on the status of these negotiations.*

**custom-built** *custom; tailored.* At least one vendor uses a custom-built database system in addition to a commercial one to speed up operations. *At least one vendor uses a custom database system in addition to a commercial one to speed up operations.*

**custom-made** *custom; tailored.* Our courses are custom-made to meet the training needs of each client. *Our courses are tailored to meet the training needs of each client.*

**custom-tailored** *custom; customized; tailored.* Customers today demand custom-tailored solutions to communications problems. *Customers today demand customized solutions to communications problems.*

**cut by (in) half** *halve.* A cooperative agreement was announced that could cut by half the amount of ozone-destroying chemicals released in the service and repair of auto air conditioners. *A cooperative agreement was announced that could halve the amount of ozone-destroying chemicals released in the service and repair of auto air conditioners.*

**cyclical** *cyclic.* The lengths of time within cyclical periods tend to vary. *The lengths of time within cyclic periods tend to vary.*

# D

**date back to** *date from; date to.* Rogation Days date back at least to the 13th century and probably to the days before the Norman Conquest. *Rogation Days date to at least the 13th century and probably to the days before the Norman Conquest.*

**day in (and) day out** *always; ceaselessly; consistently; constantly; daily; endlessly; eternally; everlastingly; every day; forever; invariably; never ending; perpetually; routinely; unfailingly.* I was doing portraits day in and day out. *I was doing portraits every day.*

**day-to-day routine** *routine.* I am greatly tired of the day-to-day routine. *I am greatly tired of the routine.*

**dead body** *body.* Lying next to him as he wrote was the dead body of his son, Lieutenant Bayard Wilkeson, who had been killed in the first day of battle. *Lying next to him as he wrote was the body of his son, Lieutenant Bayard Wilkeson, who had been killed in the first day of battle.*

**(a) decade's (year's) history of** *(a) decade (year) of.* In spite of over a year's history of unusual trading in "Inside Wall Street" highlighted stocks, BW amazingly did not alert the New York Stock Exchange or the Securities & Exchange Commission. *In spite of over a year of unusual trading in "Inside Wall Street" highlighted stocks, BW amazingly did not alert the New York Stock Exchange or the Securities & Exchange Commission.*

**decapitate ... (the) head (of)** *behead; decapitate.* I never could watch my father decapitate the heads of our chickens. *I never could watch my father decapitate our chickens.*

**(a; the) declining (decreasing; diminishing; dwindling) amount (degree; extent; part; percentage; portion; proportion) (of)** *decreasingly; less; less and less.*

**(a; the) declining (decreasing; diminishing; dwindling) number (quantity) (of)** *decreasingly; few; fewer and fewer.*

**decrease down** *decrease.*

**decreasing in** *decreasingly.*

**deductive reasoning**  *deduction.*

**deem as**  *deem.* Values are preferences, or what we deem as good. *Values are preferences, or what we deem good.* ■ The interior is comfortable and complete with numerous antiques, as well as conveniences that most modern travelers would deem as necessary. *The interior is comfortable and complete with numerous antiques, as well as conveniences that most modern travelers would deem necessary.*

**defer back**  *defer.* Although you might be able to defer back to your accountant, the best impression will be left by you if you are in command of the information. *Although you might be able to defer to your accountant, the best impression will be left by you if you are in command of the information.*

**(most; very) definitely**  *yes.*

**(a; the) ... degree of**  delete. He provides a healthy and thoughtful degree of skepticism about prospects for positive change at the national level. *He provides a healthy and thoughtful skepticism about prospects for positive change at the national level.* ■ Competitor reaction cannot be predicted with any degree of accuracy. *Competitor reaction cannot be predicted with any accuracy.* ■ This is sophisticated, suicidal and there's a degree of ruthlessness that we haven't ever seen in the use of terrorism before. *This is sophisticated, suicidal and there's a ruthlessness that we haven't ever seen in the use of terrorism before.*

**demise**  *death; end.* That access is hastening the demise of many U.S. industries. *That access is hastening the end of many U.S. industries.*

**depart**  *leave.* The president departs for Moscow this morning. *The president leaves for Moscow this morning.*

**dependency**  *dependence.* It may also be difficult for these people to make the decision to marry because of the dependency and commitment required in an intimate relationship. *It may also be difficult for these people to make the decision to marry because of the dependence and commitment required in an intimate relationship.*

**depreciate in value**  *depreciate.* He was carrying several hundred condos which depreciated between 10 and 30 percent in value. *He was carrying several hundred condos which depreciated between 10 and 30 percent.*

**derive benefit (from)** *benefit*. This suggests that many people would derive benefit from "stand-up and stretch" workbreaks. *This suggests that many people would benefit from "stand-up and stretch" workbreaks.*

**derive enjoyment from** *admire; delight in; enjoy; rejoice in; relish; savor.* Although badgers and other mammals are trapped so that their pelts can be sold, the hunters also derive enjoyment from their activities. *Although badgers and other mammals are trapped so that their pelts can be sold, the hunters also enjoy their activities.*

**derive pleasure from** *admire; appreciate; delight in; enjoy; rejoice in; relish; savor.* We derived great pleasure from their performance. *We delighted in their performance.*

**derive satisfaction from** *admire; appreciate; delight in; enjoy; rejoice in; relish; savor.* If you derive genuine satisfaction from being in a leadership role, you will obviously bring that attitude to your role as a meeting leader. *If you genuinely enjoy being in a leadership role, you will obviously bring that attitude to your role as a meeting leader.*

**descend down** *descend*. The summer months of December through February hit the mid-80s and descend down to the mid-60s at night. *The summer months of December through February hit the mid-80s and descend to the mid-60s at night.*

**describe (explain) in ... detail** *detail*. The proposal should describe in detail the procedure to be used to obtain data. *The proposal should detail the procedure to be used to obtain data.*

**desideratum** *need.*

**designate as** *designate*. Designating schools as failed or unsatisfactory could do more damage than the label of success would do good. *Designating schools failed or unsatisfactory could do more damage than the label of success would do good.* ■ It is standard convention to designate counterclockwise moment directions as positive and those in the clockwise direction as negative. *It is standard convention to designate counterclockwise moment directions positive and those in the clockwise direction negative.*

**despite the fact that** *although; but; even though; still; though; yet.* Despite the fact that all the charts are on paper rather than on-line, the bank reports that departments competed to improve their performance. *Although all the charts are on paper rather than on-line, the bank* *reports that departments competed to improve their performance.* ■ Despite the fact that often they're the only green spot in a concrete and asphalt jungle, golf courses are still targeted as threats to the environment. *Though often they're the only green spot in a concrete and asphalt jungle, golf courses are still targeted as threats to the environment.* ■ Schumer wants to break the law despite the fact that Bush administration officials say the current stockpile of Cipro is adequate. *Schumer wants to break the law even though Bush administration officials say the current stockpile of Cipro is adequate.*

**detailed (in-depth) analysis** *analysis; detail.* Apparently there are some who would discourage any detailed analysis of these weaknesses. *Apparently there are some who would discourage any analysis of these weaknesses.*

**determine the truth (truthfulness; validity; veracity) of** *verify.* Consumers cannot easily inspect software to determine the truth of a manufacturer's claims about a product's expected behavior. *Consumers cannot easily inspect software to verify a manufacturer's claims about a product's expected behavior.*

**devoid of** *dis-; il-; im-; in-; ir-; lack; -less(ness); mis-; no; non-; not; un-; want; with no; without.* Your editorial makes the term censorship somewhat devoid of meaning. *Your editorial makes the term censorship somewhat meaningless.*

**diametrical** *diametral.* The diametrical pitch is the number of teeth about the circumference divided by the diameter. *The diametral pitch is the number of teeth about the circumference divided by the diameter.*

**(five; many; several) different** *(five; many; several); different.* My parents own five different homes. *My parents own five homes.*

**different and distinct** *different; distinct.* The idea that each person's fingerprints were different and distinct from everyone else's was based on the work of Sir Francis Galton. *The idea that each person's fingerprints were different from everyone else's was based on the work of Sir Francis Galton.*

**(a; the) difficult task** *difficult; task.* The difficult task of obtaining information for marketing decisionmaking presents two overriding challenges. *The task of obtaining information for marketing decisionmaking presents two overriding challenges.*

**difficulty in (of) -ing** *difficulty -ing*. She has great difficulty in falling asleep. *She has great difficulty falling asleep.*

**diminish down** *diminish*.

**direct ... attention to** *advertise; announce; blazon; broadcast; disclose; divulge; expose; herald; indicate; make known; make public; mention; point out; point to; present; proclaim; promote; publicize; reveal; show; tell; uncover; unveil.* The Draper award is seen by some engineering leaders as a way of directing attention to the profession and making sure engineers share the spotlight with scientists. *The Draper award is seen by some engineering leaders as a way of promoting the profession and making sure engineers share the spotlight with scientists.*

**disassociate** *dissociate.* It set off calls by the faculty for nationally known conservatives to disassociate themselves from alleged Jew-baiting by the *Review,* which in the past has been accused of race-baiting and unfair characterization of women and homosexuals. *It set off calls by the faculty for nationally known conservatives to dissociate themselves from alleged Jew-baiting by the* Review, *which in the past has been accused of race-baiting and unfair characterization of women and homosexuals.* ■ Since a man does not disassociate responsibility and blame, he often refuses both. *Since a man does not dissociate responsibility and blame, he often refuses both.* ■ All you have to do is highlight the text — a range of characters if you want to disassociate them from the applied character style or one or more paragraphs if you want to disassociate it/them from the applied paragraph style. *All you have to do is highlight the text — a range of characters if you want to dissociate them from the applied character style or one or more paragraphs if you want to dissociate it/them from the applied paragraph style.*

**discomfiture** *discomfit; discomfort.*

**(in) discussion** *speaking; talking.* At Honda, managers spend up to 50 percent of their time in discussions with dealers and distributors. *At Honda, managers spend up to 50 percent of their time talking with dealers and distributors.*

**display (a; the) ... (of; to)** delete. The Task Manager displays a list of the programs that are currently running. *The Task Manager lists the programs that are currently running.*

**distinct difference (distinctly different)** *different; distinct; distinction.* We wanted to do something distinctly different. *We wanted to do something distinct.*

**divide in half** *halve.*

**divide up** *divide.* He suggested we divide up the money between us. *He suggested we divide the money between us.*

**do (a; the) ... (about; in; of; on; to)** *-(al)ly;* delete. We did a thorough search of the area and found nothing. *We thoroughly searched the area and found nothing.* ■ They'd rather build a roadway than provide a program that prevents someone from doing harm to someone else. *They'd rather build a roadway than provide a program that prevents someone from harming someone else.* ■ Are we supposed to be doing the underlining of the title twice? *Are we supposed to be underlining the title twice?*

**do away with** *cancel; destroy; end; kill; stop.*

**does not ... any** *no; none; nothing.* I do not understand any of this. *I understand none of this.*

**does not have to** *needs not.* You do not have to specify extensions when you save or load files. *You need not specify extensions when you save or load files.* ■ Of course the article does not have to be this long. *Of course the article need not be this long.*

**does not necessarily** *needs not.* A long waiting time does not necessarily mean that your doctor is smart, successful, busy, dedicated, or involved in saving lives. *A long waiting time need not mean that your doctor is smart, successful, busy, dedicated, or involved in saving lives.*

**does not pay attention to** *ignores.* We are pleased that the survey has emphasized that the existing practice of budgeting does not pay attention to its impact on women. *We are pleased that the survey has emphasized that the existing practice of budgeting ignores its impact on women.*

**does not remember** *forgets.*

**$... dollar** *$....* A single day of downtime for one of these huge generators can cost up to $1 million dollars. *A single day of downtime for one of these huge generators can cost up to $1 million.* ■ The maximum state award generally ranges between $10,000 and $25,000 dollars. *The maximum state award generally ranges between $10,000 and $25,000.*

**dollar amount** delete. The daily maximum price change is 50 basis points, which is equivalent to a dollar amount of $1,250. *The daily maximum price change is 50 basis points, which is equivalent to $1,250.*

**dollar value** *value.*

**domicile** (*n*) *home; house.*

**domicile** (*v*) *dwell; live; reside.*

**done (finished; over) with** *done (finished; over).*

**doomed to fail (failure)** *doomed.* The governor said the president's strategy is doomed to fail. *The governor said the president's strategy is doomed.*

**dosage** *dose.* If the recommended dosage does not provide relief of symptoms or symptoms become worse, seek immediate medical attention. *If the recommended dose does not provide relief of symptoms or symptoms become worse, seek immediate medical attention.*

**doubt but that** *doubt that.*

**down the line (pike; road; way)** *at length; from now; in time; later.* Ten years down the line where are you going to be? *Ten years from now where are you going to be?*

**down to a minimum of** *down to.*

**dramatical** *dramatic.*

**draw attention to** *advertise; announce; blazon; broadcast; disclose; divulge; expose; herald; indicate; make known; make public; mention; point out; point to; present; proclaim; promote; publicize; reveal; show; tell; uncover; unveil.* Our goal is to draw attention to what has been accomplished in improving the world food situation. *Our goal is to point out what has been accomplished in improving the world food situation.*

**draw (a; the) conclusion (of)** *conclude; deduce; draw; infer; reason.* What conclusions were you able to draw from your experience? *What were you able to conclude from your experience?*

**draw (a; the) inference (of)** *conclude; deduce; draw; infer; reason.* If it does not find the employer's explanation adequate then it is entitled but not compelled to draw an inference of sex discrimination. *If it does*

*not find the employer's explanation adequate then it is entitled but not com-
pelled to infer sex discrimination.*

**draw to a close (end)** *cease; close; complete; conclude; end; finish; halt;
stop.* Scientists expect to feel in the next few days a real sense of letdown as the first phase of humanity's exploration of the Earth's
neighborhood draws to a close. *Scientists expect to feel in the next few
days a real sense of letdown as the first phase of humanity's exploration of
the Earth's neighborhood concludes.*

**draw to a conclusion** *cease; close; complete; conclude; end; finish; halt;
stop.* As these tasks draw to a conclusion, the panel needs to consider
the contents of their report to the LGA Executive. *As these tasks conclude, the panel needs to consider the contents of their report to the LGA
Executive.*

**driving force** *drive; energy; force; impetus; motivation; power.* He is
especially concerned about young people and is the driving force
behind Catholic Schools United. *He is especially concerned about young
people and is the impetus behind Catholic Schools United.*

**drop down** *down; drop.*

**dualistic** *dual.* They have dualistic meanings. *They have dual meanings.*

**due to the fact that** *because; considering; for; given; in that; since.* This
procedure is impractical due to the fact that the game tree for any
interesting games is extremely large. *This procedure is impractical
because the game tree for any interesting games is extremely large.* ■ We are
unable to accept returns or issue refunds for any order due to the fact
that this is a prescription medication. *We are unable to accept returns or
issue refunds for any order since this is a prescription medication.*

**duplicate copy** *copy; duplicate.* When you want a duplicate copy of
one or more files, you use the COPY command. *When you want a copy
of one or more files, you use the COPY command.*

**during a (the) juncture (juncture in time; moment; moment in time;
period; period in time; point; point in time; stage; stage in time;
time) when** *when.* He had supported my friends and I during the
time when we retrieved the abusive pictures from the Marine in
Mississippi. *He had supported my friends and I when we retrieved the abusive pictures from the Marine in Mississippi.*

**during the course (length) of** *during; for; in; over; throughout; when; while; with.* During the course of the analysis, we suppose the array or list contains *n* elements. *Throughout the analysis, we suppose the array or list contains n elements.* ■ During the course of trying to negotiate with the gunmen, her husband was shot and killed. *While trying to negotiate with the gunmen, her husband was shot and killed.* ■ In addition, all regional students must attend one colloquium during the length of their enrollment. *In addition, all regional students must attend one colloquium during their enrollment.* ■ I wish to have my sheets replaced on a daily basis during the length of my stay. *I wish to have my sheets replaced on a daily basis during my stay.*

**during (for; over) the decade (period; period of time; span of time; time; years) (from) … through (till; to; until)** *between … and; from … through (to).* The fees and expenses of the non-interested Trustees for the period November 26, 1986 to October 31, 1987 amounted to $3,731. *The fees and expenses of the non-interested Trustees from November 26, 1986 to October 31, 1987 amounted to $3,731.*

**during the period (period of time; span of time; time; years) (that)** *while.*

**during the rule of** *under.* It was turned into a Roman colony during the rule of Augustus, around the year 20 B.C. *It was turned into a Roman colony under Augustus, around the year 20 B.C.*

**dwindle down** *dwindle.* A $10,000 gross bonus can dwindle down to a surprisingly small amount with income tax deductions. *A $10,000 gross bonus can dwindle to a surprisingly small amount with income tax deductions.*

**dynamical** *dynamic.*

# E

**each and every (one)**  *all; each; every (one).* Each and every one of these crimes was committed by a pathological killer. *Each of these crimes was committed by a pathological killer.*

**each one**  *each.* My method is to introduce the key elements of office automation and explain each one in concrete terms. *My method is to introduce the key elements of office automation and explain each in concrete terms.*

**(from) each other**  *delete.* The two dates on the printout differ from each other because the first was entered as text and the second as a code. *The two dates on the printout differ because the first was entered as text and the second as a code.*

**early beginnings**  *beginnings.*

**-ed (-en) before (earlier; previously)**  *-ed (-en).* Actually the term was used previously by Thomas Edison. *Actually the term was used by Thomas Edison.*

**edifice**  *building.*

**educational institution**  *college; school; university.* Locate and identify a newsgroup available at your educational institution related to marketing. *Locate and identify a newsgroup available at your school related to marketing.*

**effectuate**  *achieve; bring about; carry out; effect; execute; realize.* In order to effectuate this policy, the legislature imposed strict liability for all damages resulting from a failure to remove such materials on the owners of residential premises. *In order to effect this policy, the legislature imposed strict liability for all damages resulting from a failure to remove such materials on the owners of residential premises.*

**e.g. ... and others (and so forth; and so on; and such; and the like; et al.; etc.)**  *and others (and so forth; and so on; and such; and the like; et al.; etc.); e.g.; for example; for instance.* They typically have unpredictable ranges of occurrences, and they usually have related attributes (e.g., skill category, detailed skill description, etc.) that are of interest to the organization. *They typically have unpredictable ranges of occurrences, and they usually have related attributes (skill category, detailed skill description,* *etc.) that are of interest to the organization.* ■ Analyze the resulting circuit to determine the required quantities (e.g., voltage gain, input resistance, etc.). *Analyze the resulting circuit to determine the required quantities (e.g., voltage gain, input resistance).*

**egoistical (egotistical)** *egoistic; egotistic.*

**either one** *either.* The vice president doesn't like either one of them. *The vice president doesn't like either of them.*

**elect as** *elect.* Whom will you elect as president? *Whom will you elect president?*

**electrical** *electric.*

**(a; the) ... element (in; of; to)** *some;* delete. There will always be an element of doubt. *There will always be some doubt.* ■ The florid phrases and poor editing suggest some element of haste in the booklet's concoction. *The florid phrases and poor editing suggest some haste in the booklet's concoction.* ■ A common element to any system is the need for continuous top-management involvement. *Common to any system is the need for continuous top-management involvement.*

**elliptical** *elliptic.*

**emblematical** *emblematic.*

**emerge out** *emerge.* Part (d) corresponds to a time when the reflected shock waves have emerged out from the dust cloud. *Part (d) corresponds to a time when the reflected shock waves have emerged from the dust cloud.*

**empathetic** *empathic.*

**employ** *use.* Fewer than one-tenth of the small business prospects worldwide employ computers today. *Fewer than one-tenth of the small business prospects worldwide use computers today.*

**employment** *use.* The consistent employment of particular defenses leads to the development of personality traits. *The consistent use of particular defenses leads to the development of personality traits.*

**enable ... to** *let.* This enables analysts to sense the need for changes in methods. *This lets analysts sense the need for changes in methods.*

**encapsulate** *encapsule.* The responses provide a snapshot view of current U.S. efforts to use Japanese information and encapsulate some of the challenges faced by both providers and users. *The responses provide a snapshot view of current U.S. efforts to use Japanese information and encapsule some of the challenges faced by both providers and users.*

**encircle** *circle.*

**enclosed herein (herewith) is (please find)** *enclosed is; here is.* Enclosed herewith please find a letter from our client, Mr. Edward Price, which is self-explanatory. *Here is a letter from our client, Mr. Edward Price, which is self-explanatory.* ■ Enclosed herein please find a really funny romantic comedy, submitted for your perusal. *Enclosed is a really funny romantic comedy, submitted for your perusal.*

**enclosed is** *here is.*

**encounter** *find; have; meet;* delete. This support usually consists of a technical representative you can call if you encounter a problem. *This support usually consists of a technical representative you can call if you have a problem.*

**endeavor** *try.*

**end product** *product.* Each writer has his or her own process because there are different ways to make the end product. *Each writer has his or her own process because there are different ways to make the product.*

**end (final; net; ultimate) result** *result.* The end result was a series of consolidations that lasted until a single company was left to serve the market. *The result was a series of consolidations that lasted until a single company was left to serve the market.*

**engage in ... (a; the)** delete. I appreciate the straightforward way in which you've engaged in this discussion. *I appreciate the straightforward way in which you've discussed this.* ■ Known as an active force in the labor movement, the unions at the Gillette France plant are engaged in a nationwide campaign to shape public opinion. *Known as an active force in the labor movement, the unions at the Gillette France plant are campaigning nationwide to shape public opinion.*

**enter into a contract** *agree; contract.*

**enter into an agreement** *agree; contract.* Courier Dispatch Group Inc.

143

said it has entered into an agreement in principle to acquire the assets of J.A. Finn Inc. *Courier Dispatch Group Inc. said it has agreed in principle to acquire the assets of J.A. Finn Inc.*

**entirely** delete. Our competition introduced an entirely new product. *Our competition introduced a new product.*

**entitle** *title.* The report is entitled "Outlook for EFTPOS: An Executive Summary." *The report is titled "Outlook for EFTPOS: An Executive Summary."*

**enumerate** *count; list; name; numerate.*

**epidemical** *epidemic.*

**epidemiological** *epidemiologic.*

**epigrammatical** *epigrammatic.*

**epigraphical** *epigraphic.*

**equally as** *equally; as.* It was equally as difficult for me. *It was equally difficult for me.* ■ Newer categories of antidepressant drugs are equally as effective as older generation antidepressants. *Newer categories of antidepressant drugs are as effective as older generation antidepressants.*

**equitable** *fair.*

**(the) -(i)er ... of the two** *(the) -(i)er; (the) more.* Sunday will probably be the better of the two days. *Sunday will probably be the better day.*

**-(i)er ... rather than** *-(i)er ... than.* It is quicker to multiply both sides by the reciprocal of the fraction rather than by the common denominator. *It is quicker to multiply both sides by the reciprocal of the fraction than by the common denominator.*

**essential core** *core; crux; essence; gist; pith; substance.* The reviewer let himself be diverted by the book's feminist frame and missed its essential core. *The reviewer let himself be diverted by the book's feminist frame and missed its essence.*

**(an; the) essential ... for (in; of; to)** *essential to.* Homeownership is an essential part of the American dream. *Homeownership is essential to the American dream.* ■ His point is that physical contact is an essential element in everyone's life, and most people don't get enough. *His point is that physical contact is essential to everyone's life, and most people don't get enough.* ■ Toughness is not an essential ingredient for getting ahead, and it isn't the same as resolve. *Toughness is not essential to getting ahead, and it isn't the same as resolve.*

**essential prerequisite**  *essential; prerequisite.* Categorizing a given product is an essential prerequisite for a successful marketing effort. *Categorizing a given product is essential for a successful marketing effort.*

**establish**  *set up.*

**establish conclusive evidence (proof) of**  *prove.*

**established standard**  *standard.* Over the past few years, a number of spreadsheet, database, and word processing programs have become established standards in their areas of application. *Over the past few years, a number of spreadsheet, database, and word processing programs have become standards in their areas of application.*

**established tradition**  *tradition.* IBM broke established traditions and set up a special group at Boca Raton, Florida, to develop their own microcomputer. *IBM broke traditions and set up a special group at Boca Raton, Florida, to develop their own microcomputer.*

**establishment**  *business; club; company; firm; shop; store.* The state supreme court will decide whether to allow nude dancing to continue at that establishment. *The state supreme court will decide whether to allow nude dancing to continue at that club.*

**-est ever**  *-est.* That amount is the largest ever paid by the city in a civil right's action. *That amount is the largest paid by the city in a civil right's action.*

**et cetera, et cetera, et cetera (etc., etc., etc.)**  *and so forth; and so on; and the like; etc.* It quickly becomes confusing as you open one, copy what you want, find the application you want to paste it into, do the paste, go to the next application you need to copy something from, return to the one into which you're pasting, etc., etc., etc. *It quickly becomes confusing as you open one, copy what you want, find the application you want to paste it into, do the paste, go to the next application you need to copy something from, return to the one into which you're pasting, and so on.*

**eventuality**  *event; occurrence; outcome;* delete. Kodak should have prepared for this eventuality. *Kodak should have prepared for this outcome.*

**eventuate** *arise; befall; come about; happen; occur; result; take place.* What crises erupt and decisions eventuate from the moment your eyelids flutter open until the hour you fall asleep? *What crises erupt and decisions come about from the moment your eyelids flutter open until the hour you fall asleep?*

**ever and anon** *at times; now and again; now and then; occasionally; once in a while; on occasion; sometimes.*

**every day (month; week; year)** *daily (monthly; weekly; yearly).*

**every now and then** *at times; from time to time; now and again; now and then; occasionally; once in a while; on occasion; sometimes.*

**every once in a while** *at times; from time to time; now and again; now and then; occasionally; once in a while; on occasion; sometimes.* Every once in a while, I was struck by how hot it was. *Now and then, I was struck by how hot it was.*

**every single (solitary)** *all; every.* Every single solitary juvenile in these four states was examined. *Every juvenile in these four states was examined.*

**evidence in (to) support of (that)** *evidence for (of; that).* The great pay-raise debate is on, and the spectator sees very little evidence to support that higher salaries will attract and keep higher-quality candidates. *The great pay-raise debate is on, and the spectator sees very little evidence that higher salaries will attract and keep higher-quality candidates.* ■ This discovery provided evidence in support of the Copernican system and showed that everything did not revolve around the Earth. *This discovery provided evidence of the Copernican system and showed that everything did not revolve around the Earth.*

**exact (exactly) duplicate** *duplicate; exact; identical; match; (the) same.* Nothing could exactly duplicate what we just heard. *Nothing could match what we just heard.*

**exact (exactly) equivalent** *duplicate; equivalent; exact; identical; match; (the) same.* This situation is exactly equivalent to our usual neglect of the Earth's rotation when we do experiments in laboratories. *This situation is equivalent to our usual neglect of the Earth's rotation when we do experiments in laboratories.*

**exact (exactly) identical** *duplicate; exact; identical; match; (the) same.*

This pattern, though not exactly identical, tends to recur every year. *This pattern, though not identical, tends to recur every year.*

**exactly sure** *sure.* I'm not exactly sure of her name. *I'm not sure of her name.*

**exact (exactly) match** *duplicate; exact; identical; match; (the) same.* When you enter a value that doesn't exactly match one of those listed on the lookup table, the function will find the value equal to or less than the value being looked up. *When you enter a value that doesn't match one of those listed on the lookup table, the function will find the value equal to or less than the value being looked up.*

**exact (exactly) (the) same** *duplicate; exact; identical; just; match; (the) same.* He used those exact same words. *He used those exact words.*

**examination** *exam.*

**(an) example that illustrates (to illustrate)** *example (of); (to) illustrate.* Here are some examples to illustrate the benefits of word processing on a network. *Here are some examples of the benefits of word processing on a network.*

**excerption** *excerpt.*

**(a; the) excessive amount (of)** *excessive; too much.*

**(a; the) excessive number (of)** *excessive; too many.* If your failure to detect errors in the proofing stage results in a published text that contains an excessive number of errors, the costs of making these corrections in a subsequent printing will be charged against your royalties. *If your failure to detect errors in the proofing stage results in a published text that contains excessive errors, the costs of making these corrections in a subsequent printing will be charged against your royalties.*

**excess verbiage** *verbiage.* Excess verbiage befogs language. *Verbiage befogs language.*

**excruciatingly painful** *excruciating; painful.* It has been an excruciatingly painful experience for the town's 8,000 residents. *It has been an excruciating experience for the town's 8,000 residents.*

**(that) exist to ...** delete. Ample evidence exists to support the differences in investment tax shields across industries. *Ample evidence sup-*

*ports the differences in investment tax shields across industries.* ■ Believe it or not, it is freely admitted even within the ranks of psychiatry that no conclusive evidence exists to show that any form of mental illness is biologically caused. *Believe it or not, it is freely admitted even within the ranks of psychiatry that no conclusive evidence shows that any form of mental illness is biologically caused.* ■ County attorneys have broad discretion in this area, and generally do not file charges unless they are satisfied that sufficient evidence exists to prove the crime beyond a reasonable doubt. *County attorneys have broad discretion in this area, and generally do not file charges unless they are satisfied that sufficient evidence proves the crime beyond a reasonable doubt.*

**expect (expectation) and hope** *expect (expectation); hope; trust.* We're pleased with our progress and expect and hope that it will continue as our initiatives take hold. *We're pleased with our progress and expect that it will continue as our initiatives take hold.*

**expediency** *expedience.*

**expeditiously** *abruptly; apace; briskly; directly; fast; forthwith; hastily; hurriedly; posthaste; presently; promptly; quickly; rapidly; right away; shortly; soon; speedily; straightaway; swiftly; wingedly.* This problem must be dealt with expeditiously. *This problem must be dealt with quickly.*

**expenditure (of money)** *cost; expense.* He deplored the long electoral campaigns that involved heavy expenditures of money and brought the country to a virtual standstill for months. *He deplored the long electoral campaigns that involved heavy costs and brought the country to a virtual standstill for months.*

**experience** *feel; find; go through; have; know; see; sense; suffer.* According to this book, many people have experienced boredom and alienation. *According to this book, many people have known boredom and alienation.* ■ The goal was to show people all over the world laughing and having fun, and to emphasize the fact that all human beings are born with the ability to experience joy. *The goal was to show people all over the world laughing and having fun, and to emphasize the fact that all human beings are born with the ability to feel joy.*

**experience** *delete.* This magazine has experienced tremendous growth in the past two years. *This magazine has grown tremendously in the past two years.* ■ Today, nearly 50 years after I had experienced reading "colored need not apply," job segregation and discrimination still exist for African-Americans who are not trained for the better-paying jobs. *Today, nearly 50 years after I had read "colored need not apply," job segregation and discrimination still exist for African-Americans who are not trained for the better-paying jobs.*

**exploitative** *exploitive.*

**express ... (about; for; of; to)** delete. He expressed doubt whether the issue would be much of a headache on the campaign trail this fall. *He doubted whether the issue would be much of a headache on the campaign trail this fall.* ◼ Many express open admiration for women who are healthy, well-groomed, and confident. *Many openly admire women who are healthy, well-groomed, and confident.* ◼ Most top executives seem to believe strongly in the need for better human relations, but they often express distrust of the training program itself. *Most top executives seem to believe strongly in the need for better human relations, but they often distrust the training program itself.* ◼ We wish to express our sincere thanks to our special representative for her responsiveness. *We wish to sincerely thank our special representative for her responsiveness.*

**express concern (about)** *agonize (over; about); brood (on; over); dread; fear; fret (about; over); regret; stew (about; over); worry (about; over).* Some scientists express concern about the implications of splicing the genes for certain insecticides into plants. *Some scientists worry about the implications of splicing the genes for certain insecticides into plants.*

**express opposition to** *contest; criticize; disagree with; disapprove of; dispute; object to; oppose; protest.*

**express skepticism (about)** *disbelieve; distrust; doubt; mistrust; question.* But others express skepticism about those results, with some scientists' questions verging upon accusations of exaggeration. *But others distrust those results, with some scientists' questions verging upon accusations of exaggeration.*

**express sorrow (about)** *bemoan; deplore; grieve; lament; moan; mourn; regret.* At a press conference earlier in the day, he had expressed sorrow that American writers and American politics seem to occupy two different worlds. *At a press conference earlier in the day, he had bemoaned that American writers and American politics seem to occupy two different worlds.*

**extend (issue) an invitation to** *invite.* The Open Software Foundation would like to extend an invitation to you to explore the OSF/Motif user environment. *The Open Software Foundation would like to invite you to explore the OSF/Motif user environment.*

**extend out** *extend*. Press the right arrow until the highlight extends out to cell F4, and then press Return. *Press the right arrow until the highlight extends to cell F4, and then press Return.*

**extensively throughout** *all through; extensively in (through); throughout*. Our reporter has traveled extensively throughout South America. *Our reporter has traveled throughout South America.*

**(an; the) ... extent of** delete. The opening of the first permanently located fair was September 24, 1894, and it ran for an extent of six days. *The opening of the first permanently located fair was September 24, 1894, and it ran for six days.* ■ And between Coney Island and Rockaway inlet there is an extent of some five miles of beach that could be used for re-embarkations. *And between Coney Island and Rockaway inlet there is some five miles of beach that could be used for re-embarkations.*

# F

**face up to** *face.*

**facilitate** *ease; help.*

**facility** *bathroom; building; factory; hospital; jail; office; place; plant; prison; school;* delete. In 1986, hospital executives estimated that 21 percent of their facilities might close. *In 1986, hospital executives estimated that 21 percent of their hospitals might close.*

**(a; the) ... factor (in; of; to)** delete. The fact that we could not have children was a contributing factor to our divorce. *The fact that we could not have children contributed to our divorce.* ■ Knowing the consequences of obesity should be a motivating factor in losing weight. *Knowing the consequences of obesity should be a motivation in losing weight.* ■ Researchers indicate, however, that after age 50 lifestyle becomes a less influential factor in physiological change than aging itself. *Researchers indicate, however, that after age 50 lifestyle becomes less influential in physiological change than aging itself.*

**facts and information** *facts; information.* Request a full disclosure statement highlighting all the pertinent facts and information about the franchisor. *Request a full disclosure statement highlighting all the pertinent facts about the franchisor.*

**factual basis** *basis; fact; reason; truth.* People who know me know there's no factual basis to the story. *People who know me know there's no truth to the story.*

**fail to comply with** *break; disobey; violate.* The Federal Trade Commission is readying a crackdown on commercial sites that fail to comply with the law. *The Federal Trade Commission is readying a crackdown on commercial sites that violate the law.* ■ In the future, farmers and drivers who fail to comply with the biosecurity requirements are likely to be reported for prosecution. *In the future, farmers and drivers who disobey the biosecurity requirements are likely to be reported for prosecution.*

**fair (just) and equitable** *fair; just; equitable.* I support fair and equitable taxes to insure human services are funded. *I support equitable taxes to insure human services are funded.*

fair and square *fair; honest; just; square.*

false and misleading *deceptive; false; misleading.*

false illusion *illusion.*

false pretense *pretense.*

far and away *by far; much.* The judgment was for $10.3 billion, far and away the biggest ever in American commerce. *The judgment was for $10.3 billion, by far the biggest ever in American commerce.*

far and wide *broadly; widely.*

far away from *far from.* These blocks are usually physically located far away from the file's data blocks. *These blocks are usually physically located far from the file's data blocks.*

fasten together *fasten.* Screw threads provide a fast and easy method of fastening two parts together and of exerting a force that can be used for adjustment of movable parts. *Screw threads provide a fast and easy method of fastening two parts and of exerting a force that can be used for adjustment of movable parts.*

favor ... as opposed to (instead of; rather than) *favor ... over; favor ... to.* Lager is a pale, American-style beer favored by the young as opposed to the dark, traditional "bitter" English beer. *Lager is a pale, American-style beer favored by the young over the dark, traditional "bitter" English beer.* ■ He is armed, like his men, with a cut-down musket and a tomahawk, which the Rangers favored instead of traditional European edged weapons. *He is armed, like his men, with a cut-down musket and a tomahawk, which the Rangers favored over traditional European edged weapons.*

fear and trembling *anxiety; dismay; dread; fear; foreboding; horror; terror; trembling.*

(a; the) ... feeling(s) (of) delete. We describe the intensity of the feeling of anger along a four-point scale. *We describe the intensity of anger along a four-point scale.* ■ Neither of us has any guilt feelings about it. *Neither of us has any guilt about it.*

feel inside *feel.* What's most important is how you feel inside about it. *What's most important is how you feel about it.*

**fervency** *fervor.*

**few and far between** *exiguous; few; infrequent; meager; rare; scant; scanty; scarce; scattered; seldom; sparse; uncommon; unusual.* Since then the shooting stars have been few and far between. *Since then the shooting stars have been infrequent.*

**few (small) in number** *exiguous; few; infrequent; limited; meager; not many; rare; scant; scanty; scarce; sparse; uncommon.* Although the clinical trials are few in number and have small patient populations, the response rates are higher than those reported with intravenous chemotherapy. *Although the clinical trials are few and have small patient populations, the response rates are higher than those reported with intravenous chemotherapy.*

**fifty (50) percent (of)** *half (of); one-half (of).* Nearly fifty percent of the town's population is associated with the university. *Nearly half the town's population is associated with the university.*

**figuratively speaking** *as it were; in a sense; in a way; so to speak.*

**(a; the) ... figure** delete. Alan Paton has become something of a legendary figure. *Alan Paton has become something of a legend.*

**fill up** *fill.* Fill up the tank when you're in town. *Fill the tank when you're in town.*

**fill to capacity** *fill.* The auditorium was filled to capacity with the singer's adoring fans. *The auditorium was filled with the singer's adoring fans.*

**filter out** *filter.* It's very hard to filter out fact from fiction. *It's very hard to filter fact from fiction.*

**filthy dirty** *dirty; filthy.*

**final and irrevocable** *final; irrevocable.* His decision not to seek a fourth term as governor is final and irrevocable. *His decision not to seek a fourth term as governor is final.*

**final (ultimate) completion** *completion.* Because the order, timing, and costs of the individual tasks are interrelated, they all affect the total cost of the project and its final completion date. *Because the order, timing, and costs of the individual tasks are interrelated, they all affect the* *total cost of the project and its completion date.*

**final (ultimate) conclusion** *conclusion.* I haven't yet come to a final conclusion about what we should do. *I haven't yet come to a conclusion about what we should do.*

**final (ultimate) culmination** *culmination.* The Graduation Review serves as the final culmination of the MA Program in terms of review, reflection, summative integration and completed documentation. *The Graduation Review serves as the culmination of the MA Program in terms of review, reflection, summative integration and completed documentation.*

**finalize** *complete; conclude; finish.* After five or ten successful projects, you should review guidelines and begin to finalize the procedure. *After five or ten successful projects, you should review guidelines and begin to complete the procedure.*

**final (ultimate) outcome** *outcome.* We were saddened by the final outcome. *We were saddened by the outcome.*

**final (ultimate) resolution** *resolution.* The outcome of these matters is not presently determinable, but the ultimate resolution of such matters will not have a material adverse impact on NYNEX's financial position. *The outcome of these matters is not presently determinable, but the resolution of such matters will not have a material adverse impact on NYNEX's financial position.*

**final (ultimate) settlement** *settlement.*

**financial (monetary) resources** *assets; capital; finances; funds; money; resources.*

**financial wherewithal** *assets; capital; cash; finances; funds; means; money; wherewithal.* The commission also is considering whether owners have the financial wherewithal to operate the plant. *The commission also is considering whether owners have the money to operate the plant.*

**find out** *find; learn.* We found out that today's teenagers are very anxious about the future. *We learned that today's teenagers are very anxious about the future.*

**(all) fine (good) and well** *all right; fine; good; great; nice; pleasant; pleasing; welcome; well.*

**finish up** *finish.*

**firm (strong) commitment** *commitment.* Voters are not firmly committed to any of the candidates. *Voters are not committed to any of the candidates.*

**firm (strong) conviction** *conviction.* This participative process has enabled us to develop a strong conviction throughout the Company that our strategy is the right one. *This participative process has enabled us to develop a conviction throughout the Company that our strategy is the right one.*

**firmly establish** *establish; firm.* We should have resolved them earlier in the implementation of the reorganization, before structure and behavior patterns became firmly established. *We should have resolved them earlier in the implementation of the reorganization, before structure and behavior patterns became firm.*

**firm (strong) resolution** *resolution.*

**first and foremost** *chief; chiefly; first; foremost; main; mainly; mostly; primarily; primary; principal; principally;* delete. Football is first and foremost a running game. *Football is primarily a running game.*

**first and last** *only; sole.*

**first and only** *only; sole.* Was he the first and only person to have superheated ice, yet whose work has fallen into obscurity? *Was he the only person to have superheated ice, yet whose work has fallen into obscurity?*

**first ... before** *before.* You cannot print a document on the disk that has been fast-saved unless you first positioned the cursor at the end of the document before you saved it. *You cannot print a document on the disk that has been fast-saved unless you positioned the cursor at the end of the document before you saved it.* ■ The only way to prevent such occurrences is to ensure that the nodes performing the restoration first determine the type of failure before invoking their restoration mechanisms. *The only way to prevent such occurrences is to ensure that the nodes performing the restoration determine the type of failure before invoking their restoration mechanisms.* ■ Complications due to sampling and disease need to be first eliminated before firm conclusions can be made. *Complications due to sampling and disease need to be eliminated before firm conclusions can be made.*

**first begin**  *begin; start.* If you note the appropriate framework when you first begin your assignment, you will be able to relate what you know from these broader areas to the text at hand. *If you note the appropriate framework when you begin your assignment, you will be able to relate what you know from these broader areas to the text at hand.*

**first (initially) coined**  *coined.* The term *psychic distance* was initially coined by Swedish researchers at the University of Uppsala. *The term psychic distance was coined by Swedish researchers at the University of Uppsala.*

**first come into being**  *arise; begin; start.* When Social Security first came into being, relatively few people lived to the retirement age of 65, so the many were supporting the few. *When Social Security began, relatively few people lived to the retirement age of 65, so the many were supporting the few.*

**first created**  *created.*

**first ever**  *first.* This was the first-ever congressional review of the condition of wilderness areas protected from development under a landmark 1964 law. *This was the first congressional review of the condition of wilderness areas protected from development under a landmark 1964 law.*

**first initially**  *first; initially.* When he first initially got the complaint, he wrote a letter to the Human Rights Commission admitting his guilt. *When he first got the complaint, he wrote a letter to the Human Rights Commission admitting his guilt.*

**first introduced**  *introduced.* He built on some ideas first introduced by Leibniz almost 200 years earlier. *He built on some ideas introduced by Leibniz almost 200 years earlier.*

**first invented**  *invented.* The idea of a sweet treat was first invented by cavemen who ate honey from bee hives. *The idea of a sweet treat was invented by cavemen who ate honey from bee hives.*

**firstly**  *first.* Firstly, Brookside Estates is a privately managed and maintained housing complex. *First, Brookside Estates is a privately managed and maintained housing complex.* ■ Firstly, the users of system A may be convinced that system A is far superior to the universal standard. *First, the users of system A may be convinced that system A is far superior to the universal standard.*

**first of all** *first*. I would first of all ask how many of you are going to help us. *I would first ask how many of you are going to help us.*

**first off** *first*. First off, these price and yield figures are for multimillion-dollar dealer-to-dealer negotiated transactions at any given hour or day. *First, these price and yield figures are for multimillion-dollar dealer-to-dealer negotiated transactions at any given hour or day.*

**first start** *begin; start*. The market share of Searle's Calan was fairly low when we first started. *The market share of Searle's Calan was fairly low when we began.*

**first time ever** *first time*. It's the first time ever that disabled skiers were represented at the Olympics. *It's the first time that disabled skiers were represented at the Olympics.*

**fly in the face of** *challenge; contradict; defy; dispute; disregard; go against; ignore; neglect; overlook*. Although it may be morally reassuring, this tale flies in the face of historical fact. *Although it may be morally reassuring, this tale defies historical fact.*

**focal point** *center; focus*. The U.S.-Canada trade agreement has been the focal point of the campaign. *The U.S.-Canada trade agreement has been the focus of the campaign.*

**focus ... attention on (upon)** *concentrate on; focus on*. It's time we focus our attention on the plight of the poor. *It's time we focus on the plight of the poor.* ■ I was too wrapped up in my own concerns to be able to focus my attention on him. *I was too wrapped up in my own concerns to be able to concentrate on him.*

**focus (media; people's; public) attention on (upon)** *advertise; announce; blazon; broadcast; disclose; divulge; expose; herald; indicate; make known; make public; mention; point out; point to; present; proclaim; promote; publicize; reveal; show; tell; uncover; unveil*. All this has helped us focus attention on the problem. *All this has helped us publicize the problem.*

**focus ... effort on (upon)** *concentrate on; focus on*. He said the crew would focus efforts on saving baby penguins. *He said the crew would concentrate on saving baby penguins.*

**focus ... energy on (upon)** *concentrate on; focus on*. If production focuses its energies on manufacturing a product at the lowest possible cost, but the sales department is willing to accept unprofitable orders, conflict will arise. *If production focuses on manufacturing a product at the lowest possible cost, but the sales department is willing to accept unprofitable orders, conflict will arise.*

**focus in** *focus*. We're focusing in on what we have to do to achieve this. *We're focusing on what we have to do to achieve this.*

**focus of attention** *cynosure; focus*.

**focus ... time and energy on (upon)** *concentrate on; focus on*. With Bonney managing all aspects of our temporary staffing program, our HR staff is able to focus time and energy on other responsibilities. *With Bonney managing all aspects of our temporary staffing program, our HR staff is able to focus on other responsibilities.*

**fold up** *fold*. The commission folded up because the voters implicitly voted to have it fold up. *The commission folded because the voters implicitly voted to have it fold.*

**follow after** *follow*. Your META tags should follow after your <TITLE></TITLE> tags. *Your META tags should follow your <TITLE></TITLE> tags.*

**follow ... below** *below; follow*. Look at the following sentences below. *Look at the following sentences.*

**follow along the lines of** *duplicate; imitate; match; resemble*. There might be a settlement on rates by the end of this year; however, we doubt it will follow along the lines of the New York rate case moratorium. *There might be a settlement on rates by the end of this year; however, we doubt it will resemble the New York rate case moratorium.*

**for all intents and purposes** *effectively; essentially; in effect; in essence; practically; virtually*. Following the treatment with interleukin-2, the nodule for all intents and purposes disappeared. *Following the treatment with interleukin-2, the nodule virtually disappeared.*

**for all practical purposes** *effectively; essentially; in effect; in essence; practically; virtually*. For all practical purposes, there will be no expansion in existing programs. *There will be virtually no expansion in existing programs.* ■ For all practical purposes, there are but two ways to get this information. *In essence, there are but two ways to get this information.*

**for an extended (prolonged; protracted) amount of time (length of time; period; period of time; span of time; time; while)** *awhile; for a long time (while); for a time (while); for days (hours; weeks; years); for six months (three years); long.* We had observed this family for a prolonged period of time. *We had long observed this family.*

**for another (thing)** *second.* For another thing, there is still ample legal precedent for highly effective affirmative action programs that stop short of specific quotas. *Second, there is still ample legal precedent for highly effective affirmative action programs that stop short of specific quotas.*

**forasmuch as** *because; considering; for; given; in that; since.* Forasmuch as Brian and Laura have consented together in wedlock, and have pledged themselves each to the other in the presence of this company, I do now pronounce that they are husband and wife. *In that Brian and Laura have consented together in wedlock, and have pledged themselves each to the other in the presence of this company, I do now pronounce that they are husband and wife.*

**for a while** *awhile.* After this program executes for a while, procedure B is called. *After this program executes awhile, procedure B is called.*

**for awhile** *awhile.* If the program continues to run for awhile, the answer may not be so clear. *If the program continues to run awhile, the answer may not be so clear.*

**forebearer** *forebear.* Episodic reform movements were separated by long periods when many citizens, much like their Colonial forebearers, fantasized that Americans had created a near-utopian society. *Episodic reform movements were separated by long periods when many citizens, much like their Colonial forebears, fantasized that Americans had created a near-utopian society.*

**forecast ... future** *forecast; foretell; predict.* After a model is identified as being a good predictor, it is used to forecast future sales. *After a model is identified as being a good predictor, it is used to forecast sales.*

**foretell ... future** *forecast; foretell; predict.* If you choose to believe that the cards do foretell future events, the obvious follow-up question is whether events suggested by the cards are set in stone, or whether they can be avoided. *If you choose to believe that the cards do foretell events, the obvious follow-up question is whether events suggested by the cards are set in stone, or whether they can be avoided.*

**forever and a day** *always; ceaselessly; consistently; constantly; endlessly; eternally; everlastingly; everyday; forever; invariably; never ending; perpetually; routinely; unfailingly.*

**forevermore** *always; evermore; forever.* I am not naive enough to think that we will forevermore walk hand in hand with the business community to clean the environment. *I am not naive enough to think that we will forever walk hand in hand with the business community to clean the environment.*

**forewarn** *warn.* We do, however, forewarn the authorities in charge of our planet's destiny against decisions which are supported by pseudoscientific arguments or false and nonrelevant data. *We do, however, warn the authorities in charge of our planet's destiny against decisions which are supported by pseudoscientific arguments or false and nonrelevant data.*

**for example (for instance)** *say.* When the scanner reads the bar code on, for example, a can of beans, the computer looks up the product number the bar code represents and returns its name and price to the register. *When the scanner reads the bar code on, say, a can of beans, the computer looks up the product number the bar code represents and returns its name and price to the register.*

**for example ... and others (and so forth; and so on; and such; and the like; et al.; etc.; or whatever)** *and others (and so forth; and so on; and such; and the like; et al.; etc.; or); e.g.; for example; for instance.* Many other examples of the influence religion has on buyer behavior — for example, on values and norms, time, sense of self, and so forth — will be found in the following sections. *Many other examples of the influence religion has on buyer behavior — on values and norms, time, sense of self, and so forth — will be found in the following sections.* ■ For example, you may create one directory to hold word processing documents, another to hold Applesoft programs, etc. *For example, you may create one directory to hold word processing documents and another to hold Applesoft programs.*

**for fear (that; of) ... can (could; may; might; shall; should; will; would)** *lest.* Few of us know what to say to friends who are mourning, so we may avoid them for fear we'll say the wrong thing. *Few of us know what to say to friends who are mourning, so we may avoid them lest we say the wrong thing.* ■ The Arab League has meanwhile refused to transfer millions of dollars in aid to the PA for fear that top officials would lay their hands on the money. *The Arab League has meanwhile* *refused to transfer millions of dollars in aid to the PA lest top officials lay their hands on the money.*

**for free** *free.* Purchasers of 1.0 versions will receive 1.1 upgrades for free from IBM. *Purchasers of 1.0 versions will receive free 1.1 upgrades from IBM.*

**for (in; to) (the) furtherance of** *for; to advance; to foster; to further; to promote.* Neither the conspiracy itself nor the overt acts allegedly done in furtherance of it were directed toward Boisjoly. *Neither the conspiracy itself nor the overt acts allegedly done to foster it were directed toward Boisjoly.* ■ This is done in furtherance of the principle that all witness identifications be made independently. *This is done to advance the principle that all witness identifications be made independently.* ■ In furtherance of its corporate purposes, the corporation shall have all the general powers enumerated in Article 1396-2.02. *To further its corporate purposes, the corporation shall have all the general powers enumerated in Article 1396-2.02.*

**for (an) indefinite (indeterminate) amount of time (length of time; period; period of time; span of time; time; while)** *briefly; for a time; for a while; indefinitely; temporarily.* We are freezing prices and wages for an indefinite period. *We are freezing prices and wages temporarily.*

**for instance ... and others (and so forth; and so on; and such; and the like; et al.; etc.; or whatever)** *and others (and so forth; and so on; and such; and the like; et al.; etc.; or); e.g.; for example; for instance.* Use one of these labels to assign a number and perhaps a descriptive title to each disk, for instance, Disk 1: Letters, Disk 2: Spreadsheet Files, Disk 3: Reports, and so on. *Use one of these labels to assign a number and perhaps a descriptive title to each disk, for instance, Disk 1: Letters, Disk 2: Spreadsheet Files, and Disk 3: Reports.*

**for long** *long.* If top executives cannot control their responsibilities, they usually do not remain in their positions for long. *If top executives cannot control their responsibilities, they usually do not remain long in their positions.*

**form (a; the) judgment (about; as to; concerning; of; on; regarding)** *assess; conclude; decide; deduce; determine; evaluate; infer; judge; reason; resolve; settle.* Voters cannot form a judgment unless the candidates say what they mean. *Voters cannot decide unless the candidates say what they mean.* ■ The Stock Selection Guide helps you to learn the facts about a company's past and present and form a judgment as to its likely value in the future. *The Stock Selection Guide helps you to learn the facts about a company's past and present and assess its likely value in the future.*

**form (an; the) opinion (about; as to; concerning; of; on; regarding)** *assess; conclude; decide; deduce; determine; evaluate; infer; judge; reason; resolve; settle.* Just as you should not form an opinion of a person you meet based upon a fragment (first impression), so you should not form an opinion of the market. *Just as you should not judge a person you meet based upon a fragment (first impression), so you should not judge the market.*

**form (a; the) resolution (about; as to; concerning; of; on; regarding)** *conclude; decide; determine; resolve; settle.* When you rise in the morning, form a resolution to make the day a happy one for a fellow creature. *When you rise in the morning, resolve to make the day a happy one for a fellow creature.* ■ Then bring the two sides together to form a resolution to peacefully and equitably end the conflict. *Then bring the two sides together to determine to peacefully and equitably end the conflict.*

**formulate** *devise; form; make.* Have you formulated no opinion about her? *Have you formed no opinion about her?*

**for obvious reasons** *obviously.* For obvious reasons, he wants to announce his choice at the convention. *Obviously, he wants to announce his choice at the convention.*

**for one ... (be) an example (an instance)** *(be) an example (an instance); for one; one example (one instance).* The Massachusetts Industrial Services Program, for one, is an example of the kind of broad industrial extension service we think is needed to retool manufacturing facilities. *The Massachusetts Industrial Services Program is one example of the kind of broad industrial extension service we think is needed to retool manufacturing facilities.*

**for one (thing)** *first.* For one thing, a national program would have to be tailored to each state because the delivery of health care services can differ significantly. *First, a national program would have to be tailored to each state because the delivery of health care services can differ significantly.*

**for ... purposes (of)** *for; so as to; to.* The money we receive from licensing John Wayne's image is used entirely for charitable purposes. *The money we receive from licensing John Wayne's image is used entirely for charity.*

**for reasons of**  *after; because of; by; for; from; in; out of; through*. When airlines have replaced older planes, they have done so primarily for reasons of economics — newer aircraft cost less to inspect and repair. *When airlines have replaced older planes, they have done so primarily because of economics — newer aircraft cost less to inspect and repair.*

**for some time (now)**  *long*. I have enjoyed reading your articles for some time now. *I have long enjoyed reading your articles.*

**for that matter**  *also; and; as well; besides; beyond that (this); even; further; furthermore; moreover; more than that (this); still more; then; too; what is more*; delete. How can they speak up and tell the South Africans what they should do with their people or, for that matter, what the Soviet Union should do with its Jewish population? *How can they speak up and tell the South Africans what they should do with their people, or even what the Soviet Union should do with its Jewish population?*

**for that (this) reason**  *consequently; hence; so; then; therefore; thus*. For that reason, I wouldn't do it again. *I therefore wouldn't do it again.*

**for the duration (length) of**  *during; throughout*. The company intends to maintain silence for the duration of the sale process. *The company intends to maintain silence during the sale process.*

**for the first (last) time**  *first (last)*. The series of studies were presented for the first time at the three-day conference. *The series of studies were first presented at the three-day conference.*

**for the foreseeable future**  *for a time; for a while; for now; for many (several) months (years); for six (two) months (years); for some time; for the present; for the time being; temporarily*. He is one of those who believes that a recession can be avoided for the foreseeable future. *He is one of those who believes that a recession can be avoided for now.*

**for the immediate future**  *for a time; for a while; for now; for many (several) months (years); for six (two) months (years); for some time; for the present; for the time being; temporarily*. Several said they were canceling planned business trips for the immediate future. *Several said they were canceling planned business trips for the present.*

**for the most part**  *almost all; chiefly; commonly; generally; greatly; in general; largely; mainly; most; mostly; most often; much; nearly all; normally; overall; typically; usually*. Those problems for the most part have been overcome. *Those problems have been largely overcome.*

**for the (very) near future** *for a time; for a while; for now; for many (several) months (years); for six (two) months (years); for some time; for the present; for the time being; temporarily.* While the analysts expected Kraft and General Foods to exist as separate entities for the near future, they said they did not expect the honeymoon to last forever. *While the analysts expected Kraft and General Foods to exist as separate entities for now, they said they did not expect the honeymoon to last forever.*

**for the not-so-distant (not-too-distant) future** *for a time; for a while; for now; for many (several) months (years); for six (two) months (years); for some time; for the present; for the time being; temporarily.*

**for the present** *for now;* delete. Perhaps one day we shall find an Etruscan library, buried deep in the Italian countryside, but for the present, we have to make do with what we have, which is precious little. *Perhaps one day we shall find an Etruscan library, buried deep in the Italian countryside, but for now, we have to make do with what we have, which is precious little.*

**for the purpose of (-ing)** *for (-ing); so as to; to.* All deposited items are received for the purpose of collection, and all credits for deposited items are provisional. *All deposited items are received for collection, and all credits for deposited items are provisional.* ■ The mission of the Deaf Dog Education Action Fund is to provide education and funding for the purpose of improving and/or saving the lives of deaf dogs. *The mission of the Deaf Dog Education Action Fund is to provide education and funding so as to improve and/or save the lives of deaf dogs.* ■ Trade Council of Iceland was established in 1986 for the purpose of promoting exports and increasing marketing awareness among Icelandic companies. *Trade Council of Iceland was established in 1986 to promote exports and increase marketing awareness among Icelandic companies.*

**for the (simple) reason that** *because; considering; for; given; in that; since.* Normally, short-term Treasuries yield less than longer-term Treasuries, for the simple reason that investors demand to be rewarded for tying up their money in longer-term instruments. *Normally, short-term Treasuries yield less than longer-term Treasuries since investors demand to be rewarded for tying up their money in longer-term instruments.* ■ It's not a bestseller for the simple reason that people aren't brave enough to read it. *It's not a bestseller because people aren't brave enough to read it.*

**for the sake of** *for; so as to; to.* I have never found it necessary to practice "defensive medicine," if that means doing that which would not

164

otherwise be done solely for the sake of protecting oneself against possible legal action. *I have never found it necessary to practice "defensive medicine," if that means doing that which would not otherwise be done solely to protect oneself against possible legal action.*

**for the time (while) being** *for now; for the moment; for the present;* delete. For the time being, look at the current PLOT ORIGIN and the SCALE. *For the moment, look at the current PLOT ORIGIN and the SCALE.*

**for ... to come** *for.* This can go on for generations to come. *This can go on for generations.*

**forward in (into) the future** *forward; in (into) the future.* He misleads those who may be truly seeking to understand where the Jews come from and how, as Jews, they can best carry their traditions forward into the future. *He misleads those who may be truly seeking to understand where the Jews come from and how, as Jews, they can best carry their traditions forward.* ■ AgriVision will take a real and practical look at how to take UK farming forward into the future. *AgriVision will take a real and practical look at how to take UK farming into the future.*

**for (many; several) years (now)** *long.* The few policies I was able to get from SBLI have, for many years now, paid me an annual dividend, with no payment of any premium. *The few policies I was able to get from SBLI have long paid me an annual dividend, with no payment of any premium.*

**for your information** delete. For your information, links may not appear underlined, but will appear in this color. *Links may not appear underlined, but will appear in this color.*

**fourthly** *fourth.*

**frame of mind** *attitude; belief; opinion; position; posture; stand; standpoint; vantage; view; viewpoint;* delete.

**fraught with meaning (significance)** *consequential; meaningful; momentous; significant.* If nothing else, the question is fraught with significance for Democrats trying to figure out whether to mount a campaign today that will peak three years from now. *If nothing else, the question is significant for Democrats trying to figure out whether to mount a campaign today that will peak three years from now.* ■ Silly or not, the prices we settle for are fraught with meaning for they either substantiate our travel savvy or betray our gullibility. *Silly or not, the prices we settle for are meaningful for they either substantiate our travel savvy or betray our gullibility.*

**free and gratis** *free.*

**free, complimentary** *complimentary; free.* If you would like to receive a free, complimentary copy of the Samplers for each of these courses, return the enclosed self-addressed, postage-paid card and mail it today. *If you would like to receive a complimentary copy of the Samplers for each of these courses, return the enclosed self-addressed, postage-paid card and mail it today.*

**free gift** *gift.* For your free gift, fill out this form today. *For your gift, fill out this form today.*

**free of charge** *free.* All meetings are free of charge and open to the public. *All meetings are free and open to the public.*

**free pass** *pass.*

**free up** *free.* On some programs, rows and columns can be deleted to free up memory for new data on a model. *On some programs, rows and columns can be deleted to free memory for new data on a model.*

**freezing cold** *cold; freezing.* It's freezing cold outside. *It's freezing outside.*

**from (a; the) ... aspect (of)** *as (does); as for; as to; for; from; in; in that; -(al)ly; since; to;* delete. From a legal aspect, the joint venture falls under local company or corporation law when participation is in the form of equity. *Legally, the joint venture falls under local company or corporation law when participation is in the form of equity.*

**from beginning to end** *all through; completely; entirely; thoroughly; throughout; totally; wholly;* delete. I listened to the whole song, from beginning to end. *I listened to the whole song.* ■ Our surety bonding software is custom designed to meet your specific needs from beginning to end. *Our surety bonding software is custom designed to meet your specific needs completely.*

**from (a; the) ... distance of** *from; from ... away.* Most of the spectators watched from a distance of 1,300 feet, while the Soviet observers viewed the firings from a concrete bunker. *Most of the spectators* *watched from 1,300 feet away, while the Soviet observers viewed the firings from a concrete bunker.*

**from hence**  *hence.*

**from minute (moment) to minute (moment)**  *directly; momentarily; momently; presently; soon.* I expect them from moment to moment. *I expect them momently.*

**from now (on)**  *hence.*

**from ... on (onward)**  *since.* Other researchers had already confirmed that from 200 A.D. onward there had been human sacrifices of varying kinds. *Other researchers had already confirmed that since 200 A.D. there had been human sacrifices of varying kinds.*

**from one ... to another**  *between.* Moving your funds from one institution to another is easy to do, and there is no tax liability or IRS penalty at all, if you follow the correct procedures. *Moving your funds between institutions is easy to do, and there is no tax liability or IRS penalty at all, if you follow the correct procedures.*

**from (a; the) ... perspective (of)**  *as (does); as for; as to; for; from; in; in that; -(al)ly; since; to;* delete. From my perspective, trashing my system makes a lot of sense. *Trashing my system makes a lot of sense to me.* ■ From a historical perspective, there have been more than a few cases where decisions that have been rendered seem to fly in the face of the evidence. *Historically, there have been more than a few cases where decisions that have been rendered seem to fly in the face of the evidence.*

**from (a; the) ... point of view (of)**  *as (does); as for; as to; for; from; in; in that; -(al)ly; since; to;* delete. You've got to look at it from an optimistic point of view. *You've got to look at it optimistically.* ■ I try to see things from the customer's point of view. *I try to see things as the customer does.*

**from (a; the) ... standpoint (of)**  *as (does); as for; as to; for; from; in; in that; -(al)ly; since; to;* delete. From a statistical standpoint, who is most vulnerable to colon-rectal cancer? *Statistically, who is most vulnerable to colon-rectal cancer?* ■ I have had some experience with grief from a personal standpoint. *I have had some personal experience with grief.* ■ The proposed purchase price is indeed a good value from the city's standpoint. *The proposed purchase price is indeed a good value for the city.* ■ A move to Jacksonville will be highly profitable for the club and would be smart from a business standpoint. *A move to Jacksonville will be highly profitable for the club and would be smart business.* ■ From a medical standpoint, we don't have any evidence that the senator abuses alcohol. *We don't have any medical evidence that the senator abuses alcohol.*

**from start to finish**  *all through; completely; entirely; thoroughly; throughout; totally; wholly.*

**from that day (moment; point; time) (forward; on; onward)** *from then (on); since; since then;* delete. From that point on, she hasn't said a word to me. *Since then, she hasn't said a word to me.*

**from the beginning (start)** *always.* From the start, it has been a haven for those whose religions or political beliefs were not tolerated in their homelands. *It has always been a haven for those whose religions or political beliefs were not tolerated in their homelands.*

**from the fact that** *because; considering; for; given; in that; since.*

**from (in) the following year** *from (in) (1991).*

**from (in) the preceding year** *from (in) (1989).* At year-end 1987, 70,893 persons were employed within Ericsson, a decrease of 1,682 from the preceding year. *At year-end 1987, 70,893 persons were employed within Ericsson, a decrease of 1,682 from 1986.*

**from the time of ... (on)** *since.* From the time of the Elizabethan settlement on, the Church of England attempted, with varying degrees of success, to consolidate its position both as a distinctive middle way between Catholicism and Puritanism and as the national religion of England. *Since the Elizabethan settlement, the Church of England attempted, with varying degrees of success, to consolidate its position both as a distinctive middle way between Catholicism and Puritanism and as the national religion of England.*

**from this day (moment; point; time) (forward; on; onward)** *from now (on); hence; henceforth; henceforward;* delete. From this point on, elected students and faculty will be running the affairs of the school. *Henceforth, elected students and faculty will be running the affairs of the school.*

**from ... until** *from ... to.* This book is intriguing because it also concerns the role of that on-again, off-again colonial revival in popular culture from 1876 until the present. *This book is intriguing because it also concerns the role of that on-again, off-again colonial revival in popular culture from 1876 to the present.*

**from (a; the) ... viewpoint (of)** *as (does); as for; as to; for; from; in; in that; -(al)ly; since; to;* delete. From a business viewpoint, it makes good sense to free brain power from the drudgery of processing data and to engage it in finding new ways to apply that data. *It makes good sense for business to free brain power from the drudgery of processing data and to engage it in finding new ways to apply that data.*

**from whence** *whence.* From whence did he draw his strength? *Whence did he draw his strength?*

**full capacity** *capacity.* Demand for petroleum products was so strong that refineries were operating at or near full capacity. *Demand for petroleum products was so strong that refineries were operating at or near capacity.*

**full (maximum) potential (potentiality)** *potential (potentiality).* If we are to achieve our full potential, we must see beyond the routine. *If we are to achieve our potential, we must see beyond the routine.*

**full satisfaction** *satisfaction.*

**fundamental** *basic;* delete.

**fundamental (and) basic** *basic; fundamental.* These are fundamental and basic rights. *These are basic rights.*

**fundamental basis** *basis.* The fundamental basis of any relationship is truth. *The basis of any relationship is truth.*

**fundamental principle** *principle.*

**furiously angry** *angry; furious.* She's furiously angry. *She's furious.*

**further** *more.* For further information, or free form samples, contact Deluxe at their toll-free number. *For more information, or free form samples, contact Deluxe at their toll-free number.*

**furthermore** *also; and; as well; besides; even; further; still more; then; too.* Furthermore, some of the changes may reduce the extent to which issuers may issue tax-exempt bonds. *Further, some of the changes may reduce the extent to which issuers may issue tax-exempt bonds.*

**fuse together** *fuse.* Most metals, except for low- and medium-carbon steels, require fluxes to aid in the process of melting and fusing the metals together. *Most metals, except for low- and medium-carbon steels, require fluxes to aid in the process of melting and fusing the metals.*

**future developments** *developments.* Please check back regularly for updates and future developments. *Please check back regularly for updates and developments.*

**future plans** *plans.* He said future plans call for the introduction of 2-Mbs service in the switched network by 1992, which would mean videoconferences could be switched like normal phone calls. *He said plans call for the introduction of 2-Mbs service in the switched network by 1992, which would mean videoconferences could be switched like normal phone calls.*

**future projections** *projections.*

**future prospects** *prospects.* Proponents of the information center concept, Atre Consultants are not overly romantic about its future prospects. *Proponents of the information center concept, Atre Consultants are not overly romantic about its prospects.*

# G

**gather together** *gather*. In Dubai, about 400 relatives of the dead and their supporters gathered together for a memorial service at a large Shiite mosque. *In Dubai, about 400 relatives of the dead and their supporters gathered for a memorial service at a large Shiite mosque.*

**general consensus** *consensus*. The general consensus among corporations is to be cautious about 1989. *The consensus among corporations is to be cautious about 1989.*

**general public** *public*.

**general vicinity** *vicinity; area*.

**gentleman** *man*. Nothing would give me greater pleasure than to see these gentlemen put out of business. *Nothing would give me greater pleasure than to see these men put out of business.*

**geographical** *geographic*. Several large commercial banks provide economic data and forecasts for the geographical area they serve. *Several large commercial banks provide economic data and forecasts for the geographic area they serve.*

**geological** *geologic*. On-site geological studies would be needed to confirm an impact origin. *On-site geologic studies would be needed to confirm an impact origin.*

**geometrical** *geometric*.

**get married** *marry*. We plan to get married in the fall. *We plan to marry in the fall.*

**get across** *convey; explain*. There's an important element here that we need to get across. *There's an important element here that we need to convey.*

**get in touch with** *call; contact; phone; reach; visit; write (to)*. Agency representatives with reports to enter can get in touch with him at (703) 323-5711. *Agency representatives with reports to enter can reach him at (703) 323-5711.*

**give (a; the) ... (for; of; to)** delete. Give an estimate on the amount of time it will take and the number of people you will need. *Estimate the amount of time it will take and the number of people you will need.* ■ The Book of Leviticus gives a list of the women who are not available to marry certain men. *The Book of Leviticus lists the women who are not available to marry certain men.* ■ The main purpose of choosing an outside auditor is to guarantee to insiders and interested outsiders that the financial data presented in financial documents give an accurate representation of events. *The main purpose of choosing an outside auditor is to guarantee to insiders and interested outsiders that the financial data presented in financial documents accurately represent events.* ■ They work hard; they deserve to be given compensation. *They work hard; they deserve to be compensated.* ■ Did he give any indication of what he plans to do? *Did he indicate what he plans to do?* ■ I'll give you a call at the end of the week. *I'll call you at the end of the week.* ■ I hope you will give me consideration for diverse projects. *I hope you will consider me for diverse projects.* ■ Many small businesses and private individuals are giving serious consideration to their energy and resource needs for the year ahead. *Many small businesses and private individuals are seriously considering their energy and resource needs for the year ahead.* ■ Thanks to Craig for taking the time out of his busy schedule to give this book a read. *Thanks to Craig for taking the time out of his busy schedule to read this book.*

**give birth to** *bear.* The prospect that the princess might give birth to a girl has already sparked speculation that there will be pressure to change the law. *The prospect that the princess might bear a girl has already sparked speculation that there will be pressure to change the law.* ■ This dilemma gave birth to an idea that was to revolutionize the road building industry. *This dilemma bore an idea that was to revolutionize the road building industry.*

**given at (in)** *at (in).* Since all limits are given in thousandths, the values can be converted by moving the decimal point three places to the left. *Since all limits are in thousandths, the values can be converted by moving the decimal point three places to the left.*

**given the fact that** *because; considering; for; given; in that; since; when.* Given the fact that she only read 400 pages of the book, she didn't do too badly. *Considering she only read 400 pages of the book, she didn't do too badly.* ■ Given the fact that more than 90 percent of information is still in paper form, this is indeed a tall order. *Since more than 90 percent of information is still in paper form, this is indeed a tall order.*

**give offense to** *offend.* Ask them to develop a set of labels that does not give offense to any group of countries. *Ask them to develop a set of labels that does not offend any group of countries.*

**give rise to** *bear; cause.* The researchers concluded that abnormalities in the neurotransmitter system may give rise to the depression in demented patients. *The researchers concluded that abnormalities in the neurotransmitter system may cause the depression in demented patients.*

**go along with** *agree with; back; endorse; favor; support.* He was unwilling to say whether he would go along with such a recommendation. *He was unwilling to say whether he would support such a recommendation.*

**(just) goes to show** *attests; proves; reveals; shows; supports; verifies; delete.* It just goes to show that safety in driving is most important. *It shows that safety in driving is most important.*

**(it) goes without saying (that)** *clearly; naturally; obviously; of course; plainly; delete.* This may go without saying, but I also look at a person's motivation, commitment, and energy. *Naturally, I also look at a person's motivation, commitment, and energy.*

**go forward** *advance; continue; go on; happen; move on; occur; proceed; progress.* We want the project to go forward as soon as possible, and we are confident that these issues can be addressed. *We want the project to proceed as soon as possible, and we are confident that these issues can be addressed.* ∎ McVeigh prosecutors predict execution will go forward. *McVeigh prosecutors predict execution will occur.*

**good and sufficient** *adequate; good; sufficient.* We think that the safety of present plants is good and sufficient. *We think that the safety of present plants is adequate.*

**go through ... experience** *experience; go through.* I think I'm a much better person for having gone through that experience. *I think I'm a much better person for having experienced that.*

**grateful thanks** *gratitude; thanks.*

**(a; the) greater (larger) number (of)** *more.* Usually the greater number of services offered, the larger the margin needed on each side to maintain profitability. *Usually the more services offered, the larger the margin needed on each side to maintain profitability.*

**(a; the) great (large) fraction (of)** *a good (great) deal (of); a good (great) many (of); almost all (of); (nine) in (ten) (of); many (of); most (of); much (of); nearly all (of); (43) of (48) (of); (67) percent (of); three-fourths (two-thirds) (of).* Of the numerous complete fossils discovered in this quarry, a large fraction are either babies or mothers carrying young. *Of the numerous complete fossils discovered in this quarry, most are either babies or mothers carrying young.*

**group together** *group.* The Chapter command divides your Notepad pages into chapters and groups together related information. *The Chapter command divides your Notepad pages into chapters and groups related information.* ■ There have been debates for decades regarding the best ways for employees to be grouped together. *There have been debates for decades regarding the best ways for employees to be grouped.*

# H

**had ... then** *had*. Had he exhibited the kind of behavior that would have warranted such a recommendation, then it would have been made. *Had he exhibited the kind of behavior that would have warranted such a recommendation, it would have been made.*

**hale and hearty** *hale; healthy; hearty; well.*

**half (a) dozen** *six.*

**half of** *half*. The menus occupy almost half of the screen display. *The menus occupy almost half the screen display.*

**harbinger of the future (of things to come)** *harbinger; omen; sign.* I hope it is a harbinger of the future. *I hope it is an omen.* ■ This made 1989 the most stable year in terms of oil prices since 1984, and was widely interpreted as a harbinger of things to come: a more prosperous era for OPEC. *This made 1989 the most stable year in terms of oil prices since 1984, and was widely interpreted as a harbinger: a more prosperous era for OPEC.*

**hard and fast** *firm; fixed; steadfast; strict.*

**has (a; the) ... (about; for; of; on; over)** delete. If you have intentions of going, you should make your reservations now. *If you intend to go, you should make your reservations now.* ■ He has control over the entire program. *He controls the entire program.* ■ Boston has the need for a new harbor tunnel. *Boston needs a new harbor tunnel.* ■ The strategic partnering lawyer must have a firm grasp of the fundamentals of the legal principles in Europe and in the Far East. *The strategic partnering lawyer must firmly grasp the fundamentals of the legal principles in Europe and in the Far East.*

**has a bearing on (upon)** *acts on; affects; bears on; influences.* What we are learning about primates and other social species has a direct bearing on our own species. *What we are learning about primates and other social species directly bears on our own species.*

**has a (the) capability to** *can; is able to.*

**has a difference of opinion with** *differs; disagrees with; disputes; objects to; opposes.* We have a difference of opinion with the decision the judge made. *We disagree with the decision the judge made.*

**has a (the) habit of (-ing)** *tends to; will.* He has a habit of biting his nails. *He tends to bite his nails.*

**has an (the) ability to** *can; is able to.* Eighty percent of the retail deposit accounts have the ability to be accessed by a debit card even though actual usage is much less. *Eighty percent of the retail deposit accounts can be accessed by a debit card even though actual usage is much less.*

**has an (the) appreciation for** *appreciates; approves of; cherishes; enjoys; esteems; likes; prizes; treasures; understands; values.* Most people don't have an appreciation for esoteric beliefs. *Most people don't appreciate esoteric beliefs.*

**has a (the) preference for** *favors; prefers.* By now, you will have gathered that I have a strong preference for organization along functional lines. *By now, you will have gathered that I strongly prefer organization along functional lines.*

**has a (the) tendency (to)** *tends to; will.* As a community, the Basques have a tendency to be healthy and long-lived. *As a community, the Basques tend to be healthy and long-lived.*

**has (a) ... effect on (upon)** *acts on; affects; bears on; influences;* delete. Over the past twenty years, the U.S. economy has had a significant effect on the Amish way of life. *Over the past twenty years, the U.S. economy has significantly influenced the Amish way of life.* ■ Human activity is changing the composition of the atmosphere in ways that could have profound effects upon life on the Earth. *Human activity is changing the composition of the atmosphere in ways that could profoundly affect life on the Earth.*

**has got** *has.*

**has (a) ... impact (on; upon)** *acts on; affects; bears on; influences;* delete. It has a direct impact on the majority of the American people. *It directly affects the majority of the American people.* ■ Your tone of voice, expression, and apparent receptiveness to others' responses all have a tremendous impact upon those you wish to reach. *Your tone of voice, expression, and apparent receptiveness to others' responses all tremendously influence those you wish to reach.*

**has (a) ... influence on (upon)**  *acts on; affects; bears on; influences;* delete. Management was alerted to the fact that the social environment of employees had a great influence on productivity. *Management was alerted to the fact that the social environment of employees greatly affected productivity.*

**has occasion to be**  *is.* The ombudsman often has occasion to be aware of problems arising between levels and units. *The ombudsman often is aware of problems arising between levels and units.* ■ If he has occasion to be in Washington, the president likes to spend time with him. *If he is in Washington, the president likes to spend time with him.* ■ Some fifty years later I had occasion to be in the vicinity of that church and I went in, just to see. *Some fifty years later I was in the vicinity of that church and I went in, just to see.* ■ If you have ever had occasion to be deprived of your normal sleep, you know how hard it is to function when you haven't had enough rest. *If you have ever been deprived of your normal sleep, you know how hard it is to function when you haven't had enough rest.*

**has only to**  *need only.* To view any of the channels available, you have only to switch between channels. *To view any of the channels available, you need only switch between channels.*

**has reference to**  *concerns; deals with; is about; pertains to; regards; relates to.* Abase has reference to a bringing down in condition or feelings; debase has reference to the bringing down of a thing in purity; degrade has reference to a bringing down from some higher grade or from some standard. *Abase pertains to a bringing down in condition or feelings; debase pertains to the bringing down of a thing in purity; degrade pertains to a bringing down from some higher grade or from some standard.* ■ This letter has reference to the outstanding series of articles in your esteemed daily appearing in the column "Without Malice." *This letter concerns the outstanding series of articles in your esteemed daily appearing in the column "Without Malice."*

**has the effect of -ing**  delete. Such a slowdown would have the effect of easing inflationary fears. *Such a slowdown would ease inflationary fears.* ■ The Seven of Diamonds is called the Ugly Card, and has the effect of doubling the negative value of any Jacks collected by the player who wins a trick containing this card. *The Seven of Diamonds is called the Ugly Card, and doubles the negative value of any Jacks collected by the player who wins a trick containing this card.*

**has (got) to**  *must.* I have to be going. *I must be going.*

**(that) has to do with** *concerns; deals with; is about; pertains to; regards; relates to.* The first has to do with the relative merits of CD versus analog. *The first pertains to the relative merits of CD versus analog.*

**have (possess) ... in common** *share.* We have no interests in common. *We share no interests.*

**have ... in (my) possession** *have; possess.* We now have in our possession a class of machines that are right around energy breakeven. *We now possess a class of machines that are right around energy breakeven.* ■ Many of the tombstone pictures I now have in my possession represent a unique record because the original tombstones have been replaced with newer ones. *Many of the tombstone pictures I now have represent a unique record because the original tombstones have been replaced with newer ones.*

**head up** *direct; head; lead.* Bush headed up the committee that eliminated those regulations. *Bush headed the committee that eliminated those regulations.*

**heat up** *heat.* I just threw it all together and then heated it up. *I just threw it all together and then heated it.*

**(a; the) height of** *delete.* The stratosphere is one of the middle layers of the atmosphere that starts some 15 kilometers above Earth's surface and extends to a height of about 50 kilometers. *The stratosphere is one of the middle layers of the atmosphere that starts some 15 kilometers above Earth's surface and extends to about 50 kilometers.*

**help in (of) -ing** *help (-ing).* Those who have no diversions or hobbies may need help in selecting appropriate activities. *Those who have no diversions or hobbies may need help selecting appropriate activities.* ■ The work may also help in tracking down inherited influences in mental diseases. *The work may also help track down inherited influences in mental diseases.*

**help out** *help.* They're very eager to help out. *They're very eager to help.*

**help ... to** *help.* Following these guidelines may help to cut down on the amount of aspirin you need. *Following these guidelines may help cut down on the amount of aspirin you need.*

**henceforth (henceforward)** *hence.*

**hereafter**  *hence.*

**(the) here and now**  *(just; right) now; presently; the present.*

**high and dry**  *alone; helpless; powerless.*

**high and low**  *everywhere.*

**high and mighty**  *arrogant; disdainful; dogmatic; domineering; haughty.*

**(a; the) high degree (of)**  *abundant; a good (great) deal (of); a good (great) many (of); ample; great; high; many (of); marked; most (of); much (of); salient; striking; vast;* delete. One of the distinguishing characteristics of the Eurobond market is its high degree of competitiveness. *One of the distinguishing characteristics of the Eurobond market is its marked competitiveness.*

**(a; the) high level (of)**  *abundant; a good (great) deal (of); a good (great) many (of); ample; great; high; many (of); marked; most (of); much (of); salient; striking; vast;* delete. The London merchant banks have a very high level of expertise. *The London merchant banks have vast expertise.*

**(a; the) high number (of)**  *a good (great) many (of); almost all; countless; dozens (of); hundreds (of); many (of); millions (of); most (of); nearly all (of); numerous; scores (of); six hundred (twelve hundred) (of); thousands (of).* Hampton's high number of published recordings further supports the idea that he has spent several decades sharing his vibe playing with those who would listen. *Hampton's numerous published recordings further supports the idea that he has spent several decades sharing his vibe playing with those who would listen.*

**(a; the) high percentage (of)**  *a good (great) deal (of); a good (great) many (of); almost all (of); (nine) in (ten) (of); many (of); most (of); much (of); nearly all (of); (43) of (48) (of); (67) percent (of); three-fourths (two-thirds) (of).* That probably is excellent advice, if these bonds represent a high percentage of your total investments. *That probably is excellent advice, if these bonds represent much of your total investments.*

**(a; the) high proportion (of)**  *a good (great) deal (of); a good (great) many (of); almost all (of); (nine) in (ten) (of); many (of); most (of); much (of); nearly all (of); (43) of (48) (of); (67) percent (of); three-fourths (two-thirds) (of).* In the pharmaceutical industry, most companies devote a high proportion of their budgets to R&D expenditures. *In the pharmaceutical industry, most companies devote much of their budgets to R&D expenditures.*

**hired mercenary** *mercenary.*

**historical experience** *experience; history.* The quote could be miscon-strued to leave the impression that we made an explicit assumption that was at odds with recent historical experience. *The quote could be misconstrued to leave the impression that we made an explicit assumption that was at odds with recent experience.*

**historically ... in the past** *historically; in the past.* I didn't have any anxiety about being paid because I know that historically the gov-ernment always has in the past. *I didn't have any anxiety about being paid because I know that historically the government always has.*

**historical precedent** *history; precedent.* We are unaware of any histor-ical precedent that has seen a nation indefinitely borrow and con-sume its way to prosperity. *We are unaware of any precedent that has seen a nation indefinitely borrow and consume its way to prosperity.*

**historical record** *history; record.* Mr. Macdonald is too young to have known this, but neither youth nor filial piety justifies distorting the historical record. *Mr. Macdonald is too young to have known this, but nei-ther youth nor filial piety justifies distorting the record.*

**hoist up** *hoist.*

**hold a meeting** *meet.*

**hold (to) the view (that)** *assert; believe; claim; consider; contend; feel; hold; judge; maintain; regard; say; think; to; view.* Most utility regulators and economists hold to the view that electric utilities are "natural monopolies." *Most utility regulators and economists hold that electric utilities are "natural monopolies."*

**hold (to) the opinion (that)** *assert; believe; claim; consider; contend; feel; hold; judge; maintain; regard; say; think; to; view.*

**hold true** *hold.* As we age, our muscles become weaker and more eas-ily tired, and the same holds true for polio victims. *As we age, our mus-cles become weaker and more easily tired, and the same holds for polio vic-tims.* ■ If these preliminary data hold true a sample size of 2500 may be insufficient to detect a 25% change with 90% confidence. *If these preliminary data hold a sample size of 2500 may be insufficient to detect a 25% change with 90% confidence.*

**hollow tube** *tube.*

**honestly and truly (truthfully)** *honestly; truly; truthfully;* delete. I tell people what I honestly and truthfully believe. *I tell people what I honestly believe.*

**(the) honest truth** *honestly; truly; (the) truth; truthfully.* The person you're interviewing doesn't want you to discover the honest truth. *The person you're interviewing doesn't want you to discover the truth.*

**hope and expect (expectation)** *expect (expectation); hope; trust.* It is my hope and expectation that these cuts won't take effect. *It is my hope that these cuts won't take effect.*

**hopefully** *(I; we) hope; let's hope.* delete. Today, hopefully, we have some answers to these problems. *Today, I hope, we have some answers to these problems.* ■ We're looking forward to working with you on this project (and hopefully others later). *We're looking forward to working with you on this project (and we hope others later).*

**how do (you) go about (-ing)** *how do (you).* How do you go about getting an income tax extension? *How do you get an income tax extension?*

**how in God's (heaven's) name** *however; how ever.*

**how in the world (on earth)** *however; how ever.* How in the world did you manage that? *However did you manage that?*

**how is it (that)** *how come; why.*

**howsoever** *however.*

**hue and cry** *clamor; hubbub; outcry.* He moved to stem the hue and cry by saying that the House would vote next week on trimming the raise to 30 percent. *He moved to stem the outcry by saying that the House would vote next week on trimming the raise to 30 percent.*

**huge (large) throng** *throng.* At the hotel, Sitting Bull welcomed large throngs of people who simply wanted to see him. *At the hotel, Sitting Bull welcomed throngs of people who simply wanted to see him.*

**human being** *being; female; human; male; man; person; woman.* Such a statement is beneath the dignity of any civilized human being. *Such a statement is beneath the dignity of any civilized person.*

**human resources**  *employees; people; persons; workers.* If the company does not have enough human resources to meet future needs, it must begin hiring them. *If the company does not have enough employees to meet future needs, it must begin hiring them.*

**humongous**  *big; giant; grand; great; huge; immense; large; mammoth; mighty; monstrous.* It's a humongous amount, oceans and oceans of material. *It's a huge amount, oceans and oceans of material.*

**hurry up**  *hurry.*

# I

**(an) identical (identically) match**  *duplicate; exact; identical; match; (the) same.*  Make sure you have two forms of identification that are an identical match to your ticket documentation. *Make sure you have two forms of identification that are identical to your ticket documentation.*

**identical (identically) (the) same**  *duplicate; exact; identical; match; (the) same.*  The operating system assumes they are the same file because the first eight characters are identically the same. *The operating system assumes they are the same file because the first eight characters are identical.*

**I do not think so**  *I think not.*

**I don't think**  *I doubt; I think;* delete. If Dole doesn't act more civilized, he's not going to make it, I don't think. *If Dole doesn't act more civilized, he's not going to make it.* ■ Technology is not now being taxed, and I don't think it will ever be taxed in the supply of these services. *Technology is not now being taxed, and I doubt it will ever be taxed in the supply of these services.*

**if and only if**  *if; only if.*  It is agreed that the premiums stated in the Coverage Selections page are subject to recomputation if, and only if, the rates fixed and established are found not to meet the requirements of state law. *It is agreed that the premiums stated in the Coverage Selections page are subject to recomputation only if the rates fixed and established are found not to meet the requirements of state law.*

**if and (or) when**  *if; when.*  To use a program, it is not necessary for you to know all the commands because many of them are for advanced features that you learn if and when you need them. *To use a program, it is not necessary for you to know all the commands because many of them are for advanced features that you learn if you need them.*

**if by way of hypothesis (supposition)**  *assuming (that); supposing (that).*

**if ... had**  *had.*  If you had run a large number of trials, the results would be very similar. *Had you run a large number of trials, the results would be very similar.*

**if it were not for**  *but for; except for.*  The loss would have been $261 million if it were not for an accounting change related to the treatment of income taxes. *The loss would have been $261 million but for an accounting change related to the treatment of income taxes.*

**ifs, ands, or buts** *absolutely; conditions;* delete. Money in an FDIC-insured account is absolutely safe — no ifs, ands, or buts. *Money in an FDIC-insured account is absolutely safe.*

**if ... should** *should.* We will be alert to other opportunities if this one should collapse. *We will be alert to other opportunities should this one collapse.*

**if ... then** *if.* If he tells you he doesn't ever want to have children, then you will have to make a decision. *If he tells you he doesn't ever want to have children, you will have to make a decision.* ∎ If so, then you would most likely have the learning style of doing or active experimentation. *If so, you would most likely have the learning style of doing or active experimentation.*

**if that (this) is the case (situation)** *if so.* If that is the situation, please contact me for detailed information on costs and time required. *If so, please contact me for detailed information on costs and time required.*

**if that (this) is true** *if so.*

**if ... were** *should; were.* If that were the only penalty, I would settle for keeping 22 cents on the dollar. *Were that the only penalty, I would settle for keeping 22 cents on the dollar.*

**I'll (let me) tell you (something)** delete.

**illustrative example** *example; illustration.* From the Software Library, you can download illustrative code examples and the latest technical specifications. *From the Software Library, you can download code examples and the latest technical specifications.*

**I'm curious why** *why (do).* I'm curious why you want to see him. *Why do you want to see him?*

**I mean** delete.

**immunological** *immunologic.*

**impact (on; upon)** *(v) act on; affect; bear on; influence.* It's the numbers that impact on all of us. *It's the numbers that influence all of us.* ∎ This ABC program enables U.S. non-profit or public institutions to support current and future collaborative training-related research on infectious diseases that impact upon people living in tropical countries. *This ABC program enables U.S. non-profit or public institutions to support current and future collaborative training-related research on infectious diseases that affect people living in tropical countries.*

**implement** *achieve; complete; effect; fulfill; make; perform; produce; realize; set.*

**importance** *import; moment.*

**important essentials** *essentials.* There are six important essentials to having a good quality compost heap. *There are six essentials to having a good quality compost heap.*

**(an; the) important ... for (in; of; to)** *important for (to).* Because decision making is an important element of a manager's job, we need to discover anything that can improve the quality of decision making. *Because decision making is important to a manager's job, we need to discover anything that can improve the quality of decision making.* ■ Their willingness to commit capital was an important factor for success. *Their willingness to commit capital was important for success.* ■ Certainly, overall physical health is an important component in any society. *Certainly, overall physical health is important to any society.*

**in (on; with) (a; the) ... (of; that)** *-ing (that).* In the 1980s, many people made plans on the assumption that oil prices would exceed $75 per barrel by 1990. *In the 1980s, many people made plans assuming that oil prices would exceed $75 per barrel by 1990.* ■ These same people are making significant international dispositions on the expectation that Japan will continue to be the world's largest creditor. *These same people are making significant international dispositions expecting that Japan will continue to be the world's largest creditor.*

**in a bad mood** *angry; dejected; depressed; displeased; downcast; glum; grouchy; sad; unhappy; vexed.*

**in accord (accordance) with** *according to; by; following; in keeping with; in line with; in step with; to; under.* This document shall be governed and construed in accordance with the laws of the State of Utah. *This document shall be governed and construed under the laws of the State of Utah.*

**in a class by itself** *matchless; novel; peerless; singular; special; unequaled; unique; unmatched; unrivaled.*

**in a (the) ... condition**  delete. The Tenant must keep the Apartment in a clean and sanitary condition, free of garbage, rubbish, and other filth. *The Tenant must keep the Apartment clean and sanitary, free of garbage, rubbish, and other filth.*

**in actual fact**  *actually; indeed; in fact; in faith; in reality; in truth; really; truly;* delete. And, in actual fact, the copywriter who created the spots and several other people who worked on it are also Catholic. *And, in fact, the copywriter who created the spots and several other people who worked on it are also Catholic.*

**in actuality**  *actually; indeed; in fact; in faith; in truth; really; truly;* delete. In actuality, such a situation seldom occurs. *In fact, such a situation seldom occurs.*

**in addition**  *also; and; as well; besides; beyond that (this); even; further; furthermore; moreover; more than that (this); still more; then; too; what is more.* In addition, we reviewed several net present value models. *We even reviewed several net present value models.*

**in addition to**  *besides; beyond.* In addition to using words to communicate, all of us talk with our body poses and facial expressions. *Besides using words to communicate, all of us talk with our body poses and facial expressions.*

**in addition to ... additionally (also; as well; too)**  *besides; beyond; in addition to.* In addition to measuring a computer in terms of its memory and processing speed, we must also analyze the computer's ability to handle list processing. *In addition to measuring a computer in terms of its memory and processing speed, we must analyze the computer's ability to handle list processing.* ■ The cell walls of gram-negative bacteria are more complex because they have, in addition to a peptidoglycan layer, an additional layer called an outer membrane. *The cell walls of gram-negative bacteria are more complex because they have, in addition to a peptidoglycan layer, a layer called an outer membrane.* ■ In addition to the methods defined in Table 13-1, each property has both a get and set method as well. *In addition to the methods defined in Table 13-1, each property has both a get and set method.*

**in a (the) ... direction**  delete. Vertical lines are drawn along the left side of a triangle in an upward direction. *Vertical lines are drawn upward along the left side of a triangle.*

**in advance**  *before; beforehand; earlier; sooner;* delete. If I'd known in advance that out of every 100 books published, only one becomes a best seller, I wouldn't have started a book. *If I'd known sooner that out of every 100 books published, only one becomes a best seller, I wouldn't have started a book.*

**in advance of** *ahead of; before.* In advance of our first break, let me introduce Thomas Armstrong, Ph.D., a learning and education specialist. *Before our first break, let me introduce Thomas Armstrong, Ph.D., a learning and education specialist.*

**inadvertent (unintended; unintentional) oversight** *oversight.* It was an unintentional oversight that the material was not provided to the members of the Board of Massage Therapy. *It was an oversight that the material was not provided to the members of the Board of Massage Therapy.*

**in a (the) fashion (manner; way) (in which; that)** *as; like.* Zeus allows you to work intuitively in the way that you think best. *Zeus allows you to work intuitively as you think best.* ■ But such a scientific inquiry already took place years ago, in the manner provided for by law. *But such a scientific inquiry already took place years ago, as provided for by law.*

**in a (the) fashion (manner; way) characteristic of** *alike; as; like; much as; much like; much the same (as); rather like; resembling; similar to; similarly to.* In a fashion characteristic of his other work, the paintings are on scrap wood panels and other flat, rectangular materials that Young salvages from the streets. *Like his other work, the paintings are on scrap wood panels and other flat, rectangular materials that Young salvages from the streets.*

**in a (the) fashion (manner; way) similar to** *alike; as; like; much as; much like; much the same (as); rather like; resembling; similar to; similarly to.* In a manner similar to modern-day whales, ichthyosaurs seem to have frequented breeding or birthing areas. *Like modern-day whales, ichthyosaurs seem to have frequented breeding or birthing areas.*

**in a few minutes (moments)** *briefly; directly; momently; presently; quickly; shortly; soon; straightaway.* Press any key, and in a few moments, the Lotus 1-2-3 spreadsheet will appear on the screen. *Press any key, and the Lotus 1-2-3 spreadsheet will directly appear on the screen.*

**in a good mood** *cheerful; glad; gleeful; happy; joyful; joyous; merry; pleased.*

**in agreement with** *according to; by; following; in keeping with; in line with; in step with; to; under.*

**in (almost) all (every) cases (circumstances; instances; situations)** *all; almost all; almost always; always; consistently; constantly; invariably; nearly all; nearly always; unfailingly.* The actual percentage should be given in all cases. *The actual percentage should always be given.*

**in all likelihood** *likely; most (very) likely; probably; most (very) probably.* In all likelihood, it will get extended until there is a determination of the ESOP litigation. *Most likely, it will get extended until there is a determination of the ESOP litigation.*

**in all probability** *likely; most (very) likely; probably; most (very) probably.* A telephone call to the coordinator keeps the bank from stepping on its own toes by duplicating efforts and, in all probability, makes the call more effective. *A telephone call to the coordinator keeps the bank from stepping on its own toes by duplicating efforts and, most probably, makes the call more effective.*

**in a lot of cases (circumstances; instances; situations)** *frequently; most often; often; sometimes; usually.* In a lot of cases, serial killers seek power over others. *Often, serial killers seek power over others.*

**in a (the) majority of cases (circumstances; instances; situations)** *frequently; most often; often; usually.*

**in a manner of speaking** *as it were; in a sense; in a way; so to speak.*

**in a (some) measure** *partially; partly; somewhat.*

**in a minute (moment)** *briefly; directly; momently; presently; quickly; shortly; soon; straightaway.*

**in an attempt (effort; endeavor) to** *in trying to; to try to.* In an attempt to satisfy the informal group, the employee may come in conflict with the formal organization. *In trying to satisfy the informal group, the employee may come in conflict with the formal organization.*

**in an attempt (effort; endeavor) to try to** *in trying to; to try to.* In an effort to try to contain the spiraling cost of automobile insurance, a number of legislative changes have been proposed. *In trying to contain the spiraling cost of automobile insurance, a number of legislative changes have been proposed.* ■ Police administrators have begun to get law enforcement to explore alliances with private security professionals in an attempt to try to find the community roots of crime. *Police administrators have begun to get law enforcement to explore alliances* *with private security professionals to try to find the community roots of crime.*

**in and of itself (themselves)** *as such; in itself (in themselves).* The mere claim of protection asserted by a witness of his constitutional rights does not in and of itself constitute the admission of a crime. *The mere claim of protection asserted by a witness of his constitutional rights does not in itself constitute the admission of a crime.*

**in a nutshell** *briefly; concisely; succinctly; tersely.* That, in a nutshell, explains the financial community's attitude toward the crash. *That briefly explains the financial community's attitude toward the crash.*

**in any case (event)** *all (just) the same; anyhow; even so; still; still and all; yet.*

**in any fashion (manner; way)** *at all; in the least;* delete. And he personally is not obligated in any way to stand behind the $675 million bond offering, or any other debt of the project. *And he personally is not at all obligated to stand behind the $675 million bond offering, or any other debt of the project.*

**in any way, shape, or form (or fashion)** *at all; in any way; in the least; in the slightest;* delete. Can that evidence be used in any way, shape, or form? *Can that evidence be used in any way?* ■ I will never discuss this issue with you in any way, shape, form, or fashion again. *I will never discuss this issue with you again.*

**in a position to** *able to; ready to.* By the end of the year, we will be in a position to hire another person. *By the end of the year, we will be ready to hire another person.*

**in appearance** delete. They may look different in appearance, but each is built essentially with the same type of components that perform the same functions. *They may look different, but each is built essentially with the same type of components that perform the same functions.*

**in a row** *straight.* Whether the bill dies on Beacon Hill for the third year in a row or becomes law in some form, the advocates of acupuncture are pressing their case with a gentle insistence. *Whether the bill dies on Beacon Hill for the third straight year or becomes law in some form, the advocates of acupuncture are pressing their case with a gentle insistence.*

**in arrears** *late; overdue.*

**in a (the) ... sense** *-(al)ly;* delete. In a broad sense, office automation is the incorporation of technology to help people manage information. *Broadly, office automation is the incorporation of technology to help people manage information.* ■ Although there is a significant relationship in a statistical sense, the association is not strong. *Although there is a significant statistical relationship, the association is not strong.* ■ I don't mean this in a pejorative sense. *I don't mean this pejoratively.* ■ There was really nothing which could be called communication in any genuine sense. *There was really nothing which could be called genuine communication.*

**in a similar fashion (manner; way) (to)** *alike; as; like; much as; much like; much the same (as); rather like; resembling; similar (to); similarly (to).* My guess is 99 percent of the customers will behave in a similar manner. *My guess is 99 percent of the customers will behave similarly.*

**inasmuch (insomuch) as** *as far as; as much as; so far as; so much as.* Inasmuch as we can tell, you need to be direct. *So far as we can tell, you need to be direct.*

**inasmuch (insomuch) as** *because; considering; for; given; in that; since.* All seemed to share the conviction that the American educational system is far superior inasmuch as it focuses on the individual student. *All seemed to share the conviction that the American educational system is far superior because it focuses on the individual student.* ■ There are limitations to their work inasmuch as they do not have access to all the same resources that are available to federal and state police agencies. *There are limitations to their work since they do not have access to all the same resources that are available to federal and state police agencies.*

**in association with** *along with; and; as well as; combined with; coupled with; joined with; paired with; together with; with.*

**in a (the)... state (of) ...** *in;* delete. I'm in a state of uncertainty about how to travel. *I'm uncertain about how to travel.* ■ But while men's wear has been doing pretty well, women's wear storeowners are in a state of shock. *But while men's wear has been doing pretty well, women's wear storeowners are in shock.* ■ So we are left to walk the earth like robots or zombies, telling ourselves and others that everything's fine while we are actually numb, cut off from our emotions, entrenched in a state of denial. *So we are left to walk the earth like robots or zombies,* *telling ourselves and others that everything's fine while we are actually numb, cut off from our emotions, entrenched in denial.*

**in a timely fashion (manner; way)**  *by next week (tomorrow); fast; in (within) a day (year); in (on) time; promptly; quickly; rapidly; right away; shortly; soon; speedily; swiftly; timely.* Please give me your response in a timely manner. *Please give me your response by tomorrow.*

**in attendance**  *present.* Also in attendance were key attorneys and representatives on both sides of the lawsuit. *Also present were key attorneys and representatives on both sides of the lawsuit.*

**in a way**  *rather; somehow; someway(s); somewhat.* In a way, I find it intimidating. *I somehow find it intimidating.*

**in back of**  *after; behind.*

**in ... behalf (of)**  *by; for.*

**(something; somewhere) in between**  *between; in; within.* The bonds are selling at $2 bid, $4 offered for a $100 face value bond, which means that the selling price would probably fall somewhere in between that range. *The bonds are selling at $2 bid, $4 offered for a $100 face value bond, which means that the selling price would probably fall in that range.*

**in (a; the) bigger (greater; higher; larger) amount (degree; number; quantity)**  *more; more often; more so.* Apple must wait until high-quality flat-panel screens are available in greater numbers before it can release a lap-top Macintosh. *Apple must wait until more high-quality flat-panel screens are available before it can release a lap-top Macintosh.*

**in big (great; high; huge; large; overwhelming; sizable; vast) numbers**  *a good (great) many; almost all; dozens (of); hundreds (of); many; millions (of); most; nearly all; scores (of); six hundred (twelve hundred); thousands (of).* Riot police in large numbers were called in to stop the protestors. *Scores of riot police were called in to stop the protestors.*

**in both cases (circumstances; instances; situations)**  *both; for (in) both; delete.* In both cases, about 10 percent of the sales force accounted for about 90 percent of the revenues. *For both, about 10 percent of the sales force accounted for about 90 percent of the revenues.*

**in brief (concise; succinct) summary**  *briefly (concisely; succinctly); in* *brief; in fine; in short; in sum.* In brief summary, those are some of the reasons why original intention cannot be a neat solution to the problem of expounding our Constitution — and living under it. *In sum, those are some of the reasons why original intention cannot be a neat solution to the problem of expounding our Constitution — and living under it.*

**in (a; the) ... capacity (function; position; role) (as; of)** *as (a; the).* In my capacity as chairman of the Arab group, I would like to express our deep regret for the steps taken by the United States in this regard. *As chairman of the Arab group, I would like to express our deep regret for the steps taken by the United States in this regard.* ■ In his capacity as the vice president at Mindware, Mr. Chatterjee has successfully sold to and signed multiyear contracts with large to medium-size firms. *As the vice president at Mindware, Mr. Chatterjee has successfully sold to and signed multiyear contracts with large to medium-size firms.*

**incarcerate** *jail.*

**in case** *if; lest; should.* In case you've just joined us, we're talking about men's perception of the Women's Movement. *If you've just joined us, we're talking about men's perception of the Women's Movement.*

**in (a; the) ... case (circumstance; instance; situation)** *-(al)ly.* In a typical situation, the MLI command will have stored important information in an MLI data area that is used by all MLI commands. *Typically, the MLI command will have stored important information in an MLI data area that is used by all MLI commands.*

**in (the) ... case (of)** *about; as for; as to; concerning; for; in; of; on; over; regarding; respecting; to; toward; with;* delete. In the case of the airport, that role is performed by the air traffic controller and each airline's operations center. *As to the airport, that role is performed by the air traffic controller and each airline's operations center.* ■ In contrast, in the case of a married working couple without children, premature death of one income earner is not likely to cause serious financial problems for the surviving spouse. *In contrast, for a married working couple without children, premature death of one income earner is not likely to cause serious financial problems for the surviving spouse.*

**in cases (circumstances; instances; situations) in which** *if; when; where.* In cases in which improperly tested blood products had been released, Dr. Sandler said the donors were contacted for retesting to assure that no tainted blood had been transmitted. *Where improperly tested blood products had been released, Dr. Sandler said the donors were* *contacted for retesting to assure that no tainted blood had been transmitted.*

**in cases when (where)**   *if; when; where.* In cases where one topic requires knowledge of another, the required topic is cross-referenced. *Where one topic requires knowledge of another, the required topic is cross-referenced.*

**in certain (some) cases**   *at times; now and then; occasionally; on occasion; some; sometimes;* delete. In some cases, smoking does affect mental acuity. *Smoking sometimes does affect mental acuity.*

**in certain (some) circumstances**   *at times; every so often; now and again; now and then; occasionally; on occasion; some; sometimes;* delete. In some circumstances, the computer can augment or replace many of the engineer's other tools. *Now and then, the computer can augment or replace many of the engineer's other tools.*

**in certain (some) instances**   *at times; every so often; now and again; now and then; occasionally; on occasion; some; sometimes;* delete. In some instances, we lost the customer to the competition. *We lost some customers to the competition.*

**in certain (some) regards**   *rather; somehow; someway(s); somewhat.*

**in certain (some) respects**   *rather; somehow; someway(s); somewhat.* The finding is somewhat surprising since auditory information processing seems in some respects quite different from the operations required to sense visual patterns. *The finding is somewhat surprising since auditory information processing seems somehow quite different from the operations required to sense visual patterns.*

**in certain (some) situations**   *at times; every so often; now and again; now and then; occasionally; on occasion; some; sometimes;* delete. In some situations, change threatens security. *Sometimes change threatens security.*

**in character**   delete. As the market becomes more institutional in character, it will be easier for foreign companies to enter the U.S. market. *As the market becomes more institutional, it will be easier for foreign companies to enter the U.S. market.*

**in ... circumstances (conditions)**   *-(al)ly;* delete. The attack was a carefully planned military operation that ended in tragic circumstances. *The attack was a carefully planned military operation that ended tragically.*

**in circumstances when (where)**  *if; when; where.* Independent counsel might well be required prior to accepting a defendant's waiver of important constitutional rights in circumstances where there is reason to believe that independent legal advice is necessary in order to permit the defendant to decide whether to waive or to exercise his rights. *Independent counsel might well be required prior to accepting a defendant's waiver of important constitutional rights where there is reason to believe that independent legal advice is necessary in order to permit the defendant to decide whether to waive or to exercise his rights.*

**in close proximity (to)**  *close by; close to; in proximity; near; nearby.* Some who have worked in close proximity to the Oval Office in recent years support his major propositions. *Some who have worked close to the Oval Office in recent years support his major propositions.*

**including everything**  *in all; overall.*

**in color**  delete. Chalkboards are commonly black or green in color. *Chalkboards are commonly black or green.* ■ If he or she is pale, ashen (gray), or cyanotic (bluish) in color and appears anxious, frightened, or restless, suspect shock. *If he or she is pale, ashen (gray), or cyanotic (bluish) and appears anxious, frightened, or restless, suspect shock.*

**in combination with**  *along with; and; as well as; combined with; coupled with; joined with; paired with; together with; with.* This risk is now avoided by using estrogen in combination with progesterone. *This risk is now avoided by using estrogen along with progesterone.*

**in (over) (the) coming days (decades; months; weeks; years)**  *at length; before long; eventually; in time; later; one day; over time; presently; quickly; shortly; someday; sometime; soon; ultimately; with time; yet;* delete. Other schemes could emerge in coming months. *Other schemes could emerge before long.*

**in common with**  *like.* You are quite right in pointing out that I, in common with other cultural historians, have singled out but one out of several possible Adams lines. *You are quite right in pointing out that I, like other cultural historians, have singled out but one out of several possible Adams lines.*

**in company with**  *along with; and; as well as; together with; with.* If anything, the Reagan administration, in company with the Kremlin and the other big powers, has waited too long to denounce the use of chemical weapons. *If anything, the Reagan administration, as well as the*

*Kremlin and the other big powers, has waited too long to denounce the use of chemical weapons.*

**in comparison to (with)** *against; alongside; beside; compared to (with); -(i)er than; less; less than; more; more than; next to; over; than; to; versus; vis-à-vis.* The reunion's turnout was large in comparison to other reunions. *The reunion's turnout was larger than other reunions.* ■ U.S. students are inferior in their spelling ability in comparison to the other nations' students. *U.S. students are inferior in their spelling ability to the other nations' students.* ■ Dutch auction issues experience less price volatility in comparison to ARPS. *Dutch auction issues experience less price volatility compared to ARPS.*

**in comparison (in contrast) to (with) ... relatively** *compared (contrasted) to (with).* In comparison to earlier years, inflation has been relatively moderate over the last half decade. *Compared to earlier years, inflation has been moderate over the last half decade.*

**incompetency** *incompetence.* Hospitalization often makes clients vulnerable to thoughts of inadequacy and incompetency. *Hospitalization often makes clients vulnerable to thoughts of inadequacy and incompetence.*

**in compliance with** *according to; by; following; in keeping with; in line with; in step with; to; under.* In compliance with the new order, participants now receive a 2 percent discount from market prices on shares made available directly from the company. *Under the new order, participants now receive a 2 percent discount from market prices on shares made available directly from the company.*

**in conclusion** *finally; in closing; lastly.*

**in conformance to (with)** *according to; by; following; in keeping with; in line with; in step with; to; under.* Certain terms of the Agreement shall be completed in conformance to the terms of the successful proposal. *Certain terms of the Agreement shall be completed according to the terms of the successful proposal.*

**in conformity to (with)** *according to; by; following; in keeping with; in line with; in step with; to; under.* The law says a product is presumed to be free of defects when it is produced in conformity to government standards. *The law says a product is presumed to be free of defects when it is produced to government standards.*

**in conjunction** *combined; together.* The primary evidence with which the Warren Report failed to deal consists of the ballistics report, the Zapruder film, and the autopsy report, taken in conjunction. *The primary evidence with which the Warren Report failed to deal consists of the ballistics report, the Zapruder film, and the autopsy report, taken together.*

**in conjunction with** *along with; and; as well as; combined with; coupled with; joined with; paired with; together with; with.* The results of the interviews in conjunction with other supporting data are contained in the report. *The results of the interviews and other supporting data are contained in the report.*

**in connection with** *along with; and; as well as; combined with; coupled with; joined with; paired with; together with; with.*

**in connection with** *about; as for; as to; concerning; for; in; of; on; over; regarding; respecting; to; toward; with;* delete. The bank with sufficient presence and skills may be asked to work with the client's own local advisors in connection with purely domestic transactions. *The bank with sufficient presence and skills may be asked to work with the client's own local advisors on purely domestic transactions.*

**in consequence** *consequently; hence; so; then; therefore; thus.*

**in consequence of** *after; because of; by; due to; following; for; from; in; out of; owing to; through; with.* The defendants cannot claim to have suffered damage in consequence of the plaintiffs' early entry onto premises they had already vacated pursuant to a notice to quit for nonpayment of rent. *The defendants cannot claim to have suffered damage from the plaintiffs' early entry onto premises they had already vacated pursuant to a notice to quit for nonpayment of rent.*

**in consequence of the fact that** *because; considering; for; given; in that; since.*

**in consideration of (payment of; sum of)** *because of; due to; for; in return for; in view of; on account of; owing to; through.* In consideration of the foregoing and of the mutual promises contained herein, the parties mutually agree as follows. *In view of the foregoing and the mutual promises contained herein, the parties mutually agree as follows.*

**in consideration of the fact that** *because; considering; for; given; in that; since.* In consideration of the fact that Medicare payments are already deducted from my Social Security checks, am I entitled to a credit for this further deduction? *Since Medicare payments are already deducted* *from my Social Security checks, am I entitled to a credit for this further deduction?* ■ In consideration of the fact that Ownertrades.com has no credit card transaction capabilities, and maintains no credit card information or database, and in consideration of the fact that all credit card payments to Ownertrades.com and its principals are made through PayPal using their secure transaction processes, you agree to hold Ownertrades.com and its principals harmless from any losses, claims, or damages related to your credit card. *Since Ownertrades.com has no credit card transaction capabilities, and maintains no credit card information or database, and since all credit card payments to Ownertrades.com and its principals are made through PayPal using their secure transaction processes, you agree to hold Ownertrades.com and its principals harmless from any losses, claims, or damages related to your credit card.*

**in consonance to (with)** *according to; by; following; in keeping with; in line with; in step with; to; under.*

**in contrast to (with)** *against; alongside; beside; compared to (with); -(i)er than; less; less than; more; more than; next to; over; than; to; unlike; versus; vis-à-vis.* In contrast to last month, September sales of government debt are expected to be light. *Compared to last month, September sales of government debt are expected to be light.*

**in conversation with** *conversing with; speaking to (with); talking to (with).* I don't know what happened; I was in conversation with my friend. *I don't know what happened; I was talking with my friend.*

**in copious profusion** *copiously; in profusion.* As naturally and spontaneously as the notes that issue from the throat of a thrush, the melodies poured forth from Schubert's pen in copious profusion. *As naturally and spontaneously as the notes that issue from the throat of a thrush, the melodies poured forth from Schubert's pen in profusion.*

**incorporate in(to)** *add; contain; have; include.*

**in correspondence to (with)** *according to; by; following; in keeping with; in line with; in step with; to; under.*

**(a) ... increase over** *more than.* That's a 33-percent increase over last year. *That's 33 percent more than last year.*

**increasing in** *increasingly.* The seaweed treatments are increasing in popularity with both men and women. *The seaweed treatments are increasingly popular with both men and women.*

**increasingly more** *increasingly; more; more and more.* Information processing is becoming increasingly more automated through the use of machines. *Information processing is becoming increasingly automated through the use of machines.* ■ As the size and complexity of software systems increase, the task of building and maintaining these systems becomes increasingly more arduous. *As the size and complexity of software systems increase, the task of building and maintaining these systems becomes more arduous.*

**in (over) (the) days (decades; months; weeks; years) ahead** *at length; before long; eventually; in time; later; one day; over time; presently; quickly; shortly; someday; sometime; soon; ultimately; with time; yet;* delete. We expect prospects will improve over the years ahead. *We expect prospects will improve in time.*

**in (the) days (decades; months; weeks; years) gone by** *before; earlier; formerly; once; over the (years); over time;* delete. In years gone by, much has been written about perceived gains in the powers of the presidency compared with the powers of the Congress and vice versa. *Much has been written about perceived gains in the powers of the presidency compared with the powers of the Congress and vice versa.*

**in (the) days (decades; months; weeks; years) of old** *before; earlier; formerly; once; over the (years); over time;* delete. The world must have seemed a larger place in days of old. *The world must have once seemed a larger place.*

**in (the) days (decades; months; weeks; years) past** *before; earlier; formerly; once; over the (years); over time; previously;* delete. Police academy training is more extensive for new officers, providing extensive computer training, whereas in years past only a few officers would have had any experience with computers. *Police academy training is more extensive for new officers, providing extensive computer training, whereas before only a few officers would have had any experience with computers.*

**in (the) days (decades; months; weeks; years) since** *since; since then.* However, in the years since 1970, the same continent has experienced precipitation levels above the mean measurements for the reference period. *However, since 1970, the same continent has experienced precipitation levels above the mean measurements for the reference period.*

**in (over) ... days (decades; hours; minutes; months; weeks; years) time** *in (over) ... days (decades; hours; minutes; months; weeks; years).* I'm going to be visiting some Navy bases in a few months time. *I'm going to be visiting some Navy bases in a few months.*

**in (over) (the) days (decades; months; weeks; years) to come** *at length; before long; eventually; in time; later; one day; over time; presently; quickly; shortly; someday; sometime; soon; ultimately; with time; yet;* delete. We are deadly serious about making changes that will allow us to remain a viable competitor in the years to come. *We are deadly serious about making changes that will allow us to remain a viable competitor.*

**indebtedness** *debt(s).* Sales tax revenues are down because people are spending less, paying off their indebtedness, and saving more. *Sales tax revenues are down because people are spending less, paying off their debts, and saving more.*

**in defense of** *for; with.* May I please put in a word in defense of poor Livia Budai, who has been lambasted out of all proportion in your articles? *May I please put in a word for poor Livia Budai, who has been lambasted out of all proportion in your articles?*

**in defiance of** *against; despite.* Responsibility for the tragedy rests exclusively on the war criminals in the Iranian government who have elected, in defiance of the rules of warfare established for many centuries, to make regular murderous attacks on neutral merchant ships on the high seas. *Responsibility for the tragedy rests exclusively on the war criminals in the Iranian government who have elected, despite the rules of warfare established for many centuries, to make regular murderous attacks on neutral merchant ships on the high seas.*

**in depth** *deep.*

**in despite of** *after all; apart; aside; despite; even with; for all; with all.* In despite of his good looks, he has never married. *For all his good looks, he has never married.*

**indicate** *feel; hint; mention; say; show; suggest; tell.* He indicated that he would be fine. *He said that he would be fine.*

**indication** *clue; cue; hint; inkling; sign.* There are indications that Iran may have its own chemical weapons. *There are clues that Iran may have its own chemical weapons.*

**individual** *(adj)* delete. I think there are individual exceptions. *I think there are exceptions.*

**individual(s)** (*n*) *anybody; anyone; everybody; everyone; man; men; people; person; somebody; someone; those; woman; women; you;* delete. The dominant behavioral characteristic of phobic individuals is avoidance. *The dominant behavioral characteristic of phobic persons is avoidance.*

**individuals (men; people; persons; women) who are** delete. People who are obsessive-compulsive have difficulty making decisions. *Obsessive-compulsives have difficulty making decisions.*

**inductive reasoning** *induction.*

**in due course (time)** *at length; in time; later; one day; over time; someday; sometime; with time; yet.* We will consider your statement in due time. *We will yet consider your statement.*

**in duration** *last; long;* delete. Girls are at far greater risk for sexual abuse than boys, and their sexual abuse apparently is more common and longer in duration than the abuse boys are likely to experience. *Girls are at far greater risk for sexual abuse than boys, and their sexual abuse apparently is more common and lasts longer than the abuse boys are likely to experience.*

**in each (every) case (circumstance; instance; situation)** *all; always; consistently; constantly; each; each time; for (in) each; for (in) every; every one; every time; invariably; unfailingly;* delete. In every instance, the acquirer selected is the one with the best bid. *The acquirer selected is always the one with the best bid.*

**in earlier (former; prior) times** *before; earlier; formerly; once.* There was plenty of weekend ticketing in prior times. *There once was plenty of weekend ticketing.*

**in either (neither) case (circumstance; instance; situation)** *either (neither) way;* delete. In either case, a veto would have provided Democratic opponents with powerful rhetorical ammunition in light of the 80 percent approval for the legislation in public opinion polls. *Either way, a veto would have provided Democratic opponents with powerful rhetorical ammunition in light of the 80 percent approval for the legislation in public opinion polls.*

**in either (neither) event** *either (neither) way;* delete. In either event, you have a few options. *Either way, you have a few options.*

**in error** *wrong.* He will not listen, nor will he back down even when he knows he is in error. *He will not listen, nor will he back down even when he knows he is wrong.*

**in (the) event (of; that)** *if (there were); if ... should; in case (of); should (there); were (there; ... to); when;* delete. In the event that any liquid or solid object falls into the cabinet, unplug the unit and have it checked by qualified personnel. *Should any liquid or solid object fall into the cabinet, unplug the unit and have it checked by qualified personnel.* ■ Such information would be vital in the event they choose to have children. *Such information would be vital if they choose to have children.*

**in evidence** *apparent; conspicuous; evident; obvious; plain.* Little of that has been in evidence among the thrifts. *Little of that has been evident among the thrifts.*

**in excess of** *above; better than; beyond; faster than; greater than; larger than; more than; over; stronger than.* Annually, retailers lose in excess of $1.5 billion, and only about 30 percent of those losses are to shoplifters and other outsiders. *Annually, retailers lose more than $1.5 billion, and only about 30 percent of those losses are to shoplifters and other outsiders.*

**in exchange (for)** *for.* The deal would involve his gaining credibility with the administration in exchange for his helping Nicaraguan Contras in their fight against the Sandinistas. *The deal would involve his gaining credibility with the administration for his helping Nicaraguan Contras in their fight against the Sandinistas.*

**in (the) face of** *after all; apart; aside; despite; even with; for all; with all.* He persevered in the face of strong pressure within his agency. *He persevered despite strong pressure within his agency.*

**in fact** delete. Women not able to have power in the external world have in fact developed a secondary power. *Women not able to have power in the external world have developed a secondary power.*

**in (a; the) ... fashion** *-(al)ly;* delete. It is true that the records are stored in a sequential fashion. *It is true that the records are stored sequentially.* ■ I don't think I was treated in a loyal fashion by the president. *I don't think I was treated loyally by the president.* ■ Your story quotes antismokers 11 times and tobacco industry representatives only twice — and then in a disdainful fashion. *Your story quotes antismokers 11 times and tobacco industry representatives only twice — and then disdainfully.*

**in favor (of)** *for; with*. Five circuit courts of appeal have ruled in favor of testing without individualized suspicion. *Five circuit courts of appeal have ruled for testing without individualized suspicion.*

**(an; the) infinite number (of)** *countless; endless; infinite; millions (of); myriad; numberless; untold*. The voice is capable of an infinite number of sounds and pitches. *The voice is capable of countless sounds and pitches.*

**inflammable** *flammable*.

**in force and effect** *active; at work; effective; in action; in effect; in force; in play; working*. Tenant agrees to pay Landlord at the rate of $1200 per month on the first day of each and every month in advance so long as this lease is in force and effect. *Tenant agrees to pay Landlord at the rate of $1200 per month on the first day of each and every month in advance so long as this lease is in effect.*

**inform** *tell; write*. She informed me that she wants a divorce. *She told me that she wants a divorce.*

**in (a; the) ... form** *in; -(al)ly; delete*. An analyst must be able to state the assumption in explicit form. *An analyst must be able to explicitly state the assumption.* ■ Specifications of a patent must be attached to the application in written form describing the invention in detail so that a person skilled in the field can produce the item. *Written specifications of a patent must be attached to the application describing the invention in detail so that a person skilled in the field can produce the item.*

**in ... from now** *from now; in*. In about six to seven years from now, OPEC will once again be able to capture 50 percent of the world market. *In about six to seven years, OPEC will once again be able to capture 50 percent of the world market.*

**in front of** *before*. We have tough challenges in front of us. *We have tough challenges before us.*

**in fulfillment of** *to complete; to finish; to fulfill; to satisfy*. In fulfillment of its open-ended agreement, Saatchi & Saatchi will also advise the Soviets on how much they should charge for TV spots that could reach some 180 million Soviet citizens and another 30 million viewers in Eastern Europe. *To fulfill its open-ended agreement, Saatchi & Saatchi will also advise the Soviets on how much they should charge for TV spots that could reach some 180 million Soviet citizens and another 30 million viewers in Eastern Europe.*

**in furtherance of** *to advance; to further; to help; toward.* PTG is providing information and services on the Internet as a benefit and service in furtherance of PTG's nonprofit and tax-exempt status. *PTG is providing information and services on the Internet as a benefit and service to further PTG's nonprofit and tax-exempt status.*

**in general** delete. Women in general have a responsibility to one another. *Women have a responsibility to one another.*

**(a; the) -ing of** *-ing.* The taking of drugs is bad for people. *Taking drugs is bad for people.* ■ Often the initial development of a program focuses on the obtaining of some correct solution to the given problem. *Often the initial development of a program focuses on obtaining some correct solution to the given problem.* ■ It has several verification problems that can only be appreciated by a careful reading of the treaty. *It has several verification problems that can only be appreciated by carefully reading the treaty.*

**in good time** *at length; in time; later; one day; over time; someday; sometime; with time; yet.*

**in great (large) measure** *almost all; chiefly; commonly; generally; greatly; in general; largely; mainly; most; mostly; most often; much; nearly all; normally; overall; typically; usually.* Your today is in large measure a result of your yesterdays. *Your today is largely a result of your yesterdays.*

**in great (large) part** *almost all; chiefly; commonly; generally; greatly; in general; largely; mainly; most; mostly; most often; much; nearly all; normally; overall; typically; usually.* The lower cost of U.S. labor was due in large part to the drop in value of the dollar compared with most other currencies. *The lower cost of U.S. labor was largely due to the drop in value of the dollar compared with most other currencies.*

**in great (large) quantities** *a good (great) deal (of); a good (great) many (of); almost all; dozens (of); hundreds (of); many; millions (of); most; nearly all; scores (of); six hundred (twelve hundred); thousands (of).* The $2 bills are not being ordered by area banks even though the Federal Reserve has them in large quantities. *The $2 bills are not being ordered by area banks even though the Federal Reserve has millions of them.*

**in height** *high;* delete. They should be at least 18 inch in height, not encircled, and placed close to the parts they apply to. *They should be at least 18 inch high, not encircled, and placed close to the parts they apply to.*

**in (the) history (of the world)**  *ever.* Original plans called for a fleet of 132 bombers with the cost of each plane estimated at $500 million, making it the most expensive plane in history. *Original plans called for a fleet of 132 bombers with the cost of each plane estimated at $500 million, making it the most expensive plane ever.*

**in honor of**  *after; for; to.*

**in imitation of**  *after; following.*

**in instances when (where)**  *if; when; where.* In instances where the products and services being traded within the firm are unique, the cost-plus method seems appropriate. *When the products and services being traded within the firm are unique, the cost-plus method seems appropriate.*

**in isolation (from)**  *alone; apart (from); by itself; separate (from).* It makes no sense to discuss one issue in isolation from the other. *It makes no sense to discuss one issue separate from the other.*

**initial (initially)**  *at first; first.* Initially, the key was successfully marketing the fund to commercial banks. *At first, the key was successfully marketing the fund to commercial banks.*

**initially ... begin (start)**  *begin (start).* I believe he initially started as a stand-up comic. *I believe he started as a stand-up comic.*

**in its (their) entirety**  *all (the); (the) complete; completely; (the) entire; entirely; every; (the) full; fully; (the) whole; wholly;* delete. When you read the book in its entirety, you will understand my position. *When you read the entire book, you will understand my position.*

**(be) in jeopardy**  *endangered; imperiled; jeopardized.* None of us can avoid the responsibility of working in all ways open to us to shore up the democracy that is so clearly in jeopardy. *None of us can avoid the responsibility of working in all ways open to us to shore up the democracy that is so clearly jeopardized.*

**in length**  *last; long;* delete. The panel discussion itself will be two hours in length. *The panel discussion itself will last two hours.* ■ The first is genuine trading courses, usually lasting three to five days in length. *The first is genuine trading courses, usually lasting three to five days.*

**in (the) light of the fact that** *because; considering; for; given that; in that; since; when.* ■ Perhaps the notion that information has some value is a misguided one, particularly in light of the fact that most popular Web sites merely drag you in under the pretense of providing information, while in reality they are setting you up for a sales pitch. *Perhaps the notion that information has some value is a misguided one, particularly given that most popular Web sites merely drag you in under the pretense of providing information, while in reality they are setting you up for a sales pitch.* ■ Now, why would teams who are doing miserably not give him a shot, especially in light of the fact that he led his defense to the lowest points ever allowed, and followed it up with a Super Bowl Championship? *Now, why would teams who are doing miserably not give him a shot, especially since he led his defense to the lowest points ever allowed, and followed it up with a Super Bowl Championship?* ■ In light of the fact that we are the industry being self-regulated, in light of the fact that there are at least proposals that the ISPs should fund the new corporation, and in light of the fact that industry cooperation is essential to the new corporation's success, this is inexplicable. *Considering we are the industry being self-regulated, considering there are at least proposals that the ISPs should fund the new corporation, and considering industry cooperation is essential to the new corporation's success, this is inexplicable.*

**in like fashion (manner)** *likewise; similarly.* In like fashion, managers need to know how they are doing from the viewpoints of those they are paid to serve. *Likewise, managers need to know how they are doing from the viewpoints of those they are paid to serve.*

**in (a; the) ... manner** *-(al)ly; delete.* I hope future stories dealing with sensitive issues such as this will be handled in a more responsible and accurate manner. *I hope future stories dealing with sensitive issues such as this will be handled more responsibly and accurately.* ■ According to CAREI, studies have found that some families were affected in a positive manner by the start changes and some were negatively affected. *According to CAREI, studies have found that some families were positively affected by the start changes and some were negatively affected.* ■ All writing on labels must be printed in a clear and legible manner and should be in Spanish unless authorized otherwise by the DFC. *All writing on labels must be printed clearly and legibly and should be in Spanish unless authorized otherwise by the DFC.*

**in many (most) cases** *almost all; almost always; commonly; frequently; many; many times; most; most often; much; nearly all; nearly always; normally; often; typically; usually.* In most cases, the pitch can be approximated or laid off with a scale or dividers. *Usually, the pitch can be approximated or laid off with a scale or dividers.*

**in many (most) circumstances** *almost all; almost always; commonly; frequently; many; many times; most; most often; much; nearly all; nearly always; normally; often; ordinarily; typically; usually.* RISC microprocessors operate faster than CISC microprocessors in many circumstances. *RISC microprocessors often operate faster than CISC microprocessors.*

**in many (most) instances** *almost all; almost always; commonly; frequently; many; many times; most; most often; much; nearly all; nearly always; normally; often; ordinarily; typically; usually.* In many instances, the family is in a state of dysfunction and disrepair. *Often, the family is in a state of dysfunction and disrepair.*

**in many (most) regards** *almost always; largely; many; most; mostly; most often; nearly always; often; usually.*

**in many (most) respects** *almost always; largely; many; most; mostly; most often; nearly always; often; usually.* In most respects, competition among banks has been polite. *Competition among banks has been largely polite.*

**in many (most) situations** *almost all; almost always; commonly; frequently; many; many times; most; most often; much; nearly all; nearly always; normally; often; ordinarily; typically; usually.* The speed with which a modem can transmit and receive data is important in many situations. *The speed with which a modem can transmit and receive data is usually important.*

**in (our) midst** *among (us).*

**in much the same fashion (manner; way) (as; that)** *much as; much like.* Though similar in size, material, and color and fabricated in much the same way as their plainer cousins, the new tokens bore various kinds of surface markings and showed a greater variety of shapes. *Though similar in size, material, and color and fabricated much like their plainer cousins, the new tokens bore various kinds of surface markings and showed a greater variety of shapes.*

**in my assessment** *I assert; I believe; I claim; I consider; I contend; I feel; I hold; I judge; I maintain; I regard; I say; I think; I view; to me; delete.* In my assessment, the most desirable changes for commercial banks to incorporate are as follows. *To me, the most desirable changes for commercial banks to incorporate are as follows.*

**in my estimation**  *I assert; I believe; I claim; I consider; I contend; I feel; I hold; I judge; I maintain; I regard; I say; I think; I view; to me;* delete. In my estimation, the treatment is suitable to Mr. Ross's case. *I feel the treatment is suitable to Mr. Ross's case.*

**in my judgment**  *I assert; I believe; I claim; I consider; I contend; I feel; I hold; I judge; I maintain; I regard; I say; I think; I view; to me;* delete. The most critical issue confronting America, in my judgment, is how we match educational accessibility and opportunity to the demographic change. *The most critical issue confronting America, I contend, is how we match educational accessibility and opportunity to the demographic change.*

**in my (own) mind(s)**  *for myself;* delete. I had to find out in my own mind if quiet diplomacy would work. *I had to find out for myself if quiet diplomacy would work.*

**(to) ... in my (own) mind's eye**  *envisage; envision; imagine; visualize;* delete. Once you get to the gate, you need to review in your mind's eye where the engines are. *Once you get to the gate, you need to visualize where the engines are.*

**in my opinion**  *I assert; I believe; I claim; I consider; I contend; I feel; I hold; I judge; I maintain; I regard; I say; I think; I view; to me;* delete. In my opinion, the cruelest aggression is nonverbal, passive aggression. *To me, the cruelest aggression is nonverbal, passive aggression.*

**in my view**  *I assert; I believe; I claim; I consider; I contend; I feel; I hold; I judge; I maintain; I regard; I say; I think; I view; to me;* delete. In my view, most of these principles were narrow in scope. *I believe most of these principles were narrow in scope.*

**in nature**  delete. Christianity is theistic and revelatory in nature; the New Age is humanistic and generally solipsistic in nature. *Christianity is theistic and revelatory; the New Age is humanistic and generally solipsistic.*

**in no case**  *never; not; not ever; not once.* In no case would I recommend anything that could lead to the situation at Agawam. *Never would I recommend anything that could lead to the situation at Agawam.*

**in normal (ordinary; typical; usual) practice**  *commonly; customarily;*

*normally; ordinarily; typically; usually.* In normal practice, the party chairman is nominated, and the voting delegation then stands in unison to express its support. *Normally, the party chairman is nominated, and the voting delegation then stands in unison to express its support.*

**in no small measure** *almost all; chiefly; commonly; generally; greatly; in general; largely; mainly; most; mostly; most often; much; nearly all; normally; overall; typically; usually.* Our continued success is due in no small measure to their contribution on a daily basis. *Our continued success is greatly due to their contribution on a daily basis.*

**in no small part** *almost all; chiefly; commonly; generally; greatly; in general; largely; mainly; most; mostly; most often; much; nearly all; normally; overall; typically; usually.* And I continue to feel that his lifelong feelings of inadequacy and frustration stemmed in no small part from the limitations that he imposed upon his work. *And I continue to feel that his lifelong feelings of inadequacy and frustration stemmed largely from the limitations that he imposed upon his work.*

**in no time (at all)** *promptly; quickly; rapidly; right away; shortly; soon; speedily; swiftly.*

**innovative new** *innovative; new.* An innovative new product combining the latest in communications technology is being installed in courthouses and recording offices throughout the country for public use. *A new product combining the latest in communications technology is being installed in courthouses and recording offices throughout the country for public use.*

**in no way** *never; not; not ever; not once.* In no way are they meant to represent the official position of NYNEX. *They are not meant to represent the official position of NYNEX.*

**in no way, shape, or form** *in no way; never; not; not ever; not once.* In no way, shape, or form did we aid anyone or offer incentives to anyone to go to the town meeting. *Never did we aid anyone or offer incentives to anyone to go to the town meeting.*

**in number** *delete.* Nineteenth-century sweatshops are once again increasing in number. *Nineteenth-century sweatshops are once again increasing.*

**innumerable** *countless; endless; infinite; millions (of); myriad; numberless; untold.*

**in (March) of (1992)** *in (March) (1992).* The second moving year begins in February of 1984 and extends through January of 1985. *The second moving year begins in February 1984 and extends through January 1985.*

**in (the) olden days** *before; earlier; formerly; once.*

**in operation** *active; functioning; in place; running; set up; working;* delete. A large midwestern bank has had a performance monitoring program in operation since 1981. *A large midwestern bank has had a performance monitoring program since 1981.*

**in opposition to** *against; opposed to; with.* Lenin set himself in opposition to the blundering, indecisive czar; Khomeini against the blundering, indecisive shah. *Lenin set himself against the blundering, indecisive czar; Khomeini against the blundering, indecisive shah.*

**in ... order** *-(al)ly;* delete. We examine, in alphabetical order, all the MLI commands that make up GS/OS and ProDOS 8. *We examine, alphabetically, all the MLI commands that make up GS/OS and ProDOS 8.*

**in order for** *for.* Is it necessary that animals die in order for humans to live? *Is it necessary that animals die for humans to live?*

**in order that** *for; so; so that; that.* The overall dimension and the radii are given in order that their centers may be located. *The overall dimension and the radii are given so that their centers may be located.*

**in order to** *so as to; to.* In order to qualify for a heart transplant, certain criteria must be met, one of which is having less than a year to live. *To qualify for a heart transplant, certain criteria must be met, one of which is having less than a year to live.*

**in other cases (circumstances; instances; situations)** *at times; other; (at) other times; some; sometimes;* delete. In other cases, the application may be more mundane, like helping users set up newly delivered microcomputers. *Other applications may be more mundane, like helping users set up newly delivered microcomputers.*

**in other words** *namely; that is; to wit.* The directory names in the chain must define a continuous path; in other words, each directory specified must be contained within the preceding directory. *The directory names in the chain must define a continuous path; that is, each directory specified must be contained within the preceding directory.*

**in partial fulfillment of**  *to advance; to further; to help; toward.*

**in (over) (the) past days (decades; months; weeks; years)**  *before; earlier; formerly; once; previously.*

**in payment for (of)**  *for.* Connoisseurs of the region cannot help wondering what Assad could offer Washington in payment for such a favor. *Connoisseurs of the region cannot help wondering what Assad could offer Washington for such a favor.*

**in perpetuity**  *always; ceaselessly; constantly; endlessly; eternally; everlastingly; forever; never ending; perpetually.* It promised to preserve the rest of the farm in perpetuity as farm or forest. *It promised to preserve the rest of the farm forever as farm or forest.*

**in place of**  *for.* No reasonably literate person of my acquaintance says "sunk" in place of "sank." *No reasonably literate person of my acquaintance says "sunk" for "sank."*

**in point of**  *about; as for; as to; concerning; for; in; of; on; over; regarding; respecting; to; toward; with;* delete.

**in point of fact**  *actually; indeed; in fact; in faith; in reality; in truth; really; truly;* delete. The U.S. government said he wasn't working for them, but in point of fact, he was a military attaché. *The U.S. government said he wasn't working for them, but in truth he was a military attaché.*

**in preference to**  *over.* Mile's new product emphasis is on performance in preference to fashion. *Mile's new product emphasis is on performance over fashion.*

**in proportion to**  *for; with.*

**in proximity (to)**  *close by; close to; near; nearby.* The property is in proximity to metropolitan Boston. *The property is near metropolitan Boston.*

**in punishment for (of)**  *for.*

**in pursuit of**  *exploring; probing; pursuing; searching; seeking.* One would think they could better spend their time in pursuit of the pressing problems which beset the Redevelopment Authority and the city's development plans. *One would think they could better spend their* *time pursuing the pressing problems which beset the Redevelopment Authority and the city's development plans.*

**input** *clout; pull; say; voice.* I have a lot of input into what I'll wear on the set. *I have a lot of say about what I'll wear on the set.*

**input** *thoughts; views.* These style alternatives do not solicit employee input. *These style alternatives do not solicit employee views.*

**(the) ... in question** *the; that; this;* delete. Neither Phillips nor any of its subsidiaries has ever sold the chemical in question to Libya. *Neither Phillips nor any of its subsidiaries has ever sold this chemical to Libya.*

**in quick (short) order** *abruptly; apace; briskly; directly; fast; forthwith; hastily; hurriedly; posthaste; presently; promptly; quickly; rapidly; right away; shortly; soon; speedily; straightaway; swiftly; wingedly.* Surely a motivated work force could whip us back into shape in short order. *Surely a motivated work force could whip us back into shape quickly.*

**inquire (about; of)** *ask.* I inquired of the doctor why these children have distended stomachs. *I asked the doctor why these children have distended stomachs.*

**in reaction to** *after; because of; by; due to; following; for; from; in; out of; owing to; through; with.*

**in reality** *actually; indeed; in fact; in faith; in truth; really; truly;* delete.

**in recent days (decades; months; weeks; years)** *lately; of late; recent; recently;* delete. But events have not been kind to the university in recent weeks. *But recent events have not been kind to the university.*

**in recent history (memory; times)** *in days (months; weeks; years); lately; of late; recent; recently;* delete. It is the largest drop in auto insurance rates in recent memory. *It is the largest drop in auto insurance rates in years.*

**in recorded history** *on record; recorded.* Though final figures aren't yet in, as of November 1 this has been the hottest year in recorded history. *Though final figures aren't yet in, as of November 1 this has been the hottest year on record.*

**in reference to** *about; as for; as to; concerning; for; in; of; on; over; regard-*

*ing; respecting; to; toward; with;* delete. Never make any assumptions or promises in reference to product flaws, but report all instances either to customer service or the appropriate management personnel for corrective action. *Never make any assumptions or promises about product flaws, but report all instances either to customer service or the appropriate management personnel for corrective action.*

**in regard to**  *about; as for; as to; concerning; for; in; of; on; over; regarding; respecting; to; toward; with;* delete. They questioned me in regard to a 1986 bank robbery. *They questioned me about a 1986 bank robbery.*

**in relation to**  *about; as for; as to; concerning; for; in; of; on; over; regarding; respecting; to; toward; with;* delete. The researchers interviewed the survivors in relation to six areas of postwar life. *The researchers interviewed the survivors regarding six areas of postwar life.*

**in relation (relationship) to**  *against; alongside; beside; compared to (with); -(i)er than; less; less than; more; more than; next to; over; than; to; versus; vis-à-vis.* What has been done is very small in relationship to what needs to be done. *What has been done is very small compared to what needs to be done.*

**in repetition**  *again; over.*

**in resistance to**  *against; with.*

**in respect of (to)**  *about; as for; as to; concerning; for; in; of; on; over; regarding; respecting; to; toward; with;* delete. Some additional perspective is needed in respect to South Korea. *Some additional perspective is needed on South Korea.*

**in response to**  *after; because of; by; due to; following; for; from; in; out of; owing to; through; with.* The dollar yesterday fell against most major currencies in response to renewed dollar sales by central banks. *The dollar yesterday fell against most major currencies following renewed dollar sales by central banks.*

**in return for**  *for.* Switch traders are willing, in return for a fee, to find buyers for countertraded goods. *Switch traders are willing, for a fee, to find buyers for countertraded goods.*

**(the) ins and (the) outs**  *details; features; particulars; specifics.*

**in scale**  delete.

**in scope** delete. Smokeless tobacco is becoming a problem large in scope. *Smokeless tobacco is becoming a large problem.*

**in shape** delete. The true-size surface is elliptical in shape. *The true-size surface is elliptical.*

**in short supply** *meager; rare; scant; scarce; sparse.*

**inside of** *inside.* I continued to pack my gear, with pain and anger burning inside of me. *I continued to pack my gear, with pain and anger burning inside me.*

**inside (and) out** *completely; thoroughly.*

**inside the boundaries (limits; parameters) of** *within.*

**in situations when (where)** *if; when; where.* In situations where market heterogeneity limits opportunity for uniformity, the firm should actively promote global convergence of market segments. *Where market heterogeneity limits opportunity for uniformity, the firm should actively promote global convergence of market segments.*

**in size** delete. The sides range from 4 to 24 inches in size. *The sides range from 4 to 24 inches.*

**insofar as** *as far as; as much as; so far as; so much as.* As a historian, Mr. Chaudhuri is useful insofar as he recounts personal experience — for example, his accounts of the Bose brothers. *As a historian, Mr. Chaudhuri is useful so far as he recounts personal experience — for example, his accounts of the Bose brothers.*

**insofar as** *because; considering; for; given; in that; since.* Insofar as more than 98 percent of House incumbents were returned to office in the last election, it shouldn't surprise anyone that the members are turning Congress into a family business. *Since more than 98 percent of House incumbents were returned to office in the last election, it shouldn't surprise anyone that the members are turning Congress into a family business.*

**insofar as ... (goes; is concerned)** *about; as for; as to; concerning; for; in; of; on; over; regarding; respecting; to; toward; with;* delete. The president's position, insofar as negotiations are concerned, has never changed. *The president's position on negotiations has never changed.* ■ Intent, an element of the offense, may also be a factor insofar as a vehicle's recovery and condition are concerned. *Intent, an element of* *the offense, may also be a factor in a vehicle's recovery and condition.* ■ The ruling clarifies that the "orthotics" benefit in section 1861(s)(9) of the Act, insofar as braces are concerned, is limited to leg, arm, back, and neck braces that are used independently rather than in conjunction with, or as components of, other medical or non-medical equipment. *The ruling clarifies that the "orthotics" benefit in section 1861(s)(9) of the Act, regarding braces, is limited to leg, arm, back, and neck braces that are used independently rather than in conjunction with, or as components of, other medical or non-medical equipment.*

**in some fashion (manner; way)** *somehow; someway(s).* He considers it an idea that will be adopted in some fashion to meet the spiraling demands on air travel. *He considers it an idea that will somehow be adopted to meet the spiraling demands on air travel.*

**in spite of** *after all; apart; aside; despite; even with; for all; with all.* In spite of his malady, he wrote music with great skill and creativity. *Even with his malady, he wrote music with great skill and creativity.*

**in spite of the fact that** *although; but; even though; still; though; yet.* The number of deaths from asthma has doubled in the past decade in spite of the fact that treatments have improved. *The number of deaths from asthma has doubled in the past decade, yet treatments have improved.* ■ Some commentators claim that careful writers avoid the adverb *slow* in spite of the fact that it has over four centuries of usage behind it. *Some commentators claim that careful writers avoid the adverb* slow *even though it has over four centuries of usage behind it.*

**instantaneous (instantaneously)** *at once; instant (instantly); straightaway.* We fell in love with her instantaneously. *We fell in love with her at once.*

**institute** *set up.*

**institution** *building; factory; hospital; institute; jail; office; place; plant; prison; school;* delete.

**institution of higher learning** *college; school; university.* Mitchell Scholars may study or conduct research at institutions of higher learning including the seven universities in the Republic of Ireland and the two universities in Northern Ireland. *Mitchell Scholars may study or conduct research at colleges, including the seven universities in the Republic of Ireland and the two universities in Northern Ireland.*

**in such a fashion (manner; way) as to (so as to)** *so as to; to.* The light fixture had to be designed in such a manner so as to provide the maximum light to the operating area. *The light fixture had to be designed to provide the maximum light to the operating area.* ■ Further, we do not authorize any organization to use the Association's name in such a way as to imply that such a relationship exists. *Further, we do not authorize any organization to use the Association's name so as to imply that such a relationship exists.*

**in such a fashion (manner; way) so (so that)** *so; so that; such that.* Only meter stamped, return address labels may be used on single piece, special fourth-class rate or library rate mail, and these labels must adhere in such a manner so they will not come off in one piece. *Only meter stamped, return address labels may be used on single piece, special fourth-class rate or library rate mail, and these labels must adhere so that they will not come off in one piece.*

**in such a fashion (manner; way) that** *so; so that.* Export business may be structured in such a way that the buyer bears most of the risks. *Export business may be structured so that the buyer bears most of the risks.* ■ The first was the "store," designed in such a manner that numbers could be stored in 1,000 "registers," each capable of storing 50 digits. *The first was the "store," designed so that numbers could be stored in 1,000 "registers," each capable of storing 50 digits.*

**in such (a; the) ... fashion (manner; way)** *so -(al)ly;* delete.

**insufficient** *dis-; il-; im-; in-; ir-; lack of; -less(ness); mis-; no; non-; not; not enough; scant; too few; too little; un-.* There is insufficient reason for joy. *There is not enough reason for joy.*

**(a; the) insufficient amount (of)** *not enough; too little.*

**in sufficient amount** *enough.* If radon gas enters your lungs in sufficient amounts, it can emit alpha particles that attack tissue and lead to lung cancer. *If enough radon gas enters your lungs, it can emit alpha particles that attack tissue and lead to lung cancer.*

**(a; the) insufficient number (of)** *not enough; too few.* Within two years, other American cities expect a similar gridlock of hospital beds, largely because of AIDS and an insufficient number of health-care workers. *Within two years, other American cities expect a similar gridlock of hospital beds, largely because of AIDS and too few health-care workers.*

**in sufficient number** *enough.* I hope you heard from people in sufficient number to alert you to the possibility of a nationwide constituency for extended incarceration of violent felons. *I hope you heard from enough people to alert you to the possibility of a nationwide constituency for extended incarceration of violent felons.*

**in sufficient quantity** *enough.* Libya doesn't have the industrial capacity to make toxic agents in sufficient quantities to conduct warfare. *Libya doesn't have the industrial capacity to make enough toxic agents to conduct warfare.*

**in summary (summation)** *in brief; in fine; in short; in sum.* In summary, it is apparent that a country's comparative advantage situation will be vitally affected by the productivity of available factor inputs. *In sum, it is apparent that a country's comparative advantage situation will be vitally affected by the productivity of available factor inputs.*

**in support of** *for; with.* Radical environmentalists are already demanding that legal and ethical protection be extended to all of nature, and a few of them have demonstrated a willingness to fight, break the law, and even die in support of this conviction. *Radical environmentalists are already demanding that legal and ethical protection be extended to all of nature, and a few of them have demonstrated a willingness to fight, break the law, and even die for this conviction.*

**integrate together** *integrate; join.* The cost of the transmitters can be significantly reduced if all the lasers can be integrated together on a single substrate. *The cost of the transmitters can be significantly reduced if all the lasers can be integrated on a single substrate.*

**intellectual ability (capacity)** *ability; capacity; intellect; intelligence.* Tools and other remains left by Neanderthals show no indication that these creatures possessed the intellectual capacity for symbolic thought or language. *Tools and other remains left by Neanderthals show no indication that these creatures possessed the capacity for symbolic thought or language.*

**interdependency** *interdependence.*

**interestingly (enough)** *delete.* Interestingly enough, in about 50 percent of the cases involved, the professional offering an opinion believed abuse had occurred. *In about 50 percent of the cases involved, the professional offering an opinion believed abuse had occurred.*

**interlocutor**  *speaker; talker.*

**in ... terms**  *-(al)ly;* delete. They both spoke in optimistic terms. *They both spoke optimistically.*

**in terms of**  *about; as; as for; as to; by; concerning; for; in; of; on; regarding; respecting; through; under; with;* delete. In terms of safety, honesty, and trust, banks consistently score higher than life insurance companies. *In safety, honesty, and trust, banks consistently score higher than life insurance companies.* ■ How would you say you are different in terms of your personas? *How would you say your personas are different?* ■ She's more aggressive in terms of what she wants. *She's more aggressive about what she wants.* ■ Women are looking for help in terms of PMS. *Women are looking for help with PMS.* ■ Other doctors have criticized IL-2 therapy in terms of its toxicity. *Other doctors have criticized IL-2 therapy for its toxicity.* ■ The forecast level should be judged in terms of its reasonableness. *The forecast level should be judged on its reasonableness.*

**interpretative**  *interpretive.* Strategically placed U.S. nationals play an important interpretative role between the host country and the U.S. headquarters. *Strategically placed U.S. nationals play an important interpretive role between the host country and the U.S. headquarters.*

**interpret to mean**  *interpret as.* Achieving a desired standard of living must be interpreted to mean finding the pattern of consumption expenditures that yields maximum satisfaction. *Achieving a desired standard of living must be interpreted as finding the pattern of consumption expenditures that yields maximum satisfaction.*

**in that (this) case (circumstance; instance; situation)**  *here; now; then; there;* delete. No ampersand is required in this case because the argument will not be modified. *No ampersand is required now because the argument will not be modified.*

**in that (this) connection**  *about (for; in; on; to) that (this);* delete.

**in that (this) day and age**  *in that (this) age; in that (this) day; in that (this) time; (just; right) now; nowadays; then; these (those) days; today.* In this day and age of global violence, I find it interesting that the *Globe Magazine* would publish articles about two international terrorists. *In this age of global violence, I find it interesting that the* Globe Magazine *would publish articles about two international terrorists.*

217

**in that (this) direction** *toward that (this)*. That means any push in this direction would require guidance from officials of the new administration. *That means any push toward this would require guidance from officials of the new administration.*

**in that (this) fashion (manner; way)** *like this (that); so; thus*. What can she expect if she continues to behave in this manner? *What can she expect if she continues to behave like this?*

**in that (this) general vicinity** *around (near) here (there); thereabouts (hereabouts)*. There have been a lot of crimes in this general vicinity. *There have been a lot of crimes near here.*

**in (on) that (this) matter** *about (for; in; on; to) that (this); delete*. Rothko's views on this matter were very well known among his circle of friends. *Rothko's views on this were very well known among his circle of friends.*

**in that (this) regard** *about (for; in; on; to) that (this); delete*. There will be no change at all in that regard. *There will be no change at all in that.*

**in that (this) respect** *about (for; in; on; to) that (this); delete*.

**in the absence of** *absent; failing; having no; lacking; minus; missing; not having; with no; without*. In the absence of any other form of security, the shareholders of the contractor might be willing to let the company go out of business in the face of a serious problem. *Absent any other form of security, the shareholders of the contractor might be willing to let the company go out of business in the face of a serious problem.* ■ So in the absence of widespread XML+CSS rendering support, what is the importance of CSS in an XML developer's toolkit? *So without widespread XML+CSS rendering support, what is the importance of CSS in an XML developer's toolkit?* ■ The surface of the Earth is warmer than it would be in the absence of an atmosphere because it receives energy from two sources: the Sun and the atmosphere. *The surface of the Earth is warmer than it would be with no atmosphere because it receives energy from two sources: the Sun and the atmosphere.*

**in the act of -ing** *-ing; while -ing*. Archaeological investigations uncovered idols of woman in the act of giving birth or praying, figures of animals, neolithic shells and tools. *Archaeological investigations uncovered idols of woman giving birth or praying, figures of animals, neolithic shells and tools.* ■ The student need not be caught in the act of using for it to be recorded as "use." *The student need not be caught using for it to be recorded as "use."*

**in the affirmative** *affirmatively; favorably; positively; yes.* Eight members having voted in the affirmative, the vote carries. *Eight members having voted yes, the vote carries.*

**in the aftermath of** *(just; right) after; (close) behind; ensuing; following; succeeding.* In the aftermath of the assault-rifle mass murder, Americans should remain rational and not legislate away the right to own any type of firearm. *Following the assault-rifle mass murder, Americans should remain rational and not legislate away the right to own any type of firearm.*

**in the altogether** *naked; nude.*

**in the amount (sum) of** *for; of;* delete. Enclosed is a check in the amount of $900.00. *Enclosed is a check for $900.00.* ■ We are in the process of researching your claim and have issued credit in the amount of $31.49 to your above referenced account. *We are in the process of researching your claim and have issued credit for $31.49 to your above referenced account.*

**in the area of** *about; as for; as to; concerning; for; in; of; on; over; regarding; respecting; to; toward; with;* delete. The secondary gains for the phobic partner may be in the area of fulfilling nurturing needs. *The secondary gains for the phobic partner may be in fulfilling nurturing needs.*

**(something; somewhere) in the area (of)** *about; around; close to; more or less; near; nearly; or so; roughly; some;* delete. The trial is expected to run in the area of nine months. *The trial is expected to run some nine months.*

**in the assessment of** *assert; believe; claim; consider; contend; feel; hold; judge; maintain; regard; say; think; to; view; with.*

**in (within) the boundaries (limits; parameters) of** *in (within).*

**in the capacity of** *as.* Thus, a specialized or programmatic accrediting agency may also function in the capacity of an institutional accrediting agency. *Thus, a specialized or programmatic accrediting agency may also function as an institutional accrediting agency.*

**in the company of** *alongside; among; beside; during; in; with.* These children are here in the company of their fathers. *These children are here with their fathers.*

**in the context of** *in.* In the context of personal financial planning, the application of controls is even more important. *In personal financial planning, the application of controls is even more important.*

**(somewhere) in the course of** *during; for; in; over; throughout; when; while; with.* There were several suspects that came up in the course of our investigation, but Nancy Douglas was not one of them. *There were several suspects that came up during our investigation, but Nancy Douglas was not one of them.* ■ In the course of doing these exercises, students are introduced to almost all of their word processing program's features. *When doing these exercises, students are introduced to almost all of their word processing program's features.*

**in the course of events (things; time)** *at length; eventually; in due time; in the end; in time; later; one day; over the months (years); over time; someday; sometime; ultimately; with time; yet.* Continued observation of such men indicates that this is exactly what happens in many cases, and more evidence of this may show up in the course of time. *Continued observation of such men indicates that this is exactly what happens in many cases, and more evidence of this may show up over time.*

**in the days (decades; months; weeks; years) before (prior to)** *before.* In the days before LANs, if you wanted a coworker to add to a report you were writing, you copied the file to a disk and delivered it by hand. *Before LANs, if you wanted a coworker to add to a report you were writing, you copied the file to a disk and delivered it by hand.*

**in the direction of (toward)** *at; for; in; on; through; to; toward; with.* It appears it's headed in the direction of becoming a more conventional school that focuses on finances. *It appears it's headed toward becoming a more conventional school that focuses on finances.*

**in the distant future** *eventual; eventually; future; in many months (years); in time; in two (ten) months (years); later; much later; next month (year); one day; over time; someday; sometime; ultimately; with time; yet; delete.* In the distant future, the German people may regain unity through self-determination. *In time, the German people may regain unity through self-determination.*

**in the distant past** *before; earlier; formerly; long ago; long since; many months (years) ago; once; previously; delete.*

**in the estimation of** *assert; believe; claim; consider; contend; feel; hold; judge; maintain; regard; say; think; to; view; with.*

**in the eventuality of (that; this)** *if (there were); if ... should; in case (of); should (there); were (there; ... to); when;* delete. In the eventuality that someone decides not to follow a court order, what do you do? *If someone should decide not to follow a court order, what do you do?*

**in the extreme** *extremely; highly; hugely; mightily.* All three theories seem unlikely in the extreme. *All three theories seem highly unlikely.*

**in the face of** *against; before; confronted by (with); confronting; faced with; facing.* In the face of those developments, the off-farm work movement was inevitable. *Faced with those developments, the off-farm work movement was inevitable.*

**in the final (last) analysis** *finally; in the end; ultimately;* delete. In the final analysis, we are still grappling with the inherent problems of being human. *In the end, we are still grappling with the inherent problems of being human.*

**in the first place** *first; first of all;* delete. We found ourselves troubleshooting the immediate need, not addressing the larger issues that caused the problem in the first place. *We found ourselves troubleshooting the immediate need, not addressing the larger issues that first caused the problem.*

**in the following fashion (manner; way)** *as follows.* The value of *M* can be substituted in the equation in the following manner. *The value of* M *can be substituted in the equation as follows.*

**in the foreseeable future** *before long; directly; in a month (week); next month (year); presently; quickly; shortly; soon; this month (year); tomorrow;* delete. I expect in the foreseeable future we will see them looking inward and opening up to the world. *I expect we will presently see them looking inward and opening up to the world.*

**in the form of** *as;* delete. I offer these comments in the form of advice, not criticism. *I offer these comments as advice, not criticism.* ■ A pro-forma may be created in the form of a profit and loss statement or a cash flow statement. *A pro-forma may be created as a profit and loss statement or a cash flow statement.*

**in the function of** *as.*

**in (into) the future** *at length; before long; eventually; in a month (week); in due time; in time; later; next month (year); one day; over time; someday;*

*sometime; ultimately; with time; yet;* delete. All indications are that these patterns of change will continue into the future. *All indications are that these patterns will continue.*

**in the immediate future** *at once; before long; directly; immediately; in a month (week); momentarily; next month (year); (just; right) now; presently; quickly; shortly; soon; straightaway; this month (year); tomorrow;* delete. I don't anticipate any layoffs in the immediate future. *I don't anticipate any layoffs immediately.*

**in the immediate past** *a few months (years) ago; formerly; lately; not long ago; of late; previously; recent; recently;* delete. Computer software consulting firms constitute a growth node that will probably continue, but alone it cannot generate the numbers of jobs that have been generated in the immediate past. *Computer software consulting firms constitute a growth node that will probably continue, but alone it cannot generate the number of jobs that have been recently generated.*

**in the interest of (-ing)** *for; so as to; to.* The secretary took this action in the interest of ensuring an equitable investigation. *The secretary took this action to ensure an equitable investigation.*

**in the interim** *meantime; meanwhile.* In the interim, law enforcement agencies are bracing for the worst. *Meanwhile, law enforcement agencies are bracing for the worst.*

**in the interval** *meantime; meanwhile.*

**in the judgment of** *assert; believe; claim; consider; contend; feel; hold; judge; maintain; regard; say; think; to; view; with.* In the judgment of these scientists, it has hurt the effort. *These scientists believe it has hurt the effort.*

**in the least (slightest)** *at all;* delete. I don't mind in the least. *I don't mind at all.*

**in (over) the long run** *at length; eventually; in the end; in time; later; long-term; one day; over the months (years); over time; someday; sometime; ultimately; with time; yet.* In the long run, presumably fewer citizens would require Medicaid. *In time, presumably fewer citizens would require Medicaid.*

**in (over) the long term** *at length; eventually; in the end; in time; later; long-term; one day; over the months (years); over time; someday; sometime;*

*ultimately; with time; yet.* How will the two investments compare over the long term? *How will the two investments compare over time?*

**in the main** *almost all; chiefly; commonly; generally; greatly; in general; largely; mainly; most; mostly; most often; much; nearly all; normally; overall; typically; usually.* In the main, politicians have become contemptuous of voters. *Generally, politicians have become contemptuous of voters.*

**in the making** *brewing; developing; forming.* The teams go into action when computers at the National Weather Service foresee a disturbance in the making. *The teams go into action when computers at the National Weather Service foresee a disturbance brewing.*

**in (on) the matter of** *about; as for; as to; concerning; for; in; of; on; over; regarding; respecting; to; toward; with;* delete. All of these factors assume you have a choice in the matter of where you will hold your meeting. *All of these factors assume you have a choice in where you will hold your meeting.*

**in the meantime** *meantime; meanwhile.* In the meantime, I will discuss the software potential with our people and see if we can come up with some preliminary conclusions. *Meantime, I will discuss the software potential with our people and see if we can come up with some preliminary conclusions.*

**in the middle of** *amid; among; during; in; in between; inside; through; within.* Charles said that Britain was in the middle of another building boom and the important question was "whether we can get it right this time." *Charles said that Britain was amid another building boom and the important question was "whether we can get it right this time."*

**in the middle (midst) of -ing** *-ing.* We are currently in the middle of improving these signs with new panels and brighter lighting. *We are currently improving these signs with new panels and brighter lighting.*

**in the midst of** *amid; among; during; in; in between; inside; through; within.* Federal and state authorities are in the midst of a criminal investigation of whether an unreported series of leaks and spills was linked to groundwater polluted by more than 55 chemicals. *Federal and state authorities are amid a criminal investigation of whether an unreported series of leaks and spills was linked to groundwater polluted by more than 55 chemicals.*

**in the nature of** *akin to; close to; like; resembling; similar to; such as.*

These days it takes something in the nature of a reception with the Queen Mother to get the Maxwells together. *These days it takes something like a reception with the Queen Mother to get the Maxwells together.*

**(something; somewhere) in the nature (of)**  *about; around; close to; more or less; near; nearly; or so; roughly; some;* delete. The owners anticipate production to be in the nature of 3,000 gallons weekly. *The owners anticipate production to be around 3,000 gallons weekly.*

**in the (very) near future**  *before long; directly; in a month (week); next month (year); presently; quickly; shortly; soon; this month (year); tomorrow;* delete. I will visit my mother's grave site in the near future. *I will visit my mother's grave site next week.*

**in the (very) near past**  *a few months (years) ago; before; earlier; formerly; lately; not long ago; of late; once; previously; recent; recently;* delete.

**in (over) the near term**  *at first; at present; before long; currently; directly; for now; in (over) a month (week); initially; next month (year); now; presently; short-term; this month (year);* delete. That, perhaps, best sums up what to expect from AI in the near term. *That, perhaps, best sums up what to expect from AI for now.*

**in the negative**  *against; negatively; no; unfavorably.* I shook my head in the negative. *I shook my head no.*

**in the neighborhood (of)**  *close by; close to; near; nearby; neighboring.* "Everything around here shook," said a young woman who works at a restaurant in the neighborhood. *"Everything around here shook," said a young woman who works at a nearby restaurant.*

**(something; somewhere) in the neighborhood (of)**  *about; around; close to; more or less; near; nearly; or so; roughly; some;* delete. We have somewhere in the neighborhood of 6 million illegal aliens in this country. *We have about 6 million illegal aliens in this country.*

**in the next place**  *also; and; as well; besides; beyond that (this); further; furthermore; in addition; moreover; more than that (this); next; second; still more; too; what is more.*

**in the normal (ordinary; typical; usual) course of business (events; things)**  *as usual; commonly; customarily; normally; ordinarily; typically; usually.* In the ordinary course of events, they wouldn't go to court over something like this. *Ordinarily, they wouldn't go to court over something like this.*

**in the not-so-distant (not-too-distant) future** *before long; directly; in a month (week); next month (year); presently; quickly; shortly; soon; this month (year); tomorrow;* delete. We'll be coming out with some new communications products in the not-too-distant future. *We'll be coming out with some new communications products shortly.*

**in the not-so-distant (not-too-distant) past** *a few months (years) ago; before; earlier; formerly; lately; not long ago; of late; once; previously; recent; recently;* delete. In the not-so-distant past, people could have dropped out of high school and gotten a decent-paying job in manufacturing. *Not long ago, people could have dropped out of high school and gotten a decent-paying job in manufacturing.* ■ Look a little closer and you'll find that those controls appeared in an OCX listing in the not-too-distant past. *Look a little closer and you'll find that those controls once appeared in an OCX listing.*

**in the opinion of** *assert; believe; claim; consider; contend; feel; hold; judge; maintain; regard; say; think; to; view; with.* The Wall Street inside-information scandal could pull in yet another circle of white-collar criminals in the opinion of criminal lawyers and securities specialists. *Criminal lawyers and securities specialists contend the Wall Street inside-information scandal could pull in yet another circle of white-collar criminals.*

**in the opposite direction from (of)** *against.* Many bicyclists do not observe traffic signals, ride in the opposite direction of motor traffic, and fail to signal when overtaking pedestrians. *Many bicyclists do not observe traffic signals, ride against motor traffic, and fail to signal when overtaking pedestrians.*

**in the overall scope (sphere) of things** *all in all; all told; in all; overall;* delete. In the overall sphere of things, a vast majority of tax problems never reach the courts, particularly not as criminal prosecutions. *Overall, a vast majority of tax problems never reach the courts, particularly not as criminal prosecutions.*

**in the past** *before; earlier; formerly; once; previously;* delete. You said, in the past, that you weren't interested in the vice presidency. *Earlier you said that you weren't interested in the vice presidency.*

**in (over) the past few (several) days (decades; months; weeks; years)** *lately; of late; recent; recently.* Neural networks have generated much interest, not to mention hype, in the past few years. *Neural networks have lately generated much interest, not to mention hype.*

**in the position of** *as.* Even in modern times, and in the most developed countries, it is rare to find a woman in the position of a head of state. *Even in modern times, and in most developed countries, it is rare to find a woman as a head of state.*

**in the presence of** *alongside; among; beside; during; in; with.* On only one occasion was I in the presence of Jack and Sam at the same time. *On only one occasion was I with Jack and Sam at the same time.*

**in the process of** *in; while.* In the process of doing so, he threw out some good material. *In doing so, he threw out some good material.* ■ Answers to these and many other questions had to be resolved in the process of developing and implementing the new system of student assessment. *Answers to these and many other questions had to be resolved while developing and implementing the new system of student assessment.* ■ It is easy to damage or destroy evidence in the process of looking for it. *It is easy to damage or destroy evidence while looking for it.*

**in the process of -ing** *-ing.* I'm in the process of cleaning the house. *I'm cleaning the house.* ■ The company is in the process of changing the regulatory framework in most of its states. *The company is changing the regulatory framework in most of its states.* ■ No publication date has been set for the book, which is in the process of being written. *No publication date has been set for the book, which is being written.* ■ Out of the parent survey have come many ideas and from those ideas, many projects, which we are currently in the process of putting into action. *Out of the parent survey have come many ideas and from those ideas, many projects, which we are currently putting into action.* ■ We are currently in the process of reviewing the resumes of all applicants. *We are currently reviewing the resumes of all applicants.* ■ iCAST Corporation has closed down its website and is in the process of winding down the business. *iCAST Corporation has closed down its website and is winding down the business.*

**in the proximity (of)** *close by; close to; near; nearby.* Cosmic gamma ray bursts appear to originate in the proximity of neutron stars, but the sources have never been pinned down. *Cosmic gamma ray bursts appear to originate near neutron stars, but the sources have never been pinned down.*

**(something; somewhere) in the range from (of) ... through (to)** *between ... and; from ... to; to;* delete. According to a recent study by Arthur Andersen & Co., the cost of drilling new wells is in the range of $6 to $8 a barrel. *According to a recent study by Arthur Andersen & Co., the cost of drilling new wells is between $6 and $8 a barrel.*

**(something; somewhere) in the ... range (of)** *about; around; close to; more or less; near; nearly; or so; roughly; some;* delete. The price tag on the three-city shuttle was in the range of $200 million. *The price tag on the three-city shuttle was about $200 million.*

**in the realm of** *about; as for; as to; concerning; for; in; of; on; over; regarding; respecting; to; toward; with;* delete. Furthermore, in the realm of strategic nuclear weapons, he has overseen not reductions but improvements. *Furthermore, in strategic nuclear weapons, he has overseen not reductions but improvements.*

**(something; somewhere) in the realm (of)** *about; around; close to; more or less; near; nearly; or so; roughly; some;* delete. The company expects to employ somewhere in the realm of 300 people there by 1993. *The company expects to employ around 300 people there by 1993.*

**in (within) the realm of possibility** *conceivable; doable; possible; thinkable.* She said having a child is still within the realm of possibility. *She said having a child is still possible.*

**in (within) the recent past** *a few months (years) ago; before; earlier; formerly; lately; not long ago; of late; once; previously; recent; recently;* delete. The belief that we have an open society in which anyone can get ahead is less true than in the recent past. *The belief that we have an open society in which anyone can get ahead is less true than before.*

**(something; somewhere) in the region (of)** *about; around; close to; more or less; near; nearly; or so; roughly; some;* delete. That's on top of an additional estimated increase in food prices somewhere in the region of 4 percent. *That's on top of an additional estimated increase in food prices of about 4 percent.*

**in the role of** *as.* Morgan argues that a moral struggle is suggested by the juxtaposition of the hunt scenes and the bedroom scenes, with the Lady in the role of the hunter and Gawain as the hunted. *Morgan argues that a moral struggle is suggested by the juxtaposition of the hunt scenes and the bedroom scenes, with the Lady as the hunter and Gawain as the hunted.*

**in the same fashion (manner; way) (as; that)** *as (be); like; likewise; much like; so; the same as.* Though not necessarily displayed on the screen, hard carriage returns are much like other characters you enter in a document; therefore, you delete them in the same way you would other characters. *Though not necessarily displayed on the screen, hard carriage returns are much like other characters you enter in a document; therefore, you delete them as you would other characters.* ■ This strengthens the brain, in the same way that lifting weights strengthens muscles. *This strengthens the brain, much like lifting weights strengthens muscles.* ■ In the same way, the truths of our religion are strewn across the world, on two distant continents. *Similarly, the truths of our religion are strewn across the world, on two distant continents.*

**in the second place** *also; and; as well; besides; beyond that (this); further; furthermore; in addition; moreover; more than that (this); next; second; still more; too; what is more.*

**in the sense of** *that is;* delete. He is in a peculiar — in the sense of unusual — position. *He is in a peculiar — that is, unusual — position.*

**in the sense that** *because; considering; for; given; in that; since.* Foreign and domestic marketing are the same in the sense that the purpose is to create and manage profitable exchange relationships. *Foreign and domestic marketing are the same in that the purpose is to create and manage profitable exchange relationships.*

**in (over) the short run** *at first; at present; before long; currently; directly; for now; in (over) a month (week); initially; next month (year); now; presently; short-term; this month (year);* delete. The tax-cut proposal is the nutritional equivalent of a diet of beer: in the short run, it fills you up and gives you a buzz, but eventually it devastates the body. *The tax-cut proposal is the nutritional equivalent of a diet of beer: at first, it fills you up and gives you a buzz, but eventually it devastates the body.*

**in (over) the short term** *at first; at present; before long; currently; directly; for now; in (over) a month (week); initially; next month (year); now; presently; short-term; this month (year);* delete. People who can withstand fluctuations over the short term are virtually guaranteed a profit in the stock market. *People who can withstand short-term fluctuations are virtually guaranteed a profit in the stock market.*

**in (on) the subject of** *about; as for; as to; concerning; for; in; of; on; over; regarding; respecting; to; toward; with;* delete. Both authors have written widely on the subject of behavioral science research and application. *Both authors have written widely on behavioral science research and application.*

**in the support of (-ing)** *for; so as to; to.*

**in the third place** *also; and; as well; besides; beyond that (this); further; furthermore; in addition; moreover; more than that (this); next; still more; third; too; what is more.*

**in the ... through (to) ... range** *between ... and; from ... to; to.* Whether they will be willing to pay a base price rumored to be in the $3,000 to $6,000 range is one of the many questions to be answered. *Whether they will be willing to pay a base price rumored to be between $3,000 and $6,000 is one of the many questions to be answered.*

**in the unexpected (unlikely) event of (that)** *if (there were); if ... should; in case (of); should (there); were (there; ... to);* delete. In the unexpected event that those costs exceed $30 million, other joint owners would be obligated. *Should those costs exceed $30 million, other joint owners would be obligated.*

**in the vicinity (of)** *close by; close to; near; nearby.* It was last seen in the vicinity of the Abbot Street Bridge. *It was last seen near the Abbot Street Bridge.*

**(something; somewhere) in the vicinity (of)** *about; around; close to; more or less; near; nearly; or so; roughly; some;* delete. On its best day, my corporation earned in the vicinity of $2 million. *On its best day, my corporation earned around $2 million.*

**in the view of** *assert; believe; claim; consider; contend; feel; hold; judge; maintain; regard; say; think; to; view; with.* In the view of some strategists, he may lose the election unless he can reverse his fortunes on this issue. *Some strategists think he may lose the election unless he can reverse his fortunes on this issue.*

**in the wake of** *(just; right) after; because of; (close) behind; due to; ensuing; following; from; owing to; succeeding.* In the wake of an office and shopping-center boom comes an employment boom in business custodians. *Following an office and shopping-center boom comes an employment boom in business custodians.*

**in the way of** delete. This step requires that you research jobs to determine what they call for in the way of education, skills, and aptitudes. *This step requires that you research jobs to determine what education, skills, and aptitudes they call for.* ■ There is little motivation for long periods of foolishness, and there is much in the way of market discipline to prevent it. *There is little motivation for long periods of foolishness, and there is much market discipline to prevent it.* ■ A sentence such as "It is 93 million miles to the sun" does not generate much in the way of questions; it is too specific. *A sentence such as "It is 93 million miles to the sun" does not generate many questions; it is too specific.* ■ As parents, we got little in the way of help, a good deal in the way of confusion, and an infinite amount in the way of worry. *As parents, we got little help, a good deal of confusion, and an infinite amount of worry.*

**in thickness** *thick;* delete. In their theoretical analysis, Gaylord and Brennan consider a filter consisting of nine layers, each layer a quarter or a half of the electron wavelength in thickness. *In their theoretical analysis, Gaylord and Brennan consider a filter consisting of nine layers, each layer a quarter or a half of the electron wavelength thick.*

**intimately familiar** *familiar; intimate.*

**in (the) time(s) of** *amid; during; in; over; throughout.* The substantial risk of investment in junk bonds, particularly in times of economic uncertainty, is often disregarded by small investors. *The substantial risk of investment in junk bonds, particularly amid economic uncertainty, is often disregarded by small investors.*

**in ... tones** *-(al)ly;* delete. Police officers trooped into every grammar school in the city to talk with kids, explaining in dispassionate tones the use and abuse of crack. *Police officers trooped into every grammar school in the city to talk with kids, explaining dispassionately the use and abuse of crack.*

**in trade (for)** *for.*

**introduce (a; the) new** *introduce.* In 1983, Apple introduced a new, easier-to-use computer called the Lisa. *In 1983, Apple introduced an easier-to-use computer called the Lisa.*

**inure to the benefit of** *inure to.* This agreement shall be binding upon and inure to the benefit of the executors, administrators, and assigns of the Author and of the Client. *This agreement shall be binding upon and inure to the executors, administrators, and assigns of the Author and of the Client.*

**in (on; to; with) various (varying) degrees (extents)** *in part; in some way; more or less; partially; partly; rather; some; somehow; someway(s); somewhat; to some degree (extent); various; variously; varying; varyingly;*

delete. Four masters of the art of stretch management rely on varying degrees on a set of nuts-and-bolts techniques. *Four masters of the art of stretch management rely varyingly on a set of nuts-and-bolts techniques.*

**invidious discrimination** *discrimination; invidiousness.* Few would deny that ferreting out this kind of invidious discrimination is a great if not compelling governmental interest. *Few would deny that ferreting out this kind of invidiousness is a great if not compelling governmental interest.*

**in view of the fact that** *because; considering; for; given; in that; since; when.* These results are particularly interesting in view of the fact that Christian Scientists are forbidden to either smoke or drink. *These results are particularly interesting considering Christian Scientists are forbidden to either smoke or drink.* ■ In view of the fact that power supplies are being steadily reduced, this can be a serious design limitation. *Since power supplies are being steadily reduced, this can be a serious design limitation.* ■ Colon cancer is the second-leading cause of cancer deaths in the U.S. for both men and women, so in view of the fact that packaged breakfast cereals are so convenient, this is very good news. *Colon cancer is the second-leading cause of cancer deaths in the U.S. for both men and women, so given that packaged breakfast cereals are so convenient, this is very good news.*

**in view of the fact that** *whereas.*

**invited guest** *guest.*

**involve** *for; in; mean; of; with;* delete. Census II involves using several different types of moving averages to identify trends and outliers within a data set. *Census II uses several different types of moving averages to identify trends and outliers within a data set.* ■ The operation is self-sustaining and has operated with no public-sector funding involved. *The operation is self-sustaining and has operated with no public-sector funding.*

**involved in** *in; of; within;* delete. The costs involved in refurbishing the building are prohibitive. *The costs of refurbishing the building are prohibitive.*

**in (a; the) ... way** *-(al)ly;* delete. Each of these variations can be revised in a different way. *Each of these variations can be revised differently.* ■ Computer systems differ in a significant way from stereos. *Computer systems differ significantly from stereos.* ■ Every group that has scrutinized this product in an impartial way agrees it is safe. *Every group that has impartially scrutinized this product agrees it is safe.*

**in whatever (whichever) fashion (manner; way)** *despite how; however.* In whatever way it comes, the decision will be an important one. *Despite how it comes, the decision will be an important one.*

**in what (which) fashion (manner; way)** *how.* In what fashion does imaging technology offer potential competitive advantage? *How does imaging technology offer potential competitive advantage?* ■ In what ways does it create a communication problem for you? *How does it create a communication problem for you?*

**in what (which) regard (respect)** *how.* In what respect was this investment "tax free"? *How was this investment "tax free"?*

**in width** *wide;* delete. In high-performance hard disks, these tracks are roughly 1 micrometer in width. *In high-performance hard disks, these tracks are roughly 1 micrometer wide.*

**ironical** *ironic.*

**irregardless of** *despite (what); no matter what; regardless of; whatever.* Irregardless of the cause, the pressure of the spinal fluid with the ventricles must be relieved to prevent damage to the brain. *Regardless of the cause, the pressure of the spinal fluid with the ventricles must be relieved to prevent damage to the brain.* ■ We want every hospitality establishment to have the opportunity to list on our directory irregardless of their size or wealth. *We want every hospitality establishment to have the opportunity to list on our directory whatever their size or wealth.*

**irregardless of the fact that** *although; but; even though; still; though; yet.* Irregardless of the fact that she was raised by someone else, she is still my daughter. *Although she was raised by someone else, she is still my daughter.* ■ Charges resulting from Procard expenditures may be transferred from Local to State Account irregardless of the fact that the original voucher may be greater than $2,000. *Charges resulting from Procard expenditures may be transferred from Local to State Account even though the original voucher may be greater than $2,000.*

**irrelevancy** *irrelevance.*

**irrespective of (what)** *despite (what); no matter what; regardless of; whatever.* The product-first approach meant marketing the same product to all customers, irrespective of their profiles. *The product-first approach meant marketing the same product to all customers, regardless of their profiles.* ■ Irrespective of the reasons, the voters simply do not want to participate in a collaborative project. *No matter what the reasons, the voters simply do not want to participate in a collaborative project.*

**irrespective of how**  *despite how; however; no matter how; regardless of how.* The margins are retained irrespective of how many characters are printed per inch. *The margins are retained despite how many characters are printed per inch.*

**irrespective of the fact that**  *although; but; even though; still; though; yet.* Ireland Under 21 coach Ciaran Fitzgerald spoke of the value of keeping together his charges for tonight's game in Musgrave Park, irrespective of the fact that the only doubt surrounding the outcome is the final margin of victory. *Ireland Under 21 coach Ciaran Fitzgerald spoke of the value of keeping together his charges for tonight's game in Musgrave Park, even though the only doubt surrounding the outcome is the final margin of victory.* ■ Irrespective of the fact that the proposed regulations apply only to foreign workers, it means that for the first time it will be stipulated in law that those relying on social assistance loose their claim to a fundamental democratic right. *Although the proposed regulations apply only to foreign workers, it means that for the first time it will be stipulated in law that those relying on social assistance loose their claim to a fundamental democratic right.*

**irrespective of when**  *despite when; no matter when; regardless of when; whenever.* In other words, the operation of the Reserve benefits all members irrespective of when they join or leave the Scheme. *In other words, the operation of the Reserve benefits all members despite when they join or leave the Scheme.*

**irrespective of where**  *despite where; no matter where; regardless of where; wherever.* A successful company must have the necessary skill sets to meet the needs and wants of its customers irrespective of where they may do business. *A successful company must have the necessary skill sets to meet the needs and wants of its customers wherever they may do business.*

**irrespective of (the fact) whether ... (or)**  *despite whether; no matter whether; regardless of whether; whether ... or (not).* One delegate said his parish would continue to raise money for its diocese irrespective of whether the archdiocesan assessment is met. *One delegate said his parish would continue to raise money for its diocese whether or not the arch-*

233

*diocesan assessment is met.* ■ You need to procure the visas for all the countries, even the ones that the trains are passing through, irrespective of the fact whether the trains are stopping in those countries. *You need to procure the visas for all the countries, even the ones that the trains are passing through, whether or not the trains are stopping in those countries.*

**irrespective of which**   *despite which; no matter which; regardless of which; whichever.* We oppose foreign control, irrespective of which country it involves. *We oppose foreign control, whichever country it involves.*

**irrespective of who**   *despite who; no matter who; regardless of who; whoever.* Irrespective of who leads the group, one fact remains. *Whoever leads the group, one fact remains.*

**irrespective of whom**   *despite whom; no matter whom; regardless of whom; whomever.*

**... is ... (that; which; who; whom)**   delete. Batch files are files that contain commands that are executed automatically when you turn on your computer or type the batch file's name. *Batch files contain commands that are executed automatically when you turn on your computer or type the batch file's name.* ■ Domestic corporations are corporations that do business in the state in which they are chartered, and foreign corporations are corporations that do business outside their chartered state. *Domestic corporations do business in the state in which they are chartered, and foreign corporations do business outside their chartered state.*

**is able to**   *can.* Investors are able to buy and sell any quantity of securities. *Investors can buy and sell any quantity of securities.*

**is (was) accustomed to (-ing)**   *will (would).* They are accustomed to talking until late into the night. *They will talk until late into the night.*

**is a consequence of**   *arises from; results from; stems from.* The East African Rift is a consequence of tectonic motion between the African and Eurasian plates. *The East African Rift stems from tectonic motion between the African and Eurasian plates.*

**is a contribution to**   *contributes to.* This is a continuing contribution to a company's profitability. *This continually contributes to a company's profitability.*

**is acquainted with** *knows.*

**is a demonstration of** *demonstrates; shows; proves.*

**is a description of** *describes.* The attached proposal is a brief description of what I have in mind. *The attached proposal briefly describes what I have in mind.*

**is a deterrent to** *blocks; deters; hinders; impedes; prevents; stops; thwarts.*

**is advantageous for (to)** *aids; benefits; favors; helps.*

**is afraid of (to)** *dreads; fears; frets (about; over); stews (about; over); worries (about; over).*

**is a function of** *depends on; relates to.* The popularity of fixed-rate versus adjustable-rate mortgages seems to be a function of the level of interest rates. *The popularity of fixed-rate versus adjustable-rate mortgages seems to depend on the level of interest rates.*

**is a hindrance to** *blocks; deters; hinders; impedes; prevents; stops; thwarts.* A problem is any organizational issue that could be a hindrance to organizational success. *A problem is any organizational issue that could hinder organizational success.*

**is an acquaintance of** *knows.* Mr. Branch was an acquaintance of Miss Gregory. *Mr. Branch knew Miss Gregory.*

**is an illustration of** *illustrates.* I believe that these moves by Texaco are a perfect illustration of the precept that a clear and closer relationship between active ownership and management will increase productivity. *I believe that these moves by Texaco perfectly illustrate the precept that a clear and closer relationship between active ownership and management will increase productivity.*

**is an impediment to** *blocks; deters; hinders; impedes; prevents; stops; thwarts.*

**is an indication (indicator) of** *argues; attests to; bespeaks; betokens; indicates; shows; signals; signifies; suggests; testifies to; witnesses.* The Roman holiday atmosphere reportedly surrounding the event may be an indicator of the level of civilized intercourse we have attained in this so-called advanced industrial nation. *The Roman holiday atmosphere reportedly surrounding the event may signify the level of civilized inter-*

*course we have attained in this so-called advanced industrial nation.*

**is an obstacle to** *blocks; deters; hinders; impedes; prevents; stops; thwarts.*

**is applicable in (to)** *applies in (to); bears on; concerns; pertains to; relates to.* Regardless, the autocratic style is applicable in some situations. *Regardless, the autocratic style applies in some situations.*

**is appreciative of** *appreciates; approves of; cherishes; enjoys; esteems; likes; prizes; treasures; understands; values; welcomes.* We are especially appreciative of the item which appeared in the paper citing our need for volunteers. *We especially appreciate the item which appeared in the paper citing our need for volunteers.*

**is apprehensive of** *dreads; fears; frets (about; over); stews (about; over); worries (about; over).* My parents were apprehensive of my going to Iran. *My parents dreaded my going to Iran.*

**is appropriate in (to)** *applies in (to); bears on; concerns; pertains to; relates to.*

**is a (the) process that** delete. Anxiety is a process that alerts people to possible dangers. *Anxiety alerts people to possible dangers.*

**is a reflection of (on; upon)** *reflects (on).* Could it be that they felt the actions by the school would be a bad reflection on them? *Could it be that they felt the actions by the school would badly reflect on them?*

**is a representation of** *represents.*

**is a result of** *arises from; results from; stems from.*

**is associated to (with)** *correlates to (with); equates with; relates to.* The development of interest and confidence and infusions of practical, useful applications seem to be associated with success in mathematics. *The development of interest and confidence and infusions of practical, useful applications seem to relate to success in mathematics.*

**is at loggerheads (with)** *clashes with; conflicts with; contradicts; differs from; disagrees with; quarrels with; varies with.* He ran unsuccessfully for the Florida house and has frequently been at loggerheads with state and federal authorities. *He ran unsuccessfully for the Florida house and has frequently quarreled with state and federal authorities.*

**is at odds over (with)** *clashes with; conflicts with; contradicts; differs from; disagrees with; quarrels with; varies with.* She said the strong credit figures were at odds with a stream of government reports pointing toward a slowdown and did not reflect the health of the economy. *She said the strong credit figures contradicted a stream of government reports pointing toward a slowdown and did not reflect the health of the economy.*

**is attentive to** *attends to; heeds.*

**is at variance with** *clashes with; conflicts with; contradicts; differs from; disagrees with; quarrels with; varies with.* Although some of its particulars are at variance with what U.S. officials have heard, most key details tend to coincide. *Although some of its particulars clash with what U.S. officials have heard, most key details tend to coincide.*

**is a variant of** *departs from; deviates from; differs from; diverges from; varies from.* Endowment insurance policies are a variant of whole life in that, if the insured dies within a specified period, the insurance will be paid to a designated beneficiary. *Endowment insurance policies vary from whole life in that, if the insured dies within a specified period, the insurance will be paid to a designated beneficiary.*

**is aware of (that)** *comprehends; knows; realizes; recognizes; sees; understands.* If you are in the same position as most consumer borrowers, you should be aware that time is not on your side. *If you are in the same position as most consumer borrowers, you should realize that time is not on your side.*

**is based on (upon)** *rests on.* This policy is based upon three fundamental principles of competitive behavior. *This policy rests on three fundamental principles of competitive behavior.*

**is based on the assumption** *assumes.* Capitalism is based on the assumption that you can win. *Capitalism assumes that you can win.* ■ The annual percentage yield is based on the assumption that dividends will remain on deposit until maturity. *The annual percentage yield assumes that dividends will remain on deposit until maturity.* ■ This proposal is based on the assumption that qualitative research can add new insight into the real life issues that contribute to the health disparities. *This proposal assumes that qualitative research can add new insight into the real life issues that contribute to the health disparities.*

**is beneficial to** *aids; benefits; favors; helps.* Congress needs to make important decisions that will be beneficial to all Americans on a long-range basis. *Congress needs to make important decisions that will benefit all Americans on a long-range basis.*

**is capable of -ing** *can; is able to.* Obsolescence exists when a person or machine is no longer capable of performing to standards or management's expectations. *Obsolescence exists when a person or machine is no longer able to perform to standards or management's expectations.*

**is characteristic of** *characterizes; depicts; describes; designates; illustrates; pictures; portrays.* The protein tangles in brain tissue are characteristic of advanced Alzheimer's, and he speculates that A68 may be a precursor of the tangles. *The protein tangles in brain tissue characterize advanced Alzheimer's, and he speculates that A68 may be a precursor of the tangles.*

**is cognizant of (that)** *comprehends; knows; realizes; recognizes; sees; understands.*

**is coherent with** *agrees with; coheres with; concurs with; conforms to (with); corresponds to (with).*

**is comparable to (with)** *compares to (with); contrasts to (with); corresponds to (with); equates with; likens to; relates to; resembles.* This revolution in medicine is comparable in certain ways to the computer boom, but is more epochal. *This revolution in medicine corresponds in certain ways to the computer boom, but is more epochal.*

**is compatible with** *agrees with; coheres with; concurs with; conforms to (with); corresponds to (with).*

**is competitive with** *competes with.*

**is complementary to** *complements.* Banking is an obvious area for Nomura's diversification since it is complementary to the firm's securities business. *Banking is an obvious area for Nomura's diversification since it complements the firm's securities business.*

**is compliant with** *complies with.* Our emphasis is supporting the customers who have been fully compliant with the export regulations. *Our emphasis is supporting the customers who have fully complied with the export regulations.*

**is composed of** *comprises; consists of; contains; includes.* The informal organization is composed of all the informal groupings of people within a formal organization. *The informal organization consists of all the informal groupings of people within a formal organization.*

**is comprised of** *comprises; consists of; contains; includes.* The marketing infrastructure is comprised of several elements that change as a country develops its industrial and service sectors. *The marketing infrastructure comprises several elements that change as a country develops its industrial and service sectors.* ■ The sample is comprised of three modules. *The sample consists of three modules.*

**is concerned (about)** *brood (on; over); dread; fear; fret (about; over); regret; stew (about; over); worry (about; over).* Company analysts are concerned about the level of debt that the combined companies would carry if the hostile bid succeeds. *Company analysts worry about the level of debt that the combined companies would carry if the hostile bid succeeds.*

**is concerned with** *concerns; deals with; is about; pertains to; regards; relates to.* The first two complications are external and are concerned with the environment within which the company competes. *The first two complications are external and concern the environment within which the company competes.*

**is conditional (conditioned) on (upon)** *depends on; hinges on.* The willingness of VSS to proceed with the transaction is conditioned upon such an agreement. *The willingness of VSS to proceed with the transaction depends on such an agreement.*

**is conducive to** *conduces to.*

**is connected to (with)** *correlates to (with); equates with; relates to.*

**is conscious of (that)** *comprehends; knows; realizes; recognizes; sees; understands.*

**is consistent with** *agrees with; coheres with; concurs with; conforms to (with); corresponds to (with).* This approach is consistent with earlier rulings requiring actual proof even where overwhelming numerical evidence allows a reasonable assumption of bias. *This approach conforms to earlier rulings requiring actual proof even where overwhelming numerical evidence allows a reasonable assumption of bias.*

**is contemptuous of** *despises; disdains; scorns.*

**is contingent on (upon)** *depends on; hinges on.* Success is contingent

239

upon careful, continuous, global market research. *Success depends on careful, continuous, global market research.*

**is contributory to** *contributes.* Patients should also be warned of the cardiovascular and neoplastic liabilities of smoking that along with estrogens may be contributory to these disorders. *Patients should also be warned of the cardiovascular and neoplastic liabilities of smoking that along with estrogens may contribute to these disorders.*

**is conversant with** *knows.* I wonder whether he knows any of the Asian languages or is conversant with the sources I consulted. *I wonder whether he knows any of the Asian languages or the sources I consulted.*

**is critical of** *complains about; condemns; criticizes.* It's easy to be critical of others if they don't agree with you. *It's easy to criticize others if they don't agree with you.*

**is dangerous to** *endangers; imperils; jeopardizes.*

**is deficient in** *lacks; wants.* In perhaps the most troubling of its recent reports, NAEP showed that while few adults in their early 20s are wholly illiterate, most are deficient in necessary skills. *In perhaps the most troubling of its recent reports, NAEP showed that while few adults in their early 20s are wholly illiterate, most lack necessary skills.*

**is defined as** *is; means.* Management is defined as the process of setting and achieving goals through the execution of five basic management functions that utilize human, financial, and material resources. *Management is the process of setting and achieving goals through the execution of five basic management functions that utilize human, financial, and material resources.*

**is deleterious to** *damages; harms; hurts; impairs; injures; mars; wrongs.*

**is dependent on (upon)** *depends on; hinges on.* You shouldn't be dependent upon anyone else for your happiness. *You shouldn't depend on anyone else for your happiness.* ■ The position of the object of a phrasal verb is dependent on whether or not the phrasal verb is separable or inseparable. *The position of the object of a phrasal verb depends on whether or not the phrasal verb is separable or inseparable.*

**is descriptive of** *characterizes; depicts; describes; designates; illustrates; pictures; portrays.* The model is descriptive of human behavior across all cultures that we have encountered. *The model describes human* *behavior across all cultures that we have encountered.*

**is deserving of** *deserves.* I would like to believe that the trading company concept is deserving of serious treatment by a magazine as exemplary as yours. *I would like to believe that the trading company concept deserves serious treatment by a magazine as exemplary as yours.* ■ I think we're all deserving of a rain-free weekend. *I think we all deserve a rain-free weekend.*

**is desirous of -ing** *desires to; wants to; wishes to.* She is desirous of resolving this as soon as possible, so I respectfully request that you have your client consider the proposals. *She wants to resolve this as soon as possible, so I respectfully request that you have your client consider the proposals.*

**is destructive of (to)** *damages; destroys; harms; hurts; impairs; injures; mars; ruins.* It is a fact that some cats are destructive of property. *It is a fact that some cats destroy property.*

**is detrimental to** *damages; harms; hurts; impairs; injures; mars; wrongs.* The concern of the EEC is that these powerful drugs would be detrimental to the children. *The concern of the EEC is that these powerful drugs would injure the children.*

**is different from** *departs from; deviates from; differs from; diverges from; varies from.* If a phrase in the file on the disk is different from a phrase in the document on the screen, the command marks the entire phrase in the document on the screen. *If a phrase in the file on the disk differs from a phrase in the document on the screen, the command marks the entire phrase in the document on the screen.*

**is dismissive of** *dismisses; rejects.* The president is dismissive of the Republican accusations. *The president dismisses the Republican accusations.*

**is disposed to** *tends to.*

**is disrespectful of (toward)** *disesteems; disrespects.* We will not accept any story that is disrespectful toward any member of the Beatles, their families, or their associates. *We will not accept any story that disrespects any member of the Beatles, their families, or their associates.*

**is disruptive of** *disrupts.* Chapter 774 is disruptive of any sense of community because all control over its future has been removed.

*Chapter 774 disrupts any sense of community because all control over its future has been removed.*

**is distinguished from** *departs from; deviates from; differs from; diverges from; varies from.*

**is distrustful about (of)** *disbelieves; distrusts; doubts; mistrusts; questions.* Until students have assimilated these attitudes, they will be distrustful of scientific information. *Until students have assimilated these attitudes, they will distrust scientific information.*

**is doubtful about (of)** *disbelieves; distrusts; doubts; mistrusts; questions.* Many officials are doubtful about the effectiveness of Shultz's Mideast plan. *Many officials doubt the effectiveness of Shultz's Mideast plan.*

**is dubious about (of)** *disbelieves; distrusts; doubts; mistrusts; questions.* The A320 and the Concorde are the only commercial aircraft that use exclusively fly-by-wire controls, in part because U.S. aircraft companies are dubious about giving up tried-and-true cables. *The A320 and the Concorde are the only commercial aircraft that use exclusively fly-by-wire controls, in part because U.S. aircraft companies question giving up tried-and-true cables.*

**is duplicative of** *duplicates.* The Odyssey team's responsibilities are duplicative of the nursing team's. *The Odyssey team's responsibilities duplicate the nursing team's.* ■ The ownership of equipment will create a reluctance to try new services that require additional hardware that is partially duplicative of what has already been purchased. *The ownership of equipment will create a reluctance to try new services that require additional hardware that partially duplicates what has already been purchased.*

**is emblematic of** *emblemizes; indicates; represents; signifies; stands for; symbolizes; typifies.* The kind of comprehensive care the Clinic can provide to its cancer patients is emblematic of the Clinic's overall approach to medicine. *The kind of comprehensive care the Clinic can provide to its cancer patients typifies the Clinic's overall approach to medicine.*

**is (the) equal to** *amounts to; duplicates; equals; is; matches; rivals.* The value of the emperor's palace in the center of Tokyo is equal to the value of the entire state of California. *The value of the emperor's palace in the center of Tokyo equals the value of the entire state of California.*

**is equipped (furnished) with** *comes with.* The server normally is equipped with a large-capacity hard disk drive that acts as the central file depository for everyone on the network. *The server normally comes with a large-capacity hard disk drive that acts as the central file depository for everyone on the network.*

**is (the) equivalent of (to)** *amounts to; duplicates; equals; is; matches; rivals.* Ideally, the amount of this fund should be the equivalent of at least three months' income. *Ideally, the amount of this fund should equal at least three months' income.*

**is (a; the) -er (-or) of** delete. She was the originator of the company program. *She originated the company program.* ■ You should be a helper and encourager of your child's writing efforts. *You should help and encourage your child's writing efforts.*

**is evidence of (that)** *evinces; indicates; proves; reveals; shows; signifies; testifies (to).* The calls are evidence of the strong temptation in the judicial arena to seize on an array of recent findings on brain chemistry and behavior. *The calls testify to the strong temptation in the judicial arena to seize on an array of recent findings on brain chemistry and behavior.*

**is exploitative (exploitive) of** *abuses; cheats; deceives; exploits; ill-treats; mistreats; misuses; uses; victimizes; wrongs.* Surcharging is unfair and exploitative of customers. *Surcharging is unfair and exploits customers.*

**is faced with** *faces.* Dynamic high-technology strategy companies are faced with few national competitors. *Dynamic high-technology strategy companies face few national competitors.*

**is familiar with** *knows.* European participants in the computer industry know Europe extremely well, and they are familiar with the U.S. market. *European participants in the computer industry know Europe extremely well, and they know the U.S. market.*

**is favorable to** *aids; benefits; favors; helps.* In the five years during which the leveraged buyout has blossomed, the business environment has been particularly favorable to this type of transaction. *In the five years during which the leveraged buyout has blossomed, the business environment has particularly favored this type of transaction.*

**is fearful (about; of; that)** *dreads; fears; frets (about; over); stews (about; over); worries (about; over).* These leaders tend to be fearful of external forces because they may create a middle class or threaten the existing

243

social structure. *These leaders tend to fret about external forces because they may create a middle class or threaten the existing social structure.*

**is focused on (upon)** *focuses on.* Although most of the chapters in this volume are focused on incentives for educators, several authors remind us that students are the chief agent of their own learning. *Although most of the chapters in this volume focus on incentives for educators, several authors remind us that students are the chief agent of their own learning.*

**is for certain (sure)** *is certain (sure).* One thing is for certain: they'll have to deal with the governor when all this is over. *One thing is certain: they'll have to deal with the governor when all this is over.*

**is founded on (upon)** *rests on.*

**is going to** *shall; will.* We think that is a trend that is going to continue for several years to come. *We think that is a trend that will continue for several years to come.* ■ That simply means that you are going to need effective human relations skills. *That simply means that you will need effective human relations skills.*

**is harmful to** *damages; harms; hurts; impairs; injures; mars; wrongs.* It will ultimately be harmful to the state's economy in that it will make some products more expensive than anywhere else. *It will ultimately harm the state's economy in that it will make some products more expensive than anywhere else.*

**is helpful in (-ing)** *aids in; assists in; helps.* Intelligent market research will be helpful in settling which product lines to offer. *Intelligent market research will help settle which product lines to offer.*

**is hopeful** *expects; hopes; relies on; trusts.* I am hopeful that all will go well. *I expect that all will go well.*

**is identical to (with)** *amounts to; duplicates; equals; is; matches; rivals.* The objective, of course, is to ensure that directors' interests are identical with those of the company and its longer term stockholders. *The objective, of course, is to ensure that directors' interests match those of the company and its longer term stockholders.*

**is illustrative of** *characterizes; depicts; demonstrates; describes; designates; exemplifies; illustrates; pictures; portrays; represents.* Some American Feminists is illustrative of the nearly universal nature of the issues the studio examines. Some American Feminists *exemplifies the nearly universal nature of the issues the studio examines.*

**is imitative of** *imitates.*

**is in accord (accordance) on (with)** *agrees with; coincides with; complies with; concurs with; conforms to (with); corresponds to (with).* We feel that the activities of our diplomats in Nicaragua were in strict accordance with normal patterns of diplomatic behavior. *We feel that the activities of our diplomats in Nicaragua strictly conformed with normal patterns of diplomatic behavior.*

**is in agreement (on; with)** *agrees (on; with); coincides (with); complies (with); concurs (with); conforms (to; with); corresponds (to; with).* The client should be in agreement with the goals set. *The client should concur with the goals set.*

**is in attendance (at)** *attends.* Three presidents were in attendance at the graduation ceremonies. *Three presidents attended the graduation ceremonies.*

**is incapable of -ing** *cannot; is unable to.* All three companies were incapable of managing their prizes and two of them, Hershey and CBS, eventually discarded their acquisitions in dismay. *All three companies were unable to manage their prizes and two of them, Hershey and CBS, eventually discarded their acquisitions in dismay.*

**is in charge of** *controls; directs; governs; manages.*

**is inclined to** *tends to.*

**is inclined to believe (that)** *asserts; believes; claims; contends; feels; holds; maintains; says; thinks; to.* I am inclined to believe that we will receive a lot more calls when budgets make clear what cuts and fees public schools will institute. *I believe that we will receive a lot more calls when budgets make clear what cuts and fees public schools will institute.*

**is inclined to think (that)** *asserts; believes; claims; contends; feels; holds; maintains; says; thinks; to.* I am inclined to think that Windows 95 is in many ways inferior to Windows 3.1. *I think Windows 95 is in many ways inferior to Windows 3.1.*

**is in competition with** *competes with.* The WI is in competition with many other organizations that could also satisfy the needs women have for friendship, learning and all the other things our aims and objects describe. *The WI competes with many other organizations that could also satisfy the needs women have for friendship, learning and all the other things our aims and objects describe.*

**is in compliance with** *complies with; conforms to (with).* No register of deeds shall accept a deed for recording unless it is in compliance with the requirements of this section. *No register of deeds shall accept a deed for recording unless it complies to the requirements of this section.*

**is in conflict with** *clashes with; conflicts with; contradicts; differs from; disagrees with; quarrels with; varies with.* The NTIA petition refers to the information services prohibition in the Modification of Final Judgment as "a cumbersome, unnecessary layer of regulation that is in irreconcilable conflict with the Communications Act." *The NTIA petition refers to the information services prohibition in the Modification of Final Judgment as "a cumbersome, unnecessary layer of regulation that irreconcilably conflicts with the Communications Act."*

**is in conformance to (with)** *agrees with; coincides with; complies with; concurs with; conforms to (with); corresponds to (with).* A Basic Guide to Fair Housing Accessibility is an indispensable resource for architects, builders, contractors, site engineers, and developers who need to know that their work is in conformance with federal guidelines. *A Basic Guide to Fair Housing Accessibility is an indispensable resource for architects, builders, contractors, site engineers, and developers who need to know that their work conforms with federal guidelines.*

**is in conformity to (with)** *agrees with; coincides with; complies with; concurs with; conforms to (with); corresponds to (with).* As long as they're in conformity with the law, they can do business with whomever they like. *As long as they conform to the law, they can do business with whomever they like.*

**is in contempt of** *defies.* A parent who is in contempt of a custody order is playing with fire. *A parent who defies a custody order is playing with fire.*

**is in (marked; sharp) contrast to** *clashes with; conflicts with; contests; contradicts; contrasts with; differs from; disagrees with; disputes; opposes.* The findings are in contrast to those of the Higher Education Research Institute, which conducts an annual national survey of freshmen. *The findings conflict with those of the Higher Education Research Institute, which conducts an annual national survey of freshmen.*